John Willard Bruster
Library
Memphis State University
Memphis, Tennessee

CHARLESTON

A GRACIOUS HERITAGE

Other Books in the Century City Series

Illustrated by E. H. SUYDAM

CHARLESTON

A GRACIOUS HERITAGE

By ROBERT MOLLOY

Illustrations by

E. H. SUYDAM

NEW YORK & LONDON

D. APPLETON-CENTURY COMPANY, INC.

COPYRIGHT, 1947, BY ROBERT MOLLOY

PREFACE

In a civilization for which size is usually the criterion of importance, the little city of Charleston, South Carolina, retains and constantly enlarges its own peculiar prestige—a reputation for aristocratic appearance, punctilious manners, and an atmosphere of unforgettable individuality. It seems to prove that the still small voice of distinction can make itself heard in a raucous world.

However, convinced though he may be of the city's genuine claims to a very special niche in the world's temple of fame, the interpreter of Charleston is baffled for any simple explanation that will dispose of the skeptic. The physical facts are discouraging. Charleston, by all modern standards, is a very small city indeed. Its normal population (the city proper, of course) has scarcely if ever exceeded 70,000, and a large part of that, very close to half, is Negro. That portion of the city which has become so disproportionately famous could almost be exhibited in New York's Central Park or Van Cortlandt Park. Charleston's political importance, in any large sense, is almost wholly of the past. For generations it has not created an international ripple, and its only native son of world importance at the present day is James F. Byrnes. Its industrial standing is considerably inferior to what zealous business organizations would naturally like to achieve. It has but one modern wonder,

v

the vast bridge over the Cooper River. In no way does it appear to represent the American Dream.

For all that, it is doubtful if any city of its size on this continent can challenge Charleston's very particular place in the sun. Tourists, artists, authors have all tried to put into spoken and written words, onto canvas, film, drawing paper and copper plates, the singular personality of this old American town.

If one attempts to account for this, one falls back on the clichés of women's pages and travel articles. But no one set of answers will suffice. Charleston has great architectural beauties, beautiful gardens, a long, dramatic and romantic history, and a number of distinguished sons. Most literate people are at least faintly aware of its reputation for cultivated manners, of its ancestor worship, its excessive conservatism—which has been somewhat exaggerated—and the mildness of its climate. Yet none of these entirely explains the essence of the name Charleston.

Not even longevity provides the explanation of its attractions. There are older settlements even in our comparatively new land. Charleston dates back only to 1670, and its oldest building is not quite two and a half centuries old, which makes it a mere upstart in point of age.

In short, the city is the sum of so many things that it is to be doubted that any single book can present a complete picture. The author of this informal accompaniment to the late Mr. Suydam's rich and perceptive drawings certainly does not aspire to any complete reasoned apology. But perhaps the sympathetic and imaginative reader will see, through the conformities and contradictions in this account of Charleston, at least a hazy pattern of what constitutes a dignified old city's extraordinary individuality and—we might as well give in and use the word—charm. And perhaps he will understand why William Dean Howells said: "No other city has had a civil consciousness so intense and so continued."

ACKNOWLEDGMENTS

The bibliography which is appended to this volume will show how much I am in debt to the many authors and researchers who have written about Charleston, the South, and their outstanding men. My personal thanks are due to many Charlestonians who contributed in greater or less measure to the acquirement of facts and the forming of impressions. My particular thanks are due to Mr. E. Milby Burton, Director of the Charleston Museum, who generously furnished copies of the Museum's publications and has permitted me to benefit by quotations included in his *South Carolina Silversmiths;* and to Mr. Marion L. Hodges, who was extremely helpful in assisting me to obtain certain items of information.

Needless to say, the author is alone responsible for any or all errors of fact or of judgment.

R. M.

CONTENTS

LIST OF ILLUSTRATIONS

xi

*Facing
Page*

CHARLESTON

A GRACIOUS HERITAGE

CHAPTER ONE

Sights and Sounds

The traveler J. H. St. John Crèvecoeur, who visited Charleston some time before the Revolutionary War, was not the first or the last visitor to be impressed by the beauty of the city and the elegance of the life its more prosperous inhabitants enjoyed. He said of the latter that they were "the gayest in America." That might be open to question if someone said it now, for gayety, at least to the superficial eye, is hardly the striking feature of the city. But much of what Crèvecoeur actually saw is still true. He said, of the town's geography: "Its situation is admirable, being built at the confluence of two large rivers." It will be seen from this that the romantic French-born "American Farmer" was, as a grammarian, scarcely superior to the average journalist of today; but he knew a beautiful setting when he saw it. For Charleston is handsomely seated at the point where, as the hoary witticism says, "the Ashley and Cooper Rivers unite to form the Atlantic Ocean," a tilt at the egocentricity of the natives which has its core of truth.

As a matter of dry record, Charleston is on a peninsula where two estuaries come together to form its fine harbor. Seven and a half miles out lies the Atlantic proper, two stone jetties marking the point at which the rivers end and the sea takes over. The harbor channel is thirty-five feet deep at mean low water for ten and a half miles up the Cooper River (to the north), and a seven and a half mile passage of the same approximate depth has been dredged up the Ashley.

As the Hudson River commemorates its discoverer, these two rivers commemorate the man who was responsible for the founding of the settlement of Carolina, Anthony Ashley Cooper, later the first Earl of Shaftesbury, whose allegiances were, to say the least, changeable. He was the chief of the eight English noblemen to whom Charles the Second, to repay political debts, assigned the mighty tract of land that extended from the southern point of what is now Georgia to the northern point of North Carolina and all the way westward to "the South Seas"—in other words, the Pacific Ocean. Naturally, his majesty ignored the mere matter of a few Frenchmen and Spaniards and a handful of Indians, but we shall discuss that later.

Viewed from a fair distance in the harbor formed by these two rivers, and this is by long odds the finest sight of it, the city looks like a toy settlement on a level floor. Charleston is a part of what is called the Low Country, the coastal plain of the southeastern part of South Carolina, whose limits are rather inexactly defined, but whose character is precisely what the name implies. The city itself is built so low that its sewers are below water level, with an attendant effect upon the atmosphere which is ignored in polite society. But Miss Josephine Pinckney, in *Three O'Clock Dinner,* described the city's summer air as a mélange of the odors of "heavy salt, pluff mud, oleanders, and drains."

The skyline, too, is low. Possibly because of the warning implicit in the devastating earthquake of 1886, and also because of its mercantile poverty in modern times, Charleston has never broken out into the skyscrapers characteristic of modern American cities. Here the skyline is dominated by church spires, particularly by those of St. Michael's and St. Philip's churches, and by two hotels, one of which reaches the un-precedented height of twelve stories. The previous skyscraper was the People's Building, eight stories above the earth. But Charleston's skyline is nevertheless striking. Even though all other impressions of height are dwarfed by the mighty arching bridge over the Cooper River, Charleston from the harbor is a sight to remember. It is like a mellow color print.

The view of the harbor from the city, although it has called forth no such rhapsodies as those evoked by the harbor of Rio de Janeiro, also sets one to looking for adjectives. From the East Battery sea wall one's gaze is arrested by the soaring bridge, which, by the way, honors the memory of one of Charleston's most distinguished chief executives, John P. Grace. Beyond it, and clearly visible on a good day, are Mount Pleasant and Sullivan's Island, on which is Fort Moultrie. Access to these and to the Isle of Palms, a magnificent beach, is speeded by means of the bridge, the alternative being a ferry trip. On a small island almost directly to the east is Castle Pinckney, undertaken as a fortification when war with France was feared, but now set aside as a national monument and as a proposed site for a memorial to the Revolutionary Generals Moultrie and Thompson. The little fort played a small part in the Civil War as a place of confinement for Union prisoners after the first battle of Manassas.

Also to the east is Fort Sumter, a reddish-brown wall with the top of a house just visible above the ramparts. Northeast of this is the harbor mouth, the "iron gate" which withstood two major sieges. To the right, just barely southwest of Fort Sumter to the eye, is heavily wooded James Island, with the site of old Fort Johnson at its tip. This was the fort from which the firing on Fort Sumter began in the fateful April of 1861. It is now the site of the United States Quarantine Station.

From this standpoint on the Battery the water is a brownish yellow merging into a greener tint; and with the green of the horizon, the reddish brown of Fort Sumter, the blue of the sky, and the white foam which is stirred up by the almost ceaseless breeze, a more fitting gateway to the color-splashed city could scarcely be imagined.

First impressions of the city vary greatly, depending upon the taste and experience of the traveler and the point at which he enters—for Charleston's entries by land are no more prepossessing than those of other cities. It is a pity that everyone could not approach the city by means of a vessel which would dock on the Battery. But once in the southeast portion of Charleston, the traveler will be quickly persuaded to forget the unedifying approaches.

Putting aside personal reactions to architecture and atmosphere, it seems likely that most visitors will be impressed similarly by the brilliance of the light. For this is a city of sunshine. Statistics have been adduced to show that it is second only to Los Angeles in days of sunshine per year. Conversely, the shadows are heavy and the contrasts intense; the shade at midday is blue-black and the sun can be like a lightning flash. St. Michael's spire glistens; so does the white woodwork of piazzas, one of the chief characteristics of Charleston's architecture and one that moves many travelers to recall the West Indies, until, noting the colors of the houses, they murmur about little French towns, or spotting a balcony may for a moment think of New Orleans—until, finally, they are no longer able to pin their impressions down to any reminiscences, and inevitably conclude that Charleston is Charleston and has its own individual style—as close students are quick to point out.

In this older section of the city, west of East Battery and "South of Broad"—the latter being, so to speak, the holy land of Charleston, although the irreverent will remind you that its initial letters suggest something considerably less edifying— the pervading impression is one of stateliness. This is a country of high-walled gardens and imposing gateways and doorways, long verandas (but you must call them piazzas), pastel-colored plaster reduced to a soft tone by time and salt air, brick that time has colored, delicate iron-work, tiled roofs which are unfortunately becoming rarer, quaint and graceful chimney pots, palmetto trees (South Carolina is the Palmetto State) and live oaks. The streets are uncrowded in these residential sections, and that is fortunate, for with the exception of Meeting Street they are narrow for modern purposes, so narrow, indeed, that automobiles have to make a particularly sharp turn at the corners which is not undisconcerting to strangers. These narrow streets are an indication, if any indication were needed, of Charleston's age. They were not particularly narrow for their period.

Not only are these streets for the most part semi-deserted, but they are almost wholly free from any signs of haste. Nobody seems to be in a hurry. The automobiles move rapidly where they can find room, but people afoot and occasional bicyclists are apparently indifferent to the passing of time. Haste would be out of place in these majestic streets, under those imposing porticoes and gateways, just as a strident voice would be inappropriate.

It is all very easy on the nerves. It is the expression of a way of life in which people have found better things to do than hurry, where you can stop on the sidewalk to talk—and Charlestonians frequently do—without being jostled every few seconds by some precipitate passer-by intent on making every moment count. Are these leisurely saunterers the descendants of the people described by Crèvecoeur as "the gayest in America"? Well, he also said, "The climate renders excess of all kinds very dangerous," and you would conclude from the leisurely air of these streets that Charleston had taken his remark very much to heart and had determined never to indulge in excesses of pedestrian speed. We ought to complete

Crèvecoeur's strictures; he added, "particularly those (excesses) of the table; and yet, insensible or fearless of danger, they live on, and enjoy a short and merry life; on the contrary, the women, from being abstemious, reach to a longer period of life, and seldom die without having had several husbands." Charlestonians do love to eat. I do not know the statistics relevant to the prevalence of widowhood, although, come to think of it, I have known of a good many widows. Maybe the American Farmer was right, and Charleston men do eat themselves to death; it is obvious that they don't rush themselves to death.

And if gayety is not very apparent to the casual onlooker, it is easy to see that these Charlestonians are a pleasant lot. They will nod to you on the street, whether they know you or not, and answer you fully and cordially if you venture on a question. They will not push you aside, either on the sidewalk or in stores or on the buses. I spent almost a month in Charleston in the spring of 1946 without encountering a gruff answer or overhearing one, either in the streets or in the shops. This affability has its limits, of course. Charleston does not fling open its street doors to the passer-by; it has even been accused of a lack of hospitality. But it is undoubtedly a courteous city.

One might be tempted, after a bit, to think that this carefreeness about time and these lazy ways may explain, at least in part, the genteel shabbiness of much of the city. However, that is not the result of mere indolence. The salt air is no respecter of paint and plaster, and there have been periods of poverty when the people of Charleston, as a group, simply could not afford such luxuries as the persistent and regular application of paint. Another of those local jokes describes the natives as "too poor to paint and too proud to whitewash." At any rate, whatever the causes, that patina achieved by weathering gives a character and richness to Charleston that might be spoiled by a too great insistence upon the spic and span. It is "tourist" signs that spoil such a city, not bare spots on plaster and wood-work or a few weeds sprung up on the walks. And it must be remembered that many of the old houses were built of heart pine and cypress. The lack of paint at times hasn't affected Charleston's survival value.

Survival —perhaps that's the one word that, more than any other, explains the city. It has grown slowly in modern times, too slowly to catch up with the rapid enlargement of other Southern cities, and it has been only a static industrial back-water since the Civil War. The wonder is that the city is still in existence. It has been besieged in two major wars and bat-tered by the besiegers. Historic fires have swept it; malaria, yellow fever, and smallpox ravished it in earlier days; it has suffered a series of hurricanes, one of terrific force having struck as recently as 1938; it has had disastrous floods, and one of the worst earthquakes ever recorded in this hemisphere shook it almost to bits in 1886. All this has happened to Charleston in a little over two hundred and fifty years of its life, and it has withstood and endured. It has even survived the tourist craze of the past quarter-century, the acquisitive-ness of rich collectors, and the type of twentieth-century com-mercial ambition that would raze indiscriminately in order to rebuild. Considering all this, one marvels that the city isn't a ghost town.

Yes, Charleston is a survival, but a survival with a differ-ence. It is not a survival where people creep around amid the ruins, or a museum. If it has derived a large amount of its income in the recent past from the attractiveness of its land-marks in the eyes of strangers, it still operates as a city with commercial ambitions, however frustrated. Its inhabitants even live in the landmarks, some of them houses which are in-trinsically priceless. Some of the famous houses have been con-verted to ignominious uses, but comparatively few; and if some fine old dwellings have become lodging houses in the course of time, well, people must live somewhere and somehow. It is significant, however, that only two of Charleston's fine old dwellings have actually become public property as relics—the Heyward-Washington house on Church Street and the Manigault House on upper Meeting Street. Many fine buildings have, in a long experience with the necessity of making do, achieved a new usefulness.

People actually live in Charleston. The folk there have not found it necessary to dress themselves up in costumes of the eighteenth century and turn spinning-wheels in the attempt to achieve quaintness. You may peer into their gardens and stand shamelessly before their houses, but they go on eating dinner or whatever it is they are doing. And they enjoy themselves. They have a distinct pattern of life, although to metropolitan devotees of night clubs, their doings will probably appear tame. They have learned to live, and in doing so to compromise with many things. The city is hot in the summer, but the indigenous piazzas take a good deal of the sting out of the summer heat and encourage the southwestern breezes that spring up every afternoon. If one lives and works in the city proper, getting to and fro from business is a comparatively easy matter. Even the heat is made to do double duty. Charlestonians point with pride to an annual mean temperature of sixty-seven degrees; this attracts tourists under the heading of a marvelous winter climate. It also serves to excuse the unprogressiveness of a section of the population and to account for that *dolce far niente* which more or less characterizes the life of the community.

Of course the heat explains that leisurely way of getting around. After generations of becoming acclimatized to long summers, Charlestonians know better than to be in a hurry. There is plenty of time to do everything. There is lots of shade, and there are always friends to help one pass the time. Old friends, too; sometimes the friendships are hereditary. (That's true, no doubt, of enmities also.) As in many smaller cities, but in an even greater degree, you've known these people and their families ever since you were born, and your parents and grandparents and great-grandparents and even farther back than that. . . . They know your history, just as you know theirs. You don't gain anything by trying to impress one another. As the artist, Elizabeth O'Neill Verner, remarks in her book of prints *Mellowed by Time,* it does little good in Charleston to put on side. People knew you when. They will forgive you a good deal, but they won't be impressed by pretenses to which you have no right.

I think it may still be said, as it was in my childhood, that there is no dollar aristocracy in Charleston. This makes for an agreeable lack of snobbishness in many things. It does no harm whatever to your standing to be a clerk in a bank or a hotel or a store. Charlestonians have been poor for a long time, and they are really quite realistic about the necessity for earning a living. Renting rooms in historic houses, acting as guides to the city—these things don't matter. Mr. Thomas Wolfe's hero, in *Look Homeward, Angel,* was tormented at having had to deliver newspapers in his boyhood. Charleston's most distinguished literary figure, a descendant of the best in the city's lineage, delivered papers too in a poverty-stricken boyhood, but there is no record that he was humiliated or tormented by having to do so.

Not that false pride has been a stranger to Charleston. Far from that. Any Charlestonian can tell you of some pathetic examples. There were, for instance, two dear old gentlewomen who were obliged to sell the milk of their cow. (There used to be cows in Charleston's back yards not so many years ago before sanitary regulations put a stop to it.) These old ladies had devised a singular system of face-saving. The prospective purchaser of milk left a pitcher or other vessel before a kind of wicket, along with the necessary money. After a suitable interval, a hand would snatch (well, no, not snatch—no Charleston lady ever snatched anything) would take the vessel away and the money, and would later return the former with the milk in it. But neither of these two ladies was ever seen engaging in trade. Ridiculous, of course, and nowhere more than in Charleston, some of whose most distinguished families were founded by merchants.

It was even more difficult to make a present, particularly of money. There is a case in point, that of one old gentleman who worked as a clerk. When he and his maiden sister removed to the North, he occupied the same sort of position. Their house was somewhat bare and their table fare somewhat lean, but they joked about such trifles as that. Troubled by the obviously painful plight of these kindly and charming people, one relative, while on a visit, resolved to do something to help them. To make an offer of aid was obviously impossible, so she hid a small sum of money in a jar in the pantry so that they would come across it and (she hoped) think they had lost or misplaced it themselves. If they ever concluded that it was a surreptitious gift, the chances are that they put it into the poor box on the very next Sunday.

Of course, that was foolish, too, but I think I can explain something of what lay behind such behavior. These people were not ashamed of being poor. Not at all. But, they reasoned, if you allowed people to see that you really *needed* something, to the extent that they were impelled to offer it to you, then you were deficient in character. You weren't bearing yourself well in the face of adversity. And probably they knew only too well what charity can do to people. They didn't want to forget their sturdy independence. Their actions did not proceed from the same silly putting on of airs that used to impel some music teachers, for instance, to refuse to accept money directly from their pupils and to compel the latter to place it on a table in the hall. I've known that to happen, and it wasn't in proud Charleston. It was in undeluded New York.

Charleston's society was founded on the activities of the well-to-do and leisurely. That was natural. It was not a frontier, at least not after the first few years. (It was very poor after the Civil War.) But even in the heyday of its social glitter, money was not the prime requisite. Mrs. St. Julien Ravenel, who wrote that incomparable personal history of Charleston, *Charleston, the Place and the People,* tells of a Mrs. Holland whose soirées were attended by everyone who counted. Mrs. Holland had only one large room to live in, and not enough furniture to fill that when guests were numerous. They sat on soap boxes and liked it. Nowadays, too, the hat that is raised to you may be somewhat shabby, but it will come off with grace. Charleston has pretty manners, appropriate to their setting, but by no means limited to South of Broad Street.

This street, which does not really separate sheep and goats as much as it is supposed to, is the professional street of Charleston and its financial center. Here are the banks, the legal offices, the real estate firms, and the insurance houses. Below Meeting Street, however, Broad is residential. East Bay, which, as its name suggests, runs along the east waterfront, is the wholesale and shipping center, a long street curiously compounded of down-at-heel buildings and some really distinguished edifices. At its southern end, which joins East Battery, there has been considerable restoration of old dwellings, under the influence and supervision of Susan P. Frost, owner of the famous Pringle House and founder of the Society for the Preservation of Old Dwellings. Here old houses have been made to bloom in gay new colors.

The East Battery, which made Howells think of Venice, and the Murray Boulevard are Charleston's esplanade. Once the South Battery was the waterside companion of the East Battery, but the philanthropy of a wealthy citizen, the late Andrew B. Murray, made possible the reclamation of a large tract of marsh to the south of the city, and the boulevard enclosing this reclaimed land bears his name. It is a handsome driveway, bordered by houses which have not quite the richness of the really old ones.

Another famous street is Meeting, so called because of the original White Meeting House which stood on it. Below Broad Street it is loftily residential except for the South Carolina Society Hall. It meets Broad at the most famous corner in Charleston, where are St. Michael's Church, the City Hall, the Post Office, and the Court House. Just north of Broad Street are the noble Hibernian Hall, the Gibbes Art Gallery, the Timrod Inn, and the St. John's Hotel.

The city's chief shopping street is King Street, which, like Meeting, is residential below Broad Street. Here are to be found the Pringle House, the house where the artist Charles Fraser lived, and other distinguished dwellings, as well as one or two rather less impressive. After passing Broad Street, King Street becomes a hodgepodge of shops, some of them fine examples of architecture. All of it is exceedingly narrow. Finally, above Calhoun Street, which used to be called Boundary Street before it was renamed to honor South Carolina's favorite son (his monument stands on the near-by Marion Square or Citadel Green), King Street begins to look like New York's lower East Side. East and west of this portion of it are to be found some fine houses, intermingled, in the fashion of Charleston, with Negro slums and tumble-down areas.

Outside of a few curiosities and landmarks the extreme northern end of the city has little to offer the visitor. It has yielded to "developments," chiefly for war workers. Charleston's better suburb is on the west bank of the Ashley River,

along the road to Magnolia and Middleton Gardens, and a
bit south of the original settlement on the west bank which
was called Albemarle Point.

In the West End of the city are the imposing new Citadel—
the Military College of South Carolina—Hampton Park, the
air field and yacht basin and the fine new Roper Hospital. The
Ashley River, too, is spanned by a modern bridge, the approach to which is through an unattractive street, just as is
the case with the Cooper River span.

The visitor is usually more than willing to return to the old
city. Here the beauties of Charleston are concentrated, and
here, most of all, the quiet that is characteristic of all but the
very busiest parts of the town seems to have ensconced itself.
An occasional child's voice is usually the loudest sound one
hears, or a piano played softly. At regular intervals the chime
of St. Michael's Church sounds with a somewhat antiquated
sweetness, its tone just a trifle fuzzy. In the mornings the fish
and vegetable vendors—fewer, it seemed to me, than formerly
—sing out their long-drawn calls. There is a crescendo as the
vendor comes nearer, and then, as he moves off, the corresponding diminuendo, and quiet reigns once more in the narrow streets. Now it is hard to believe in the excitement that
pervaded Charleston in critical times, or in those people that
Crèvecoeur called the gayest in America. You do not think of
public affairs, even though you are virtually walking through
the pages of history, but of privacy. It must have been a determined taste for this privacy that led to the typical placing
of "single houses" so closely identified with the city, which
turn their sides to the passer-by and show him their false doorways opening on to the long piazzas, the real front door being
in the center and facing the garden. This desire to be free
from the public eye shows in the high walls, too, and in the
tall gateways that seem to shut out the world—with, however,

the occasional symbolic pineapple atop the posts as a reminder of hospitality. And it all can be summed up in Irwin Edman's remark about the aesthetic monuments of the Continent: "What meets the eye of the tourist once served the needs of men."

CHAPTER TWO

Rhapsody in All Colors

Charleston has innumerable admirers, and it is not too aloof to be pleased by what the more famous ones have said and written. But inevitably it has its critics and detractors. The old-time drummers, so I have heard, used to time their visits in such a way as to reach the city in the morning, transact their business, and leave on the evening of the same day. Evidently the accommodations and pleasures afforded were not to their presumably robust tastes.

The young sailor with whom I happened to talk while having dinner in a restaurant belonged to the less enthusiastic group of visitors. He suggested, in fact, that coming ashore in Charleston was rather akin to being marooned. He said it was all right for people of about fifty.

"But it's a handsome old town," I remarked, hoping to draw him out.

"Oh, yes, the city is pretty in the springtime," he conceded.

Even the most remorseless critic could scarcely deny that. Charleston's blossoms are profuse and varied; it is like a land of flowers. The very earliest travelers were impressed by the richness of the flora of the Low Country. Just two years after the establishment of Charles Town, that is, in 1682, Thomas Ashe, the clerk of the *Richmond,* mentioned in his account that the colonists were laying out their gardens. In its very first year the South Carolina *Gazette,* founded in 1732, published advertisements of garden seeds. The formal gardens were flourishing in the middle of the eighteenth century.

The visitor benefits by this long history of cultivation the first time he looks around the city. The soil is hospitable and the season is long. Before winter is well out there are snow-drops and narcissus, followed rapidly by wisteria that drapes itself over the walls and gateways, lilies, azaleas. Bignonia splashes its yellow over fences, banksia roses, freesias, ca-mellias burst into flower. Velvety, thick-petaled violets, of a rich dark color, come early. The air is scented everywhere. The tourists—no wonder—almost swoon with pleasure.

Unfortunately, the azaleas, like many of the good things in this life, do not last very long. By the first week of April they are on the way out, and usually so are the tourists. But later, when the visitors have departed, leaving the natives, as Alex-ander Woollcott remarked, "with no one to despise but them-selves," the oleanders come into their own. They have a very dark foliage and a four-petaled flower, and the colors are white, yellow, and all shades of pink, all of which show to added advantage against this somber background. I have heard Charlestonians dismiss them almost as if they were a pest or too common to be noticed. They hang over fences, they border driveways, they are clustered thick around the little pond on Rutledge Avenue. Most of the varieties have a delicate per-fume. I recall a performance of *Romeo and Juliet* by the Foot-light Players, one of the city's amateur groups, during the intermission of which everyone stood out in the courtyard talking and smoking and cooling off. Over a brick wall, under the lights, a huge oleander flung masses of white blossoms, and I couldn't help thinking what a setting that would have been for the Capulets' garden.

At this season, too, the roses become so thick that they

HISTORIC ST. PHILIP'S CHURCH, SHOWING THE NORTH
AND WEST PORTICOES AND EAST AND WEST CHURCHYARDS,
DIVIDED BY CHURCH STREET. IN THE BACKGROUND IS THE
SO-CALLED PIRATE HOUSE

THE WEST PORTICO OF ST. PHILIP'S—GATE OF THE WEST
CHURCHYARD—AND THE PIRATE HOUSE

actually seem to be struggling for a place on the bushes and trellises. Where they are trained they form a screen of white and red. Out come the fiery red blooms of the pomegranate trees, and overhead the great cream-white blossoms of the towering *Magnolia grandiflora* burst upon the air. As for the humbler flowers—lantana, pansies, bordering plants, the pink wild roses—there is simply no end to them; add jessamine, sweet peas, honeysuckle, morning glories. Many of the gardens have the most surprising way of coming into view around the corner of a fence, off in a back yard, through a hedge. You look out of a second-story back window and there is a garden next door, a mass of rainbow hues.

The Garden Club and the City of Charleston have collaborated in the establishment of one of those tours through gardens which is aptly called the Gateway Walk. This one leads through eleven gateways and a number of gardens. Entering the churchyard of St. John's Lutheran Church, you progress to the grounds of the Unitarian Church, then across King Street and into the gardens of the Charleston Library Society; then to the Gibbes Memorial Art Gallery on Meeting Street. Crossing the street, you go through the grounds of the Circular Congregational Church and then you reach the cemeteries—yes, there are two, divided by Church Street—of St. Philip's.

The Charleston Free Library, housed in a magnificent mansion on Rutledge Avenue and Bull Street, once the city home of a planter, has a fine garden which you can hardly fail to see, overhung by great magnolias. Among the private gardens is one just two blocks away on a southeast corner of Rutledge Avenue adjoining a beautiful old white house with piazzas on front and side. St. Michael's Place is full of flowers, and not far away, on Longitude Lane, there are wild strawberries, not quite as wild as the unfounded legend about this having been the site of one of the first rice fields.

The Pringle House, which is open to the public at certain hours, has a lovely old rambling garden, and the Heyward-Washington House, a museum adjunct, has a charming formal one in which all the flowers set out are those which could have been in bloom on this continent at the time of George Washington's visit there in 1791.

Not everyone in Charleston has taken advantage of the hospitality of the soil and glorified his property with flowers. Once upon a time, not so long ago, the typical Charleston back yard was admittedly a dismal affair, often heaped with brickbats and trash and ashes, and some of these still exist. But there are comparatively few spots where some glow of color cannot be seen. Even in abandoned yards the little pink dwarf roses—I believe they are some variety of moss pink, but the Charleston children all learned to call them "primroses"—grow uninvited. Once upon a time, too, there were lots of opopanax shrubs, a variety of acacia with puffy golden yellow spheres all over them. They used to be a favorite sachet, but they are no longer plentiful.

There is another, and a humble, variety of garden, too, not limited to this particular city but a characteristic part of it. That is the tomato-can kind, chiefly devoted to the culture of geraniums and almost wholly a Negro undertaking. And there must be numerous backyard conservatories with ferns and flowering plants set in old tubs and kegs. Our nurse had a striking example, all her own, and among its prizes was a night-blooming cereus. When, after years of patient pampering, this signified its readiness to produce at last, our entire family sat up to witness the blessed event. It was over thirty years ago that we did so, but I still recall the sight of that flower as worth the long vigil. Perhaps that is because the affair was incorporated with the permission to sit up late, but I prefer to think that I really enjoyed the rare flower.

Charleston has botanical traditions beyond those of mere

ornamentation, too, and shares in the name of two very distinguished flowers. The poinsettia, favorite Christmas merchandise of florists and despair of all who receive a potted specimen because it dies so swiftly, is named after Joel R. Poinsett, world traveler, unofficial ambassador, collector, and adviser to the organizers of the Smithsonian Institution. Poinsett, who was born in Charleston, brought the plant home with him from Mexico—along with the life he had risked in quieting a mob by an oration from the balcony of the American embassy in Mexico City. The gardenia, associate of evening glamour, bears in its name a tribute to the famous botanist and scientist, Dr. Alexander Garden (the friend and pupil of Linnaeus) who lived and worked in Charleston, and whose son wrote two entertaining books of anecdotes of the American Revolution. Stephen Elliott, first president of the Bank of South Carolina, long a resident of Charleston, wrote a standard work, *The Botany of South Carolina and Georgia.* And some Charlestonian, according to legend, was the first person to eat a tomato, until that time considered a poisonous fruit. What a debt the salad enthusiast owes to that intrepid, anonymous citizen—and where would spaghetti sauce and tomato pilau be without him? I like to imagine his emotions, when he first swallowed the juicy pulp, as similar to those of Juliet when she drank off Friar Laurence's soporific, or to those of the Swedish scientist who ventured to drink "heavy" water.

A practical botanist was that remarkable man, Henry Laurens—merchant, president of the Council of Safety, ambassador to Holland, opponent of slavery. He once laid out four acres, in what was then Ansonborough, with domestic and rare plants. He had olives, capers, limes, ginger, strawberries, raspberries, blue grapes, and so forth. That was in 1755, and his garden was away out of town. Even in 1743, there was a farm at the corner of Broad and King Streets, the property of a gentleman with the Christmassy name of Hollybush. And the French botanist, André Michaux, spent ten years in Charleston, collecting and propagating plants for the French government. He bought one hundred and twenty acres, near the site of the present Municipal Airport, and developed a botanic garden there.

Before we discuss the great gardens outside the town, mention should be made of Hampton Park, which is handsomely planted, and of the historic Magnolia Cemetery where Charleston's Confederate dead were buried.

As for the garden showplaces, Magnolia Gardens and Middleton Place, both are world-famous and rightly so. Charleston, for all its reputed self-sufficiency, is reasonably grateful for approval, and is proud of the fact that in the Baedekers of pre-war times Magnolia Gardens was one of the only three spots in the United States which received the coveted highest rating. Guidebooks point out, too, that at Kew Gardens in London a sign advises the traveler that the most glorious azaleas are to be found in Magnolia Gardens near Charleston, "in the United States." If you want to know what some others have said about them, look in Owen Wister's novel *Lady Baltimore* and in the July issue of the old *Century Magazine* (1921) in which John Galsworthy fairly let himself go.

I suppose many gardens have been the cause of a sore throat or have been blamed for it. Magnolia Gardens, however, is the result of a sore throat. The sore throat in question belonged to the Reverend Mr. John Grimké Drayton. The Reverend Mr. Drayton's physician advised him to abandon holy orders and to live more in the open. He had inherited his grandfather's estate, Magnolia on the Ashley, which had come down from Thomas Drayton, who arrived in South Carolina in 1671 and married the daughter of Stephen Fox, owner of a vast tract of land of which Magnolia was only a portion. So, in the early 1840's, the Reverend Mr. Drayton began to plant the *Azalea indica,* a recent importation, and introduced the *Camellia japonica,* of which there are now more than three hundred varieties in the gardens.

To enjoy the result of his enthusiasm, the visitor has only to take a pleasant short ride along U.S. 17 after crossing the Ashley River via the new Memorial Bridge, and then turn into State Road 61. This trip leads past the site of the first settlement, Albemarle Point, and into the rice country. You speed along under the somber overhanging Spanish moss, which droops beardlike from the great oaks, and which was once thought to be a source of malaria, until you come to a fairly conspicuous sign. You turn into a commodious parking area after buying your tickets, and you enter the gardens without any fuss at all, surrender your ticket, and follow the route marked out by small wooden signs. The Reverend Mr. Drayton's taste was in favor of what I suppose would be called contour gardening, in contrast to the formal ordering of plots which had come to England by way of France and Holland, and the twenty-five acres of Magnolia Gardens are laid out in winding lanes and banks of azaleas along the lake which reflects them like a great glass. To avoid rhetoric, which is a temptation here, let us simply say that the effect is overpowering in its richness and splendor and perhaps just a trifle monotonous in the arrangement of vistas. It was my impression that you couldn't see far enough from most points, so that you were in a mass of flowers most of the time. The walks are carefully marked for the most efficient route, or you might spend a good deal of time finding your way out—unless you did the unspeakable and cut across the plantings.

Azaleas are, of course, the glory of these gardens, with the *Camellia japonica* a close second, but these two flowering shrubs did not exhaust the enthusiasm of the founder of the plantings. The botanical-minded will find this a happy hunting ground. Cryptomeria, such trees as the magnolia from which the spot is named, California redwood, Chinese yew, long-leaf pine, and cypress are among the many varieties of native and exotic growths, not to mention the ever-present live oaks and their festoons of Spanish moss. The sights here are almost wholly horticultural, but there is, down by the river's edge, an elaborate marble tomb of one of the Drayton family who lost his life in a hunting accident. The sculpture is the work of an Italian artist, brought to this country by Robert Morris to carve ornaments for his own residence, sometimes referred to as "Morris's Folly." And although this is merely incidental, there *is* the sort of quiet here that broods over a cemetery; the only sound is the occasional subdued laughter of one of the groups of Negro caretakers who are forever removing fallen leaves and petals from the beds and walks, keeping the entire twenty-five acres in a state of perpetual neatness that would do credit to the tiniest of front yards.

Middleton Place, which is reached along the same route as Magnolia Gardens, has landscapes considerably older than the latter's. The lands of which it is a part were originally granted in the seventeenth century to the Williams family, but it soon after passed to the Middletons and has been owned by them and their descendants ever since.

The gardens were begun early in the life of the plantation, but the formal landscaping that has made them famous dates back to 1740, very shortly after the building of the great house. At that time Henry Middleton, later president of the Continental Congress, imported a European landscapist, a disciple of Petin. The landscape artist and a hundred slaves spent nine years in the completion of the walks, terraces, lakes, and rivulets, and here is certainly one case where what Veblen would have called "conspicuous consumption" appears to have been well worth the cost. Later, it is believed, André Michaux had a hand in the establishment of the *Camellia japonica,* for whose introduction to the continent of North

America he was largely responsible, and tradition adds that three of the four plants he himself set out are still living.

The estate is set upon a low bluff which slopes down to the waters of the Ashley River, and the visitor enters the gardens by way of the ruined steps of the house, of which only the south flanker, used as a residence by the present owners, remains. This wing repays a good look for its curiously rounded gables and the chimneys which emerge from the center of the peak of the roof. It is part of the addition made by Henry Middleton in 1755.

Arthur Middleton, one of the signers of the Declaration of Independence, seems to have cared little for the house which passed into his hands and in whose gardens he lies buried under a great tomb. The story is that one day, while he was out walking in the gardens, the message was brought to him that the house was afire and that, although the flankers were safe, the original part in the center was endangered. Satisfied, he remarked, with that classical calm which is probably to be attributed to eighteenth-century education, "Let it burn," and went on walking among his flowers. However, the house was saved, for a time. It escaped with only slight damage from the customary British vandalism when it was occupied during the Revolution; the invaders left the building intact after ruining furniture and works of art. The continentals also occupied it, and it was the scene of the negotiations for the final departure of the British from the colony. The Federal troops, in the course of General Sherman's famous tour, put the torch to the hall. The remaining south flanker was rebuilt in 1868 and has since been restored and modernized.

From the old steps the sightseer gazes down on the magnificent symmetrical terraces which lead down to the "butterfly lakes" and the plantation dock. The effect is extraordinary in its sweep and grace, and no less striking when seen from the river end, looking up. For Middleton Place Gardens, though

richly sown with roses, azaleas and camellias, impress chiefly
by their symmetry. At the extreme south end is an old rice
mill. At the northeast end are formal gardens, one in the form
of a wheel, the vast "Great Oak," a Methuselah among trees,
and the tomb of Arthur Middleton, surmounted by his arms.
At the northern end of the gardens is a great rectangular reflection pool, adjacent to which, and at right angles, is a
smaller, irregularly shaped one. Whoever was responsible for
the designing (one tradition says that the original landscape
architect was an Englishman, an ancestor of the novelist William Gilmore Simms) must have been thoroughly satisfied
when he surveyed his creation. Imagination must serve for an
idea of how the terraces looked when the entire house, with
its three detached parts, stood above them. If I had to make
a choice between Magnolia Gardens and these completely different formal ones, I believe Middleton Place would win by
a narrow margin. But fortunately one does not have to arrive
at such a decision. It would be a pity to miss the sight of either.

And, since we are now on the subject of gardens, we ought
to leap over to the Cooper River country for a few moments.
Here, on U.S. Route 52, twenty-four miles north of Charleston, are the Cypress Gardens. As Magnolia differs from Middleton Place, so do the Cypress Gardens differ from both the
others.

They are a strange and beautiful sight; endless acres of
black water, stained by the innumerable cypresses which
stand sentinel over them, reflect, as in a mirror of black
marble, the great swollen-kneed cypresses; the garlands of
Spanish moss; azaleas, camellias, *Daphne odora,* narcissus,
lilies, iris, daffodils—the flowers, of course, depending upon
the earliness of the season. As a skilful young Negro boatman
guides you among the innumerable trees, you feel as if you
were floating in a vast pool of ink, and if you entertain morbid
fancies as you glide along, that is understandable.

Cypress Gardens is a modern development. The lake, originally a fresh body of water, was later used to flood the adjoining rice fields but was abandoned years before the Civil
War. Its present use was the idea of a New Yorker, Benjamin
Kittredge, who acquired the property in the early years of this
century. He is one of a fairly large group of non-Charles-
tonians who have been active in restoring the beauty of neglected and crumbling plantations of the Low Country. But that
is another story and we shall speak of it later. Mr. Kittredge
has provided travelers to the Low Country with their very
oddest experience, one as far removed from the Georgian and
Palladian stateliness of old Charleston as could be conceived.

CHAPTER THREE

Beginnings

The most superficial description of Charleston would not go very far before it began to allude to the facts of history. At every turn the describer would find himself saying that this place belonged to so-and-so, who did this or that in some critical period of America's development. So let us briefly review that history. And, though they have left no actual traces, we must, in order to understand the struggles of the colony, first take a look at the Spanish and French attempts to gain a foothold in the region.

The Spaniards considered the coasts of what are now Georgia and South Carolina as part of their territory of Florida. In 1526 the Spaniard Ayllón, misled by the glowing reports of his scouts, came with a fleet and a patent to settle Chicora, "the land of the giant King." He attempted a settlement at the mouth of the Peedee (some say Santee) River. A severe winter and the resulting privations were fatal to many, and when Ayllón died, the leaderless and hungry remainder began to quarrel. They had brought Negro slaves from the West Indies (evil omen!) and these set fire to the houses. When fewer than a third of the original complement were left alive, it was decided to abandon the colony. A number of the company froze to death on their ships, and the vessel bearing Ayllón's body sank. A miserable relic of the settlers finally reached the West Indies, a sad ending to the first attempt at colonization in the South Carolina that was to be.

In 1540 the ill-fated De Soto, on the march through Florida and Georgia, was told by the Indians, who probably wanted to get rid of him, that not far distant was a land of gold ruled by a beautiful Indian "queen." Crossing the Savannah River, the expedition reached what is apparently the present Silver Bluff and were cordially received by the *cacica* and her people. (There is a charming reconstruction of the scene in the Charleston Museum.) The *cacica* gave De Soto a pearl necklace and told him of many more like it—at a distance.

De Soto overruled his men, who would have stayed out their welcome, and set off. Spanish fashion (or shall we simply say white fashion) he repaid the generous *cacica* by forcing her to go along as guide—"not a proper return" for her hospitality, remarks the Gentleman of Elvas in his narrative. She later escaped.

Since there was no gold to be found, the Spaniards were not interested in settling this part of the New World, and the French took the lead in the attempt to do so. In 1562, the French Huguenots having decided to seek a refuge from persecution along this coast, Admiral Coligny sent Jean Ribaut to found a settlement there. Ribaut came to the magnificent harbor which he called Port Royal, and on Parris Island, site of the present Marine Base, he built a little fort which he named Charlesfort after the King of France. On nearby Lemon Island he set up a stone marker, brought from France for the purpose, and leaving a detachment to preserve his French majesty's new possession intact, returned to his troubled country.

The colony did not prosper. Even in this fertile land, the men neglected farming in favor of cadging food from the

Indians. When fire destroyed the provisions Ribaut had left, they quarreled. Their captain hanged one rebellious soldier and sent another to a desert island to starve. The band mutinied, murdered the captain, and rescued their comrade.

Food ran short, and when the Indians rationed their gifts, the Frenchmen resolved to decamp. They contrived a clumsy vessel, caulked it with Spanish moss and rosin, and made sails for it of their linen. To speed the parting guests, the Indians furnished rope made from bark and a supply of food. All set sail except a youngster named Guillaume Rufin, who with true French canniness chose the company of the Indians in preference to a voyage in the wretched *bateau* his mates had assembled.

The sequel proved that Rufin was no fool. The ship was promptly becalmed, and yawed about for some three weeks, taking in water at a great rate while the crew were slowly starving. Finally the soldier they had rescued suggested the last resort of castaways. By an odd turn of fate the lots fell to him, and the gallant fellow promptly cut his own throat. This ghastly expedient enabled the ship's company to survive until they were picked up, shortly afterward, by an English vessel.

The idea of a French settlement in his dominions—and Protestant French, too—did not set well with Philip the Second of Spain. He ordered the Governor of Cuba to do something about it. Don Hernando Manrique de Rojas was sent to oust Ribaut. He found only the boy Rufin, whom he took with him after burning Charlesfort.

Meanwhile, Ribaut had been unable to return. Before the news of the colony's fate had reached France, Coligny sent René Laudonnière with three ships to relieve it. Laudonnière settled on the St. John's River in Florida, built Fort Caroline, and called the surrounding country *Carolana,* a pronunciation still preserved outside of Charleston. Laudonnière was not very discreet, and was soon in trouble with the Indians. His men complained, and in 1564 Ribaut was sent back. Just before he left, Coligny informed him that Philip the Second, not wholly out of patience, had sent the adventurer Pedro Menendez de Avilés to wipe out the French settlement and to replace it.

Menendez, who was to be made governor of a huge territory, sailed from Cadiz with a fully equipped expedition, numbering in all over 2,500. Arriving near St. Augustine, he gave that name to the spot and sailed after Ribaut. Ribaut defied him and fled. Menendez returned to the site of St. Augustine, and founded the settlement there, where Ribaut decided to attack him. Ribaut's ships were blown out to sea, whereupon Menendez made for Fort Caroline, butchered Laudonnière and his men, and when on his way back he found more of the French cast ashore, murdered them too, except for a few Catholics. Ribaut and the rest of his force, halted in their march overland by an unforeseen inlet, were caught and treated as the other "Lutherans" had been.

A fiery Gascon, the Chevalier de Gourgues, set out to avenge his countrymen, and did so; but he made no settlement. Menendez built Fort San Felipe on the site of the former Charlesfort, and there, harassed by hostile Indians, a Spanish garrison hung on for ten years, always hoping for gold. After most of the males had been massacred by the natives, the survivors sailed away to St. Augustine, and the red men put the torch to San Felipe.

But Philip the Second, like that famous editor whose reporter was flung down a flight of stairs, was not to be intimidated. He gave orders for the building of a bigger fort, and his orders were obeyed. Fort San Marcos was the result. The Indians thereafter were held off, but the king, having had his way, wearied of the whole business. He had too many other troubles on his hands dealing with England and France, and

Fort San Marcos was the victim of a cut in the imperial budget.

This was the last effort at Spanish colonization in South Carolina. We are decidedly not through with the Spaniards and French, but it is now time to skip the better part of a century and follow the fortunes of the English settlers.

The unfortunate Charles the First had, in the year 1629, granted to Sir Robert Heath a large tract of territory in the New World south of Virginia. After the Restoration, Charles the Second, by the Grace of God King of England, Scotland, and Ireland, anxious and obliged to reward several gentlemen who had aided him to regain his throne, was persuaded to abolish the old grant and to make a new one.

The two chief factors leading to the arrangement were the desire of certain English noblemen to establish a post for trading with the West Indies, and the fact that Barbados, home of a prosperous slave-holding colony of planters, was becoming too small for its population. There was need of new land. Sir John Colleton and his friend Anthony Ashley Cooper, first Baron Ashley and later the first Earl of Shaftesbury, discussed the possibility of obtaining a grant of such lands, and with the aid of influential persons convinced the king that a settlement on the coast of Carolina would be a profitable investment. His majesty thereupon entered into an agreement with eight gentlemen—Anthony Ashley Cooper, who, after various changes of allegiance, died in exile in 1683; the Duke of Albemarle, otherwise the famous General George Monk, who had fought for the Crown in the Civil War, been imprisoned, served Parliament and the Cromwells, and then become instrumental in the restoration of the throne; the Earl of Clarendon, father-in-law of James II and grandfather of two queens, Mary and Anne; also the Earl of Craven, Lord Berkeley, Sir William Berkeley, Sir John Colleton, and Sir George Carteret, hereinafter the Lords Proprietors.

The grant was surely one of the great real estate transactions of our era. It gave to these eight men a tract of land extending from the southern boundary of Virginia to the mouth of the St. John's River, and westward to "the South Seas," in other words, to the Pacific Ocean. That was in 1663. Arrangements were immediately made in Barbados to send out an exploring party, and Captain William Hilton, who has given his name to Hilton's Head, looked things over and reported favorably on what he found. The Barbadians were ready and willing, but the Proprietors wanted more latitude, figuratively and literally. They wanted some hundred miles more north and south, and the right to re-divide the grant at their own discretion.

The parley dragged on, and it was 1665 before the terms were agreed upon, although a year before that the Barbadians had essayed a small settlement at the mouth of the Cape Fear River. In 1665, however, the newly knighted Sir John Yeamans was commissioned Governor of Carolina and sent from Barbados to explore the Carolina coast and establish a colony there. With fewer than a hundred men, Yeamans set out. He found the Cape Fear settlers in trouble and tried to help them —in vain, for after two years they were to abandon the settlement—and then, empowering Robert Sandford to do the exploring for him, he returned to Barbados.

Sandford, whose report was just as favorable as Hilton's, stopped at the harbor of Port Royal and recommended it as the place for the settlement. A young surgeon in his company, Henry Woodward, took the notion to be left behind with the Indians in order that he might learn their language and lay the foundations for friendship and trade. This he did, after many vicissitudes, and was a tremendous help to the early colonists.

Woodward's desire to remain with the red men coincided with the wish of the Indian cacique to send his nephew away

with the white men, and Sandford left him as a kind of hostage
for the young Indian, whose mother was generously included
in the transaction as Woodward's squaw. Woodward was just
becoming acclimated when the Spaniards got wind of his presence and set out to capture him. They locked him up in St.
Augustine, and but for the fortunate intervention of the English buccaneer Searles, who was plying his trade in the vicinity,
they might have kept him there indefinitely. Searles raided
St. Augustine and set Woodward free, and Woodward signed
up as surgeon on a privateer in the hope of either making his
way back to the mother country or to Barbados; but instead
it was his fate to roam up and down the seas until, in the year
1669, he was cast ashore on the island of Nevis in the West
Indies.

Meanwhile the character of the future colony had been affected by a change of attitude on the part of the Barbados
gentlemen. They had become actively interested in the possibilities of Jamaica, wrested from the Spaniards in the time of
Cromwell, and they had lost a great deal of their interest in
the Carolina proposition. It became apparent to Ashley that
outfitting a voluntary company was going to be difficult. Carolina, under the terms of the grant, had to be settled immediately, and Ashley sought a plan to add to the attractiveness
of participation. It is not difficult to imagine him falling back
on his Virgil and muttering *"tantae molis erat...."* This, at
any rate, was his suggestion:

The charter expressly forbade the use of English titles in
the colony. Why not create new ones—barons, cassiques, and
landgraves? Each Proprietor would have 96,000 acres or
eight "baronies"; a landgrave would have 48,000, and a cas-
sique 24,000 acres. At a penny an acre, this ought to attract
title-hunters and prevent the growth of "a too numerous
democracy."

The Proprietors agreed to the suggestion, and a "funda-

THE COLLEGE OF CHARLESTON : LODGE AND CENTRAL
PORTICO

GRACE CHURCH: LOOKING EAST ON WENTWORTH STREET

mental constitution" was drawn up. It is one of the little surprises of history that the man who did the drawing up, then Ashley's secretary, was the later famous philosopher John Locke. There is, by the way, a contemporary facsimile of the document in the Charleston Library.

These titles, be it said to the credit of the colonists' sense of humor, did not persist overlong, although the expression "barony" is still used in reference to some famous old holdings. The "aristocracy" of South Carolina was self-made, but not by the purchase of fancy titles. Fortunes grew rapidly in the New World, and good wine needed no bush. It was not long before some of the early settlers, by means of trade and planting, had built up a residue of wealth and had fine houses and a retinue of servants; they sent their sons to England to acquire an education. Obviously a great many of them were very superior people, and with the aid of leisure and wealth they developed, under the aegis of the mother country, a culture which, if derivative and synthetic in many of its aspects, was nevertheless considerable. This is not meant as a sneer at the origins of Charleston or of South Carolina either, but is just for the purpose of clearing the air and avoiding the suggestion, still prevalent, that since the Proprietors were cavaliers and the result of their undertaking was a polished civilization, a group of bewigged and richly attired noblemen had set up the first colony in South Carolina. W. J. Cash, who wrote *The Mind of the South,* says plainly that the myth of Southern aristocracy by descent was a myth and nothing else; and in his biography of John Rutledge, "dictator" of South Carolina during the Revolutionary War and one of the chief designers of the Constitution, Richard Barry asserts: "No one of noble birth, legitimate or illegitimate (unless one of the rumors about Nicholas Trott was true) ever lived in South Carolina." But the common-sense evidence in the matter is one of the strongest points. The coast of Carolina, mild though the climate was by comparison, was no place for anyone without a strong back and a hard hand. And that fear of the Proprietors concerning "a too numerous democracy" must have had something behind it. Not that there were not gentlemen among those first settlers; the handful of Barbadians, for instance, who built the earliest plantations. But many were indentured servants.

Returning to our entrepreneurs, each of the Proprietors put up five hundred pounds sterling, which considering the richness of the colony's possibilities seems an inexpensive way of getting in on the ground floor, and an expedition was prepared in London. Three vessels, the *Carolina,* the *Albemarle,* and the *Port Royal,* were outfitted, and in 1669 they set sail, with a company of one hundred and fifty colonists, for the coast of Carolina, with Barbados as a first stop. Joseph West was in charge; he bore a blank commission which Sir John Yeamans might either take up for himself or assign to some one he deemed fit to be governor. Yeamans once more backed out. He commissioned as governor William Sayle. Sayle was then about eighty years old and had been governor of Bermuda; he was a hasty choice.

In the harbor at Barbados, the ships had been separated by a storm which crippled the *Carolina* and the *Port Royal* and drove the *Albemarle* on the rocks. It had to be replaced by *The Three Brothers,* and it was December of that year before the ships again set out. Forced by another storm to seek shelter, the ships put in at Nevis, and there, dramatically enough for any taste, they found Woodward. After another storm had driven *The Three Brothers* to the coast of Virginia, the battered colonists at long last reached Carolina at what is now called Bulls Bay, some twenty miles north of Charleston harbor, and then sailed down to Port Royal. It was March, 1670, and they had been on their way since the previous summer.

Even at Port Royal their wanderings were not at an end.

The friendly cacique of Kiawah met them there and advised a settlement farther to the north. He warned them against the Indians in the vicinity of Port Royal, and assured them that they would find friendly red men and a greater measure of safety from the Spaniards if they would choose a point on the Kiawah (Ashley) River. His advice was taken, and a town was laid out at Albemarle Point on the west bank. Approximately opposite the new Citadel, the site is the one you pass close by on your way to Magnolia Gardens. Its marks probably the last time Charlestonians took any outsider's advice about anything.

Albemarle Point was hurriedly fortified and then gardens were planted, for the length of the journey had reduced the ships' stores. Henry Woodward went into the interior to establish relations with the Indians and to lay the foundation for the Indian trade, one of the colonists' first sources of income and one which was to add a picturesque note to the early life of Charles Town. Then two of the ships left to fetch settlers and provisions—the *Carolina* set sail for Virginia and *The Three Brothers* for Bermuda.

The Spaniards were not of a mind to take this intrusion lying down, and the departure of the ships gave them their opportunity. They came down like a wolf on the fold, but their Indian supporters were terrified by the colonists' little cannon; and the arrival of the *Carolina* in the very nick of time persuading the Spaniards to think better of what they had set out to do, they prudently retreated.

It did not take the colonists long to realize that they had come to Canaan, if early reports, which of course were partly aimed at luring more settlers, are to be believed. These early documents fairly glow with accounts of fertile soil, easy crops, variety of timber and game and fish. There were three shortcomings, chiefly: the hostile Indians, the envious Spaniards, and the Lords Proprietors, who from the first casually discounted the other two. These handicaps were not to be despised, but it does seem odd that in this land of plenty the colonists had for a while to depend on shipments of food. Many things were yet to be done, but the new settlement was on its way. The Church of England was immediately established, and thus the ground was prepared for what Ellen Glasgow, in speaking of certain Virginians, called "a rich Episcopalian flavor."

Governor Sayle was old and feeble, and before the year was out he was dead. His lieutenant, Joseph West, was an able man; he now took over for the first of three stints of substitution, in which he acquitted himself well. He was the logical candidate for the official commission, but the Barbadian planters had now begun to flock to the colony they had earlier neglected, and their influence became strong enough to bring about the appointment of Sir John Yeamans, who assumed office in March of 1672. It is worthy of note that he brought a batch of Negro slaves with him—there had been only four in the first ships.

Yeamans was not popular, and he had plenty of trouble with the colonists for the rest of his brief remaining life, but before his death in 1674 he had laid out the new settlement on the neck of land between the Etiwan River, renamed the Cooper, and the Ashley, and which was then known as Oyster Point. The land for the new site was surrendered to the council by one John Coming and his wife Affra. Ten years actually elapsed before the colonists, under West's guidance, occupied the permanent site of their city of Charles Town, but Yeamans lived long enough to be scolded by the Proprietors for the amount of money he had put into laying out the new site. There was no pleasing the Lords Proprietors, from the very first.

It is possible to see at this point two of the germs of the future of South Carolina; the attempt to avoid "a too numer-

ous democracy" by the bestowal of titles and by such provisions in the charter as that forbidding lawyers to charge a
fee, thus keeping the law on an aristocratic basis of *noblesse
oblige*—and at the same time a determination to run things
their own way, and be independent. Indeed, it might almost be
said of the colonists, as Chesterton said of his younger
brother, that they "immediately began to argue"; but right
was on their side. The Lords Proprietors, to state the case
mildly, had no adequate notion of the difficulties involved.
They grumbled at the expenditure of a few pounds and the
failure of the colonists to send lumber as agreed, whereupon
the colonists replied sharply that they were too busy with the
Indians, the Spaniards, and their crops to be bothered. When
the Proprietors cut off the shipment of food, the settlers
rioted; Yeamans, to pacify them, sent two ships for food, and
the watchful Spaniards once more attacked. But, as before,
they were driven off by the providential appearance of the
ships. West finally mollified the Proprietors—for a time—and
the colonists went on laying the foundations of their fortunes.

More settlers came; there were Quakers, taking advantage
of the freedom of worship allowed all Protestant faiths. And
the Huguenots, having failed over a century before to effect
a settlement, came now and rooted themselves forever.

Charleston is considered an excessively clannish city, and
perhaps that is true now. One of the numerous stories told
at the town's expense, and probably, like all good stories of
the sort, the invention of a native, is that many years ago a
ten-year-old boy was brought there. He grew up into a man,
took his place in the community with some distinction, and
found the salubrious atmosphere (Chamber of Commerce
please note) so favorable to his well-being that he was well
into his eighties before he breathed the last of it. When he
was buried with proper ceremony, a headstone was erected
over his grave. The inscription recited in detail all the interest-

ing facts of his long career in his adopted city, and then, in a burst of approval, added: "Our Most Beloved Stranger."

It's a good story, but that headstone, like the grave of Rhett Butler, is one of the things you will seek in vain in Charleston. For the city has received a good many strangers and assimilated them. And that's the reason why you will probably also look in vain for a pure Anglo-Saxon Charlestonian of one of the old families.

The Huguenots were the first of these exotic groups to mingle with the original English blood of the settlers; there were some very early Dutch importations, too. And so it is that an architecture of French and Dutch influence sprang up in the Low Country, and that to this day visitors are surprised at the prevalence of names that have apparently no place in an Anglo-Saxon community. Ruthlessly anglicized for the most part, these names give an individual air to Charleston's nomenclature. There is, for instance, Legaré, which is pronounced like the name of the rascally overseer in *Uncle Tom's Cabin;* Gaillard, which is "gill'yard"; DeSaussure, which is "des'as so'," with the heavier accent on the first syllable; Huger, which is "you gee." On the other hand, Ravenel and Porcher are pronounced in the French manner, as is Horry, which sounds like "o ree." This French tinge is not always reliable in indicating origins—for instance, the case of an Irish name like DeVeaux, or a Walloon one like Mazÿck; and other French names entered late in the eighteenth century with the coming of the Santo Domingan refugees. But that is ahead of our story.

The point is that these Huguenots grafted themselves so securely on the Charleston family trees that you will scarcely find one of the old families without a Huguenot branch. They founded a church as early as 1681, when the new settlement on the present site was just a year old; and they took part in government after a brief interval of non-recognition. Even the Dissenters and Baptists faced loss of their office-holding privileges when in 1704 an attempt was made to pass a new religious act requiring all members of the Commons to be Episcopalians. This blew over, after a stormy period in which Dr. Marston, rector of St. Philip's, protested so violently that he lost his charge as a consequence; but this was the last crisis of its kind. However, it was to have later repercussions.

An example of the impractical notions of the Proprietors may be derived from their instructions for the setting out of the new town. They called for at least "six score squares of three hundred feet" and a chief street one hundred and twenty feet broad, with lesser streets a minimum of sixty feet wide. Anyone who cares to compare these figures with the original streets, which included Broad, Elliott, Tradd, Church and Stoll's Alley, will infer that West apparently acted on the principle that what the Proprietors did not know would not hurt them. It is said, however, that the streets were not narrow for their time. Indeed, the same Thomas Ashe of the *Richmond* whom we have quoted earlier described the town as "regularly laid out in broad and capacious streets."

The new site was on low land, irregularly broken by creeks and marshes which gave some of the city's streets their odd breaks and winding turns. In the eighteenth century it was still possible for a boy to swim along Vanderhorst's Creek to Broad and Meeting Streets where the City Hall now stands; and when Lord William Campbell, the last Royal governor, fled from the house at 34 Meeting Street when he saw that the time had come, he did so by stepping into a boat that had come up a part of Vanderhorst Creek and was virtually in the back yard of the house. Much of the topographical history of Charleston is one of reclamation; one of the most spectacular feats of this kind was the filling in of the marshy area south of the city which is now known as Murray Boulevard.

But, as will be seen, many governors had their troubles long before Campbell, Yeamans having, so to speak, set a precedent. It happened that the new settlers had included a large group of Scots Dissenters, and this group had become so strong in the colony that the Proprietors were led to replace West with Joseph Morton, one of the Dissenter chiefs. This was ungrateful to West; but here, as in other ways, the Proprietors were unacquainted with the temper of the colonists. The latter made good use of the Commons House established under the constitution to fight for their rights. Morton lasted only two years; the Irish nobleman appointed to succeed him lived only a month; the settlers' Council chose one man and the Proprietors, refusing to confirm him, reappointed West. He also found the going difficult, resigned, and left the province. Dominated by the Dissenters, the Council now chose Morton and the Proprietors consented, only to replace him a year later with Sir James Colleton, son of one of the original eight Lords Proprietors.

The new governor arrived with the handicap of having been preceded one year before by the king's tax collector, sent to make sure that the colonists shipped their goods only in English vessels and paid duties on imports. This official had been distinctly *persona non grata;* there were twenty-five hundred of the colonists now, and they were becoming rich and feeling their oats. And there was trouble afoot. A band of Scots had attempted a settlement at Port Royal and from the first had irritated the settlers by interfering with the town's Indian trade. They made the further mistake of stirring up the Indians against the Spaniards; and the Spaniards retaliated by razing the Scotch settlement, Stuart Town. They then came north and scoured Edisto Island, but the settlers' blood was up and the Spaniards were forced to retreat. The people of Charles Town determined to retaliate and organized an expedition against the Spaniards under the command of James

Moore. In the midst of preparations for departure, enter Sir James Colleton; and one of his first official acts was to put his foot down and forbid the expedition.

Colleton, not unlike a number of governing Englishmen then and later, was sure of himself and impatient of advice. He attempted to thrust his instructions down the throats of the colonists, and the councils opposed him until he resolved not to call any more of them. The result of this failure to reach a meeting of minds was a state of anarchy during the tenure of which laws expired, tax collections came to a dead stop, and the fiscal affairs of the colony were in a mess. With the backing of a few supporters in the form of a petition, Colleton called out the militia and the militia ignored him. The petitioners immediately lost their enthusiasm and withdrew their signatures.

At this juncture revolution was averted by the arrival of Set Sothell, who had bought out one of the original Proprietors, and who, according to the constitution, stood above the governor when in the colony. Sothell took over the authority from Colleton; he called an assembly and the assembly promptly banished the governor. But the colonists put up with Sothell only briefly. Accused of graft, he was succeeded by Philip Ludwell, who may be said to have married into his position by espousing the widow of Sir William Berkeley, another of the original eight grantees.

Ludwell reorganized the voting by counties, and this is significant for two reasons. First, it recognized the right of the Huguenots to vote; and second, it stirred up the Commons, who, irritated at what they considered an unfair disposition of the votes, passed a resolution embodying the grievances of the settlers—America's earliest Bill of Rights.

After a brief stay Ludwell was succeeded by Landgrave Smith, who lived only a short while. (The mortality among governors was high.) When Smith died in 1694, Joseph Blake was elected. He took one good look at the situation and appealed to the Proprietors to send one of their own number. They complied by sending Sir John Archdale to pour oil on the troubled waters. Archdale seems to have been a man of sense and ability, and he succeeded in his mission, although his readjustment of the voting by counties once more excluded the Huguenots. Blake succeeded him, first as his deputy and then by buying him out; and he brought about the naturalization of the Huguenots in 1697, eleven years after the main body had arrived.

The remainder of the century was politically uneventful. The colony's economy was beginning to take a very definite shape. The Indian trade flourished, and skins in great numbers were shipped to England. A few years earlier Henry Woodward had introduced the planting of rice, and this crop had begun to assume major importance, as had its corollary, slavery. The harbor was full of ships; freebooters spent money lavishly; there was prosperity on every hand. The Commons allotted the funds for a free library, the first of its kind in America.

However, the end of the century brought other troubles worse than bungling overlordship. There were bad outbreaks of smallpox, malaria and yellow fever, and the first of the great natural catastrophes which were to afflict the city arrived in the shape of a tremendous storm, which blew down houses right and left and flung the sea over the town. Fatalities were few, but the population had been greatly reduced and weakened by the fevers and there was open discouragement. It is said that the settlers would have removed to Philadelphia had it not been for the fact that yellow fever was raging there, too.

In the new century warfare occupied the colony. France was pushing her interests in the New World, and the Spaniards continued to threaten. James Moore had been elected governor in 1700. He was a man of decision and action. When

the Spaniards and French along the Mississippi joined forces
to move against the Carolinians, Moore determined to beat
them to the draw. A force was sent by land against St. Augustine, and Moore, with a small fleet, undertook to conduct the
siege by sea. His cannon, however, were too small to have any
effect on the new fort—which Colleton's stupid meddling,
years earlier, had given the Spaniards a chance to finish; and
after two months, sighting two Spanish vessels off the coast,
he decided to let well enough alone, burnt his ships, and returned to Charleston overland.

Moore naturally wanted to recover the loss of prestige
which had resulted from the failure of his expedition; but as
Colleton had handicapped him once, so his election (he was a
Churchman) over the head of the powerful Dissenter Morton
retarded him now. The Dissenters spiked his guns by staying
away from the Commons meeting that was to vote the funds
for another expedition. Fortunately, his successor as governor,
Sir Nathaniel Johnson, supported him; and Moore was able to
produce eyewitnesses of French and Spanish activities along
the Mississippi whose testimony frightened the Commons into
asking the governor for action. After considerable bickering,
Moore, whose heart was in this thing, resolved to spend his
own money. Collecting a handful of white men and about a
thousand of the friendly Creek Indians, he thoroughly quelled
the Apalachees whom the Spaniards had incited.

Governor Johnson was now aware that a crisis was approaching. He enlarged the fortifications around the town and
built a new fort on James Island, the original of that Fort
Johnson from which the first shot was fired on Fort Sumter.
Lookouts were posted on Sullivan's Island. In August of that
year, 1706, they gave warning that a fleet of enemy ships was
in the offing. Another of those attacks of yellow fever had left
the city's manpower weakened, but everyone who was able
sprang to the defense. Colonel William Rhett made his first

mark in history by sailing out to meet them with a fleet of six vessels, captured one enemy ship, and drove the others away. French and Spanish soldiers who had been landed were captured, and the city rejoiced at its first major victory. The brave Moore was a victim of the yellow fever, and it is of record that he died penniless.

The first extant architectural landmark of Charleston dates from this uneasy period—the quaint little powder magazine on Cumberland Street, built in 1703.

Meanwhile, the French had continued to press their advantages with the Indians. In 1711 the Tuscaroras broke loose in North Carolina and butchered several hundred of the settlers there. Colonel John Barnwell set out at the head of a force to aid the young sister colony, had some small success, and effected a peace. He had been wounded, and when he was still convalescing at home, the Tuscaroras erupted again. The governor at that time was a man who rejoiced in the inauspicious name of Craven, but he stirred up the Assembly to do something about it. Another force, under the leadership of James Moore, son of the Indian fighter, expelled the Tuscaroras from North Carolina. The Indian traders breathed more freely for a bit.

However, it was the Indian trade, naturally, that was responsible for these bloodlettings. Anyone wanting a good proof that warfare is economic need look no farther. The westward push of the Carolina traders irked the French on the Mississippi, the Spanish were allied with them in resisting further encroachment, and worse still, the trade itself contained the seeds of trouble. Enslaving the Indians was expressly forbidden, but the business was profitable and the temptation was great. What was more natural than that unscrupulous traders would keep the tribal pot boiling, so that they could buy the captives from the victors and send them into slavery? As late as the nineteenth century this led to an Indian uprising. It is, by the way, one of the ironies of history that these Indian captives were sent into slavery not only to the West Indies but to New England.

Credit was another cause of trouble. The laws forbade the extending of credit to the Indians, except with the consent of a chief, but there were probably many ways around this. The Indians, very humanly, disliked those to whom they owed money.

The Spanish and French were acute enough to take advantage of these grievances to stir up the red men. Finally, the suspicion and hatred they had inspired in the Indians broke forth in the formidable Yemassee War. The Creeks had hitherto been friendly, but now they and the remnant of the Apalachees joined the Yemassees. They massacred ninety settlers at Pocotaligo, not far from Charles Town, and instantly there were thousands of them on the warpath. Refugees, on the way to safety in Charles Town, choked the lanes and roads. Governor Craven himself joined in the march against the Yemassees and solicited help from North Carolina and Virginia, which came, too little and too late. The British could not send aid, because the stiff-necked Lords Proprietors refused to waive jurisdiction in the colony, and this is significant as one of the counts against the Proprietors that was to lead to their downfall. For the present, however, it is sufficient to note that the Yemassees were finally subdued.

But the war with them had cost the Carolinians a good deal in men, goods, and money. The Indian trade, so profitable and so picturesque—one thinks of the packloads proceeding along Broad Street, the caravans, the Indians themselves being received at the merchants' houses and entertained—this Indian trade was ruined. South Carolina was experiencing its first economic depression.

During this emergency the Proprietors had been busy quibbling over the financial return from the colony. The long history of dissatisfactions with the Proprietors was drawing to a logical and dramatic conclusion. But first the colonists had to rid themselves of another incubus. And that was piracy.

At first the buccaneers had been at least tacitly encouraged, for they harried the rival Spanish shipping, and their money was welcome. In fact, doubloons were among the first coins used in the colony. The pirates roistered about Charles Town virtually at will—and there is a strong presumption that, when they finally cleared out, they left something besides foreign money and a feeling of relief. As their antecedents were more or less questionable, this adds a fascinating speculation to the ethnical puzzle of Charleston.

Experiments in the planting of rice had resulted so well that the grain became the prize crop of the Low Country. When shipments reached thousands of barrels per year, it became obvious that the pirates, who were meddling with the rice ships, would have to be checked.

A crisis is always needed to dramatize a struggle. The pirates finally overstepped themselves by one outrageous act, and this led to their downfall.

In the year 1718 Edward Teach, or Thatch, who under his nickname of "Blackbeard" was the bugbear of the seas, had been driven away from the Bahamas and was roaming the waters of the Atlantic outside Charleston with four vessels. He seized a ship which numbered among its passengers Councilman Samuel Wragg and his four-year-old son William, took them as hostages, and sent a boat to Charles Town with an imperious demand for medicines for the sick men of his crew. Failing to receive these, he said, he would send the heads of the captives to Charleston. The incumbent of that uneasy gubernatorial chair, Robert Johnson—"the good Governor Johnson"—had of course no alternative. He sent the medicines, but the boat was too slow in returning for the impatient Blackbeard, and he was about to butcher his prisoners when it finally hove into view. The pirate chief contented himself with robbing them and setting them ashore virtually naked, after which he sailed off northward.

The colonists were frightened, for it was no joke to have the ferocious Blackbeard around. He did not molest the city, but when shortly afterward word came that the gentleman adventurer Stede Bonnet was in Cape Fear harbor, preparing to descend on Charles Town's ships, there was action. Colonel William Rhett, who had already sallied forth against the Spaniards, equipped two vessels and started out after Bonnet. His vessels ran aground within sight of Bonnet's ship, the *Royal James,* but that night the tide floated them off. In the morning they gave chase to the pirate's vessel and Bonnet, attempting to get away, ran aground in turn. There must have been plenty of bad seamanship about in those days, for both Rhett's vessels immediately did the same thing, one of them in such a position that she was completely at the mercy of Bonnet's cannon. Against these odds Rhett and his crew fought for five hours, losing almost half their number, and then the flood tide favored Rhett. It floated his ship first, and the pirates, seeing that the jig was up, surrendered. They were taken to Charles Town and put in the old Guard House at the head of Broad Street, where the Exchange now stands.

A week before their scheduled trial, Bonnet escaped to Sullivan's Island with his captain, but Rhett took a group of men in pursuit and recaptured him. Meanwhile the city had learned that another pirate, the desperate Moody, was outside the harbor with a strongly armed ship and two hundred men. Governor Johnson, at the head of several vessels disguised as merchantmen, went forth to battle him. The ruse worked; the leader of the pirates, who turned out to be not Moody, but Richard Worley, one of the very worst of his kind, was killed with the majority of his men. Twenty-four who remained alive were brought back to be tried with Bonnet and his men.

At the trial the presiding justice was Nicholas Trott, according to some views as big a rascal as the pirates (and also the codifier of the laws of the colony) and after a thoroughly summary proceeding the lot of them were found guilty and were sentenced to be hanged. They were executed at White Point, now the Battery, and tradition has it that they were buried at a spot coinciding with the low watermark. A tablet calls the attention of the passer-by to their story.

Having accomplished this much, Governor Johnson, not for the first time, appealed to England for help in ridding the coast of the buccaneers, but this was no longer necessary, as it turned out. The power of the pirates had been broken without aid from the mother country. Their failure to provide assistance did not enhance the Proprietors' case, which was now at its worst.

In addition to financial disputes and dissatisfactions with the governors appointed by the Proprietors, the colonists had been roused by the attempt to foist that religious bill upon them at the very time when the French were preparing to attack. They had fought this bill to a finish with the aid of Daniel Defoe, whose swingeing brief persuaded the House of Lords to kill the measure; and their representative in England, Joseph Boone, at that time petitioned the Board of Trade to abolish the Proprietors' charter. The obstinacy of the Proprietors in the matter of the Indian wars added to the popular indignation.

Finally, in 1719, after the pirates had been driven out, the storm broke. Although Governor Johnson was liked and admired, the Assembly informed him that they were going to take over the government themselves, and appointed James Moore governor. The situation led to some amusing contretemps; there was, for instance, some uncertainty about who should sign such documents as wedding licenses. But Johnson did not treat it lightly. The two vessels promised as aid against

AN OLD HOUSE AND GATEWAY, LEGARÉ STREET

THE MILES BREWTON OR PRINGLE HOUSE

the pirates came tardily into the harbor, and Johnson ordered them brought up close to the city and announced that he would open fire if the rebellious citizens did not yield. Moore had mounted guns on the waterfront bastions, and his answer was a defiance. Johnson then withdrew.

The "first Revolution" was over. South Carolina had won a long political battle, the forerunner of three more struggles against unwanted government, and the reign of the Lords Proprietors had come to an end.

CHAPTER FOUR

Royal Colony

When in 1719 South Carolina exchanged the rule of the Proprietors for that of the Hanoverians, it was a colony of about 17,000 souls, of which some 10,000 were slaves. Although its trade had been severely depressed and its financial status impaired by the struggles with the Indians, its natural riches were unimpaired. Some merchants had begun to make fortunes, and the pattern of plantation life was becoming set. Such plantation houses as Mulberry, Medway, and Middleburg had been erected before the close of the seventeenth century, and John Lawson, the Surveyor General of North Carolina, who visited the colony in 1709, asserted that country life was polite and luxurious. Edward McCrady, in his history, says that society was, at the time of the ending of proprietary rule, still rather primitive. Rooms were uncarpeted, walls were of unpainted wood, and chairs had rush seats. According to Landgrave Smith, in his courting days dinner had been served at noon, and young men visited their young ladies at three and were expected to leave at six, for some families retired at seven o'clock in the winter and at eight in the summer.

Colonel Rhett had built a large and handsome house outside the town, the first beyond the town walls, in 1716. It still stands on Hasell Street, a large and imposing example of the

double house; of course it has undergone considerable alteration, some of it recent. The town had a library as early as
1698, and a free school system had been inaugurated in 1710.
As a sign of early prosperity, there were silversmiths working
in Charles Town at the end of the seventeenth century; Lucas
Stoutenburgh, one of the best known and the earliest whose
work is preserved, had just set up shop. The second St. Philip's
Church, opened for services in 1723, was an imposing edifice
with porticoes, a belfry, and a spire with two courses. It contained three aisles and was provided with an organ. Colonel
Rhett, who did not live to see it finished, gave a communion
service of silver plate which is still in use.

It is difficult to visualize the town in those years. Only the
Rhett house and the powder magazine are now left, and old
prints are muddy and disproportionate. A "platt" or map of
1725 shows that the extreme boundaries of the town were the
east side of what is now Rutledge Avenue, the south side of
the present Beaufain Street, and the East and South Batteries
of today. There were six churches, and the stores and houses
of the merchants, but nothing is left of them today. And Mrs.
Poyas, the chronicler who wrote *Days of Yore,* says that in
1731 there were between five and six hundred houses. A few
were lordly mansions, but the greater portion were apparently
"clumsy, miserable huts, constructed of wood, a frame covered
with clapboards without and plastering it with lime within,"
the lime being made from oyster shells.

The harbor was busy, the Indian trade and its caravans were
again flourishing, and the citizens were as independent as ever
when Sir Francis Nicholson, the first provisional Royal governor, took office in 1721. Nicholson was hot-tempered, pro-
fane, and intolerant of all opposition. He battled with Colonel
Rhett, who was in charge of the fortifications and such works,
he fought with the Commons and he threatened prison for the
merchants who ventured to petition against his financial ar-

rangements. Nevertheless, he improved the colony's finances, furthered preparations to protect the colony against the Indians, and encouraged education. He did not long outlast Colonel Rhett, who had died of apoplexy in the second year of his administration—there is no suggestion that Nicholson had anything directly to do with this—and when his health failed, he resigned the office in 1725.

Arthur Middleton, president of the council, then managed the affairs of the colony for five years and struggled with the financial difficulties he had inherited, handicapped by the fact that the Board of Trade was busy arranging a final settlement with the Lords Proprietors. Ten years in all elapsed before the purchase of the colony by the Crown was actually arranged, and eleven before Robert Johnson, the same who had fought the pirates and been deposed by the people, assumed office as the first official Royal governor. In his five years in office, the financial affairs of the colony were adjusted to the general satisfaction and the way was opened for prosperity. The boundaries of the colony were shrinking, for North Carolina had been lopped off in 1729, and a further slice was removed in 1732 when the colony of Georgia was established. Charles Town, unable to look forward to the trade rivalry of the twentieth century and unaware that economically it was taking a viper to its bosom, contributed liberally toward the new settlement and entertained General Oglethorpe lavishly.

This led indirectly to a jurisdictional religious dispute. The Reverend Mr. George Whitefield, on his way to evangelize Georgia at Oglethorpe's prompting, was cordially received in Charles Town by the Reverend Mr. Alexander Garden, deputy of the Bishop of London, and immediately upset the apple cart by his method of preaching. Garden, unable to check him, finally called an ecclesiastical court to judge Whitefield, who lost his case and was suspended from office and denounced, undoubtedly to the great edification and encouragement of Methodism.

That does begin to sound rather like the Charleston with which we are familiar today; and it is true that the city began to point in other ways to its modern development. First of all, there was the founding of the South Carolina *Gazette* in 1733. The publisher was Louis Timothée (anglicized to Timothy) who was aided by his wife. In its first dress, the *Gazette* was a quaint enough little periodical, beginning as a sheet a little bigger than a piece of typewriter-size paper, with two columns and shortly afterward with three. It cost three pounds (South Carolina currency) per year and at once set up as the chronicler of all the events of the town. It was graced in 1735 by its first woodcut, which W. L. King says "could be identified with some difficulty as that of a horse." Its advertisements were notable; many of them had to do with legal matters and the problem of runaway slaves, who appear to have been commonly dressed in something called "Negro cloth." Notable, too, were the early announcements of marriages, in which the bride received fulsome compliments, and which sometimes added a worldly note about the size of the dowry. The announcement of the marriage of the daughter of Jeremiah Theus, the painter, refers to him as a "limner."

An unexpectedly intimate note occurs at the time of Timothy's death, when Mrs. Timothy inserted a note asking for the continuation of good will and expressing a hope that the subscribers would "be kindly pleased to continue their favors and good offices to his poor afflicted widow and six small children, and another hourly expected." We know it was forthcoming, for the *Gazette* continued. Although it occasionally changed its name and format, it is, through an unbroken succession, the legitimate ancestor of the present *News and Courier*.

Meanwhile, in 1729, the Scots had established the St. Andrew's Society; German Lutherans had come in 1734, perhaps the most independent of the non-British groups, for German was the only language besides English ever to gain a foothold in Charleston, and there was at one time in the nineteenth century a German newspaper. German names, by the way, are common in Charleston.

Not to be outdone by the Scots, the French Protestants founded the South Carolina Society. This began in 1736 as a charitable organization and was later expanded to include social and cultural activities.

In that same year Charleston had a theater—the Dock Street Theatre—where such plays as Farquhar's *The Recruiting Officer*, Addison's *Cato*, and *The Orphan, or the Unhappy Marriage* were performed. No subterfuge, such as was later used in New England to accomplish the presentation of plays in the guise of moral improvers, was ever necessary in the fun-loving little city of balls and horse-racing.

We must not forget, either, that this was the period in which Eliza Lucas Pinckney, mother of Charles Cotesworth and Thomas Pinckney, was beginning her career as a writer of charming letters and experimenting with the planting of indigo, long an important source of the colony's income.

In the same year that Charles Town's fighting men went forth once more to fight the Spaniards at St. Augustine—1740 —the first of Charleston's great fires destroyed a large part of the southeastern end of the city and led to the building of new dwellings, some of which, like the Robert Pringle house on Tradd Street, still stand, and some of which endured until the early years of this century. And a forthright, somewhat humorless Scotsman, James Glen, was preparing for his role of governor, during which he was, among other things, to criticize the colonists for the luxuriousness of their ways and establishments; which certainly sounds like Charleston of the great days.

Glen was such an interesting character that it may not be

amiss to take a closer look at him. He may not unfairly be referred to as an early specimen of the go-getter. Apprised in 1738 of his appointment as governor of South Carolina, he put in five years of study to fit himself for his task, and took over the office with high ambitions and very little doubt of himself. It is pleasant to record that he was not greatly disappointed in either.

He arrived at Charleston in the month of December, 1743. Although the office had been filled by Lieutenant-Governor William Bull for eight years and Bull was a resident of the town and popular, Glen was heartily received, and the townsfolk did as well at welcoming him as could be imagined without Grover Whalen. The South Carolina *Gazette* was on hand to record the reception. As Glen's ship, the *Tartar,* passed Fort Johnson, the fort saluted with five guns. The Charles Town regiment was drawn up on East Bay. When the ship docked the clerk of Council and the master in chancery escorted his excellency ashore, and two members of the Council, Edward Aitkin and Charles Pinckney (in whose house he was to take up residence) conducted him to the Council Chamber. There, having produced, so to speak, his credentials, he was escorted in state to the Granville Bastion on Meeting Street, his commission was read to the populace, cannon and musketry boomed and crackled in his honor. He returned to the Council Chamber to take the oath of office, and then he was led to Shepheard's Tavern to be entertained.

He had not come to lie on any bed of roses, however. He found the city, in his own phrase, "in ashes, defenceless, declining." He was not a man to mince matters, and he also found himself in the midst of a quarrel between the Commons, which held the purse strings, and his majesty's Council. He was often thereafter at loggerheads with the Council; it is said, however, that he never lost his temper. But he appears to have been quite thick-skinned; he insisted, for instance, on being present when the Council deliberated, and once, to get rid of him, that august body was compelled to take refuge in the attic.

Governor Glen was optimistic over the future of the colony, and predicted great things for it. Nevertheless, he was unfavorably impressed by the prevailing luxury. It obviously shocked his thrifty Scottish soul to find all sort of fripperies being imported in a quantity and quality "ill calculated for the circumstances of an Infant Colony." He wrote that he had "endeavored to restrain and correct the bias of extravagance and luxury." No doubt he objected to the plays at the new Dock Street Theatre, too. For all that, he was a leader in society.

He served at an interesting time. The French and Indian Wars began a year after his assumption of office, but he seems to have been equal to the emergency. He learned to know the Indians by traveling frequently among them, earned their friendship by instituting the custom of paying them for their lands, and pacified them. During his time trouble with the red men was kept at a minimum; and if the basis for the trouble was not eradicated, so that his successor inherited difficulties with the natives along with the chair of governor, it is at least apparent that Glen did his best.

He provided fortifications for the protection of both the Low Country and the Up Country, and in the interest of doing the job properly brought the engineer DeBrahm to the colony. But DeBrahm's plan for strengthening strategic points was considered too costly, although in 1755, when the French threatened, he was recalled.

In line with his interest in seeing that the city was restored after the great fire, Glen investigated the possibilities of preventing the outbreak and spread of others. Once, during a blaze, he actually joined the bucket brigade, thus becoming one of the first celebrated American firebuffs.

Posterity is indebted to him for *A Description of South*

Carolina, a book which omitted no detail, including even reports of weather and tides and the observations made by Dr. John Lining, the apothecary and correspondent of Franklin. He sent his book to England and even had copies distributed among the German Protestants, whom he wished to attract to South Carolina.

During Governor Glen's administration, too, occurred the founding of the first Jewish congregation in Charleston—Beth Elohim—which traces its history from 1750. Not altogether consonant with the colony's devotion to freedom was the grand jury's hearing of Peter Timothy for printing a letter of attack on Governor Glen.

But to return to our man: he had to contend not only with Indian troubles and with the results of the 1740 fire, but also with the havoc wrought by a hurricane and tidal wave which visited the city in 1752, the year of the laying of the cornerstone of St. Michael's Church. The flood, like the fire, brought improvement, for this time the work of restoration included the filling in of numerous creeks and marshy spots which had added to the distress caused by the storm when they overflowed.

Glen had the longest term of any governor of the colony. He stayed twelve years. To the city he left "fair, fortified, and flourishing" came the new appointee, William Henry Lyttleton, to remain only four years. Lyttleton was personally much admired and is held to have been a good civil administrator; he settled the hapless Acadians who had landed at Charles Town, which must have taken some tact, for they were Catholics and as such were not acceptable in the colony; but he was unfortunate in his dealings with the Indians.

The struggles between the French and the English had left unfinished business in this department. The chief grievance now of the Indians was the encroachment of the Up Country settlers. The Cherokees, in particular, objected to being pushed off their own lands by ambitious Swiss, Germans, Huguenots, Scots, Scotch-Irish, and Welsh, and finally they gave expression to their discontent by killing two white men.

This roused Lyttleton to action. There was nothing of the pacificator about him, and when the younger William Bull, who had inherited his father's talent for serving as lieutenant-governor, tried to tell his superior how to treat with the Indians, Lyttleton spurned his advice. He told the Cherokees that he would bring them to submission at the point of the bayonet. He also made the egregious mistake of holding the ambassadors as prisoners, which infuriated the red men. Then, with a mob of men, he tried to impress the Indians by mere numbers, and signed a treaty with the cunning Attakullahkullah, "The Little Carpenter," so called because of his skill in arranging terms. The Little Carpenter persuaded Lyttleton to give up his hostages and also persuaded him that he had settled the affair. Just as if he had concluded a really memorable peace, Lyttleton was received in Charles Town with tremendous enthusiasm; an orator chosen by the recently formed Library Society pronounced a speech worthy of the annals of the Pickwick Club in which he hailed the governor as the colony's "governor and protector."

Shortly after the conclusion of this worthless pact, Lyttleton was transferred to Jamaica, but the Cherokees did not even have the grace to let him depart with a clean slate. They rose, ambushed the officer in charge of Fort St. George, where Lyttleton had sent the Indian prisoners, and then, when the men in the fort paid them back in kind, went on the warpath. Appealing to Lord Geoffrey Amherst, the British commander-in-chief in the colonies, Lyttleton left the colony in the care of Lieutenant-Governor Bull, who, although he acted several times as provisional governor, was never to have the office in his own right, for colonists were not favored for the post.

Under Bull's guidance, and with the aid of a couple of military victories which helped to season a number of South Carolinians who were later to make their mark in the Revolution, the colonists finally reduced the Cherokees to the point of suing for peace. The threat of the French was now positively a thing of the past. The town that rice and indigo had built, now a beautiful city of noble Georgian houses, social delights, and luxurious living, the resort of planters from the nearby countryside, and one of the chief centers of American culture and graces, had fourteen glorious years of peace ahead of it. During ten of them, however, it was to spend a good deal of energy in preparing to effect the end of British rule.

Dr. George Milligen, who visited Charles Town in the early 1760's, published a report of it which has now become a rather rare little volume. The semi-official nature of the report is attested by the clinical discussions of bodily functions at certain seasons as recorded by Charleston's scientifically inclined pharmacist, Dr. Lining, the inclusion of directions for the cultivation of indigo, and topographical observations. But the little book is interesting for its estimate of Charles Town at that period. Milligen was interested in many things; he praised the view from the harbor, and he found the streets "broad, straight, and uniform." He states that the town consisted of some eleven hundred dwellings "generally incumbered with Balconies and Piazzas." He was evidently impressed by the social accomplishments of the inhabitants, and he describes a "dancing-assembly in Charles Town, where is always a brilliant appearance of lovely well-dressed women. We have likewise a genteel Playhouse, where a very tolerable set of actors, called the *American* Company of Comedians, frequently exhibit; and often concerts of vocal and instrumental music, generally performed by Gentlemen." He found "the ladies, I mention it to their credit, are extremely temperate, and generally drink water . . . which," he adds with obvious distaste "is very unwholesome in Charles Town."

In those days Charleston must have been charming. Enough of the pre-Revolutionary houses have survived to show how the typical architecture had developed—such Georgian houses as the Heyward House on Church Street, the Miles Brewton (Pringle) House on King Street, which were "double" houses; and such characteristic "single" houses— dwellings one room wide and with their sides turned to the street—as the Brewton House on Church Street (which, however, has now lost its piazza), or the beautiful narrow houses at 23-25 Meeting Street. St. Michael's had been opened for worship in 1761; the Exchange building, looking somewhat different from its present aspect, stood at the head of Broad Street. Mr. John Rutledge's imposing mansion stood on Broad Street, and the tasteful little Izard house to the east of it had been built. These all give a suggestion of what the town must have looked like before the early Georgian and West Indian influence began to share importance with the Adam styles and the Greek revival. It is worthy of note that the prevalence of the single house in Charleston is due to the necessity of building for the sake of coolness rather than to any deeply-rooted esthetic prejudices.

A good many of the extant plantation houses—although, of course, additions and alterations here will confuse the impression—were built during this colonial period. Crowfield, Hampton, Fenwick Hall, and the Palladian Drayton Hall are among them. Life was rich, for the rich at least; there were plenty of good books in the gentlemen's libraries, and there was the St. Cecilia Society to provide good music, and balls and dinners and suppers kept the social ball rolling. The Crown paid a bounty on indigo, the colony's rice was shipped to various parts of the world, the gentlemen's sons went to British universities. And the civilization of Charleston, on its higher levels, was similar to that of England, leaving nothing to be desired in comfort and elegance.

Why, then, did South Carolina take a leading part in the breaking of ties with England?

CHAPTER FIVE

Throwing Off the Yoke

The origins of revolution in Charlestown and South Carolina seem neither more nor less sharply defined than in the other colonies. There were, of course, actual disadvantages to the Low Country, as has been suggested in the previous chapter. These were so apparent to a large group that the latter remained loyal to the mother country throughout the conflict.

There were intangible causes, difficult to estimate. The winds of republican doctrine were blowing strongly in the latter half of the eighteenth century. Probably, in the well-stocked libraries of the great houses of Charleston, were to be found the works of the Frenchmen who had been speculating about such matters as democracy and equality. Probably, also, a number of those young men who had gone to England for their education had picked up whispers of Whiggish heresy —and William Oliver Stevens has keenly suggested that perhaps their incitement to revolt came from hearing themselves described as "those Americans."

More definite was the long tradition of scuffling with the Proprietors and the Royal government. There was resentment, naturally, over the favoritism shown in the matter of appointment to office. Colonials of ability were passed over and British-born men were appointed almost exclusively.

But, after all, men are needed to stand as the embodiment of grievances and to spearhead revolt. George the Third stood as the embodiment of a grievance. His predecessors, half-German as they were, had managed the colonies chiefly through their ministers. But as every American schoolboy used to know, the British-born George III was of another sort.

His accession was celebrated with great enthusiasm in Charlestown, but it may be significant that a year earlier the Royal governor, Thomas Boone, had made an enemy of a relentless fighter, Christopher Gadsden.

It is one of the not too subtle connections of history that the French and Indian War, which was fought for the sake of the colonies, trained a number of colonials in the art of fighting, and led to the very Stamp Act that was so important in impelling them to use that knowledge against Great Britain. And this first overt art of the new and long-reigning monarch and his ministers brought Christopher Gadsden into the limelight.

Gadsden was the son of that Gadsden who, according to legend, had lost at cards a huge parcel of land on the east side of the city to the world-traveler, Captain Anson, when the latter was in Charleston (on which he has left such traces as Anson Street and the district known as Ansonborough). The story is that, when a mere boy, Christopher Gadsden had vowed to buy the land back, and later did.

In 1746, at the age of twenty-two, Christopher Gadsden returned from the pursuit of an education and immediately began to prosper. Within fifteen years he was a solid citizen, with stores in town, a store in the country, and a plantation. Nine years after that he built the immense wharf on the Cooper River which is still called Gadsden's Wharf. But that is getting ahead of the story.

He had been elected to the Assembly in 1757, and for thirty years he remained a member of that body, with one interlude.

In 1761 Thomas Boone, the governor, was quarreling with the citizens over the election laws, and, probably to make an example, he declined to recognize the election of Gadsden, even though this had been ratified by the Assembly. Next year Gadsden was again elected, and the Assembly insisted upon his right to occupy his seat. Neither side would give in, and legislative affairs reached an impasse which lasted for two years and resulted in Boone's sailing off to England with his salary in arrears. He had made an issue, and the citizens were not backward in discussing it.

When the notorious Stamp Act was promulgated, for the laudable purpose of paying off the costs of the French and Indian War, Charlestown was not slow to indicate her distaste. When the stamps first arrived in the town, the tax collector was hanged in effigy, "Liberty" was unceremoniously buried with St. Michael's bells tolling for greater dramatic effect, and mobs searched the houses where they suspected the stamps were hidden.

A group of diligent seekers even broke into the house of Henry Laurens, "one of the noblest Romans of them all," and demanded the hated stamps. Laurens calmly told the mob that he had not the stamps, and asked them not to disturb his wife, who was ill, and not to trample his flowers. The rioters actually went away with expressions of sympathy for Mrs. Laurens and hope for her recovery. Later it was learned that William Bull, the perennial lieutenant-governor-in-charge, had spirited the stamps away to prevent trouble.

Massachusetts, it will be remembered, now invited South Carolina to send delegates to the Stamp Tax Congress in New York. Alone among the Southern colonies, South Carolina responded. Gadsden was one of the delegates. He had fairly got the bit in his teeth now.

Chiefly by grace of William Pitt's eloquent opposition, the odious tax was repealed. There was great rejoicing, and the enthusiastic citizens voted that a statue of their champion be ordered, which was done. Gadsden, however, was not satisfied. The "firebrand of the Revolution" continued to harangue his mechanics under the old Liberty Tree. He foresaw more trouble; and when the new Royal governor, Charles Greville, Lord Montagu, arrived with tidings of a token tax on tea, lead, glass and painters' colors—just to show that England had the right to levy any tax it pleased—Gadsden was able to say, "I told you so." Once more South Carolina joined in the general protest.

Meanwhile, the case of John Wilkes, the member of Parliament and pamphleteer who had been arrested under a general warrant for seditious libel, added a fillip to popular dissatisfaction. In the surge of popular indignation, South Carolina and Charlestown joined. The Commons voted a fund for the defense of "British and American liberty." The affair helped to crystallize popular feelings in the city.

There was, not so many years ago, a famous German motion picture which telescoped history to such an extent that it led directly from the cavortings of Louis XV and his court to the French Revolution. Without meaning to subscribe to such condensations, we must pass rather hastily over this pre-Revolutionary decade in Charlestown, if only in the interests of perspective.

When the British began to enforce the trade laws requiring that all goods be exported from the colonies in British ships and that all manufactured goods be bought from England alone, South Carolina joined in the non-importation agreements. The colony was in such a position that it really stood to lose very little under such a law; its agricultural products, even though they might have to go in British ships, could go anywhere, and as we have seen the Crown paid a subsidy on its indigo. Nevertheless, South Carolina backed up the New England boycott. Gadsden, for example, was a planter and a

THE JOHN STUART HOUSE. PRE-REVOLUTIONARY

A TYPICAL SCENE ON THE COOPER RIVER WATERFRONT.
NOW WHOLLY ALTERED

OLD HOUSE ON MEETING STREET. NORTH EUROPEAN
INFLUENCE

CHARACTERISTIC SINGLE HOUSES, SHOWING
EARTHQUAKE RODS

merchant, and he faced heavy losses if rice were included in the list of products to be withheld; nevertheless, he advocated its inclusion, vainly as it happened, for rice was exempted. Not every offering on the altar of principle was as great as this one, but everybody suffered in greater or less measure. There is one incident of the period which puts Gadsden in a rather pathetic light. His wife died just at this time, and, because of the non-importation of British goods, there was no mourning available for her funeral. That sounds trivial in print, but in view of the customs of the time it represented a genuine hardship to dispense with such an established rite.

As the rift widened, the situation of more and more men and women became acutely unhappy. The decision to break, or retain, the strong ties of culture and sympathy with England, posed a heart-rending choice for many men of principle. Such a man, for instance, was the younger William Bull, born right in the Low Country and a lifelong servant of its interests.

His father had been lieutenant-governor of the colony before him. William Bull the younger was born at Ashley Hall, a great plantation on the Ashley still more or less intact under the name of Kennerty Farms, although the house was destroyed by fire in the nineteenth century. Bull had the distinction of being the first native-born American to receive a medical degree. He took his at Leyden in 1734, his thesis being on the subject of lead colic; he attributed the prevalence of this ailment in his home province to the custom of storing gentlemen's liquor in lead bottles. This, of course, made the disease virtually an occupational one for gentlemen.

When young Dr. Bull returned to South Carolina, he did not practice medicine, but devoted his energies to planting and politics. At twenty-six he was justice of the peace, and he was shortly afterward elected to the Assembly and became its speaker in 1740. His experience in Indian affairs was invaluable to the royal governors he regularly supported in his subordinate capacity; so well known was he for this knowledge of how to deal with the aborigines that he journeyed to Albany in 1752 to serve on the commission that established peace between the Iroquois and the Catawbas. A treaty made with the Cherokee chief Attakullahkullah, which endured until the Revolution, was signed in a little building on Ashley Hall plantation. Bull's prominence in these matters is commemorated in a group in the Charleston Museum. This miniature shows a room in the John Stuart house on Tradd Street. The year is 1775. Bull is seated; beside him is Captain John Stuart, the famous Indian agent. Another figure is Alexander Cameron, still obstinately wearing kilts; and a fourth is Ouconnastotah, the Cherokee chieftain, bowing very low. The subject of the conference thus commemorated was the status of relations with the Indians in view of the crisis. Bull, by the way, was instrumental in founding the Charleston Museum, for as president of the Library Society he urged the appointment of a committee to assemble historical materials, and this committee was the nucleus of the museum.

Bull served five terms of varying lengths as lieutenant-governor in charge of South Carolina, but he was never honored by appointment to the office of governor. Despite this treatment, he remained a Loyalist; but the treatment was symptomatic.

Bull's tact is revealed by his official sequestration of the tax stamps, and the citizens, part of whom had behaved in a fairly Gilbertian manner at Henry Laurens' house, showed their respect for Bull when, in 1775, they seized the arms and powder stores in Charlestown by doing it in the dead of night so that he might not be embarrassed. For Bull was fated to be in the saddle when the horse was running away. The youthful Lord Montagu, not quite thirty, decamped in 1773, unable to control matters, and although Lord William Campbell, who had married a Low Country heiress, was appointed that year, he did not take over until 1775. The difficulty of Bull's position is also illustrated by the fact that he was obliged to remove from the Royal Council his own nephew, William Henry Drayton, afterwards the Chief Justice, because of his incendiary speeches. By the time the dashing Campbell arrived, with the war virtually begun, there was little left to do but go through the motions. Campbell's stay was also brief, from June 17th to the following September 15th, and when he unceremoniously fled to the *Tamar,* taking the Royal seal with him as a last gesture, Bull again held the bag. This time his lieutenant-governorship was purely nominal, anyway, for Henry Laurens' Council of Safety had been in virtual command of the state since early summer.

Bull, Tory to the end, remained in America until 1782. One of his last acts was to have himself taken in a litter to plead with Lord Rawdon for the life of Isaac Hayne. The usual penalties imposed on Loyalists were overlooked in his case and his property was restored after the Revolution, but ill-health kept him in England and he never saw his home again.

Bull was not alone in being a Loyalist. Disaffection was widespread in the colonies, as we all now know, and although South Carolina had taken the lead in bringing about the break with England, there were plenty of men to cling to the status quo. Even such patriots as Henry Laurens regretted the break; it is said that Laurens actually wept when the Declaration of Independence was read, and there is a hint that when young Edward Rutledge came home after signing the Declaration, he was almost afraid to face his older brother John. The latter, long after hostilities were in progress, resigned the governorship of the state upon the formulation of a new constitution which, he felt, made reconciliation impossible. William Henry Drayton, too, had found it difficult to make up his mind.

But these men, after all, did become Revolutionists. There was a strong and active Tory group in Charleston. In fact, a section of the old city was known as "Tory Row." The Up Country was even more seriously divided. Political jealousy, never to be completely stamped out in the state, was deadly then. There had been actual battles between the patriot militia and the Loyalists at Ninety-Six and in Greenville County, and British triumphs in the state brought immense satisfaction to a large part of the population, and a rush for cover to another part.

In March, 1776, South Carolina inaugurated a new government, with John Rutledge as president, and Charlestown prepared for war. Mr. Gadsden's introduction of the works of Thomas Paine into the discussions may have aroused denunciations, along with his bold advocacy of complete separation, but events were on his side.

In May, by means of an intercepted letter, it was learned that a British fleet was coming to subdue the Southern colonies. A fort of palmetto logs on Sullivan's Island, begun earlier in the year, was half complete at this time. The warning news brought a fever of activity and work on the fort proceeded at emergency speed. Colonel William Moultrie, after whom it was later named, was in command. At Fort Johnson, on the other side of the harbor mouth, the aging but indefatigable Gadsden, now fifty-four, was in charge. At the other end of Sullivan's Island Colonel Moses Thompson had a force of about one thousand men, all sharpshooters. Property was demolished to provide material for barricades; window weights were scrapped to be melted into musket balls.

On the thirty-first of May the British fleet was reported a score of miles away, and on the first of June the half-hundred vessels dropped anchor. Sir Henry Clinton's proclamation was sent under a flag of truce to warn the people of the desperateness of the step they were taking, and to promise a free pardon to those who would submit. General Charles Lee, meanwhile, disapproved of the determination to defend Fort Moultrie and favored Haddrell's Point, nearer the city. President Rutledge here asserted himself and refused to give the order for the fort's evacuation. Lee continued to harass Moultrie, who stuck to his guns, and was about to remove him when, after a long delay, the British fleet, on the 28th of June, sailed in to the attack. All Lee had accomplished was to deprive the fort of more than half its five tons of powder.

The British fleet poured its heavy fire into the little fort, but sandbags and palmetto logs took the sting out of the bombardment. In this battle Sergeant William Jasper, of the Second Regiment, immortalized himself by one of those small acts of heroism which seize the imagination more strongly than great campaigns, when he leapt to the rescue of the state flag and replaced it on a staff.

Meanwhile, three thousand British soldiers were landed on what is now the Isle of Palms. Colonel Thompson's force was only one-third as large, but his crack shots made their fire count, and the British retreated. The fleet, unable to make any impression on the palmetto fort, withdrew with less damage than they might have sustained had Lee seen to it that Moultrie had sufficient powder. It was a significant victory—a major engagement, won against heavy odds, before the actual signing of the Declaration of Independence—and a marvelous thing for the morale and prestige of the colonies, although it may have made them over-confident. Only St. Michael's Church failed to observe the following Sunday as a day of thanksgiving; the vestry had closed the church for that day because the rector had refused to take the oath of allegiance to the new constitution. Another Episcopalian minister, however, read the Declaration when it finally reached the city in August. As may be imagined, the day was a torrid one, and the reverend gentleman was protected from the rays of the sun by a large umbrella and was fanned by a black slave— which prompted a squib from a British onlooker in which it

was suggested that it was not very *civil* for the parson to encourage treason while being fanned by the *Devil* (pronounced
to rhyme with civil).

For the next three years the city and state enjoyed a peaceful life within their own boundaries. The city was prosperous
from the business of supplying the products of neutral coun-
tries to the other states, and although British ships along the
coast offered some hindrance, they were harried by American
privateers. There were some bad fires, very likely of incendiary
origin; and there was, for some small measure of excitement,
a supposed Popish plot.

Catholics had not shared in the general religious freedom
of the colony, and if there were any, such as the Acadian
refugees, they kept their convictions very quiet, for there were
penal laws in full force against them even in 1776, and even
the new state constitution of 1778 excluded them from office.
When two live Irish Catholics were discovered in the city in
1775, they were at once accused of conspiring with the Negroes against the patriots, and they were condemned to be
tarred and feathered and banished from the state.

But when the fires had been put out and this powerful Papist
nucleus had been removed from the sacred soil, there was
tranquillity until 1778, when the town had a bad scare. General Prévost, having attacked Port Royal, moved rapidly on
Charlestown, and the city prepared itself for battle.

More earthworks were erected at the vulnerable North
End of the city. They were just above the Line Street of the
present day. The lines were considered worthless by military
engineers. Despite this, Generals Moultrie and Laurens were
all for giving battle, but Rutledge, computing the chances,
ordered them to wait until General Lincoln's forces should arrive. Rutledge even went further. He was convinced that re-
sistance without aid was impossible, and made a suggestion for
which he has been both commended and censured. He offered

to make the state of South Carolina neutral for the duration of the war—a sort of Switzerland, except that it possessed seaports—which would be used by both sides. Certain that the city would be a pushover, the British refused. Rutledge's proposal had the effect of a delaying action; by the time it had been acted upon, forty-eight hours had gone by, and the enemy, having intercepted a letter from General Lincoln to General Moultrie, promising his immediate arrival, quickly retreated. It is possible that Lincoln's army, combined with the forces in the city, might have wrought havoc with the British, but he had delayed too long, and Prévost was able to waste the countryside on his way back to Savannah, setting an example, if any example was needed, to a later exponent of the technique, Sherman.

The city had so far got off very lightly. But in 1780 the same fleet that had been driven off in 1776 returned, this time with an army of formidable size. Against Washington's advice, Charlestown again prepared to resist, and was thoroughly battered before Gadsden and other die-hards yielded to military expediency and the city was surrendered.

Probably a number of readers, now in early middle age, can recall those boyhood classics, "The Boys of Liberty Library." After some thirty years I can still remember the beginning of a chapter from one of these romances, which was about Francis Marion: "The joy of the British knew no bounds when the Queen City of the South, Charleston, fell into their hands," though I would hesitate to insist that I have quoted with absolute word-for-word accuracy. That was exactly the situation; and the Tories rejoiced, too.

The Continental soldiers were made prisoners of war; the militia were paroled. For three years Charlestown was under British control, with all the insolence and brutality the word connoted. Clinton took up headquarters at the Miles Brewton house on King Street, where he was succeeded by the notorious

Tarleton, and Cornwallis ensconced himself at Drayton Hall on the Ashley. He is said to have behaved very well except for the fact that he was extremely stingy about food allowances to the family and servants.

For the three years of their stay, the British were in undisturbed possession, and their behavior alone may be said to have brought their downfall in the state. When they began to revoke paroles, and when the Tories up-state began a civil war, the patriots boiled over. Two of them, absent from the siege of Charlestown by chance, were to be immortal for their exploits. One was Virginia-born Thomas Sumter, whose plantation home the British burned while his wife lay seriously ill, and who, in the role of militia leader which earned his nickname, "The Gamecock," later made life miserable for the invaders. The other was the Huguenot Francis Marion, whose subsequent career hinges upon an odd accident.

How Marion chanced to be absent from Charlestown and thus escaped having to give his parole, is a strange story. He was dining with friends in the city before it fell to the British. Marion was a man of abstemious habits, and those were the days of heavy drinking. The host had followed the jolly custom of locking the doors so that his guests could not leave until they had become thoroughly potted. To avoid argument and unpleasantness, Marion took the course usually adopted by young men who are anxious to avoid, not intoxication, but marriage; he leapt out of the window, landed badly, and broke his leg. It is thought by some that the house he fled from was the Stuart House at the corner of Tradd and Orange Streets, but this has not been settled.

When the siege began, Marion, incapacitated by his injury in the interests of temperance, left the city. As soon as he was able to get about, he reported to Governor Rutledge, who gave him a commission as colonel. With a group of ragged men and boys whom he had recruited, Marion sought out

General Gates (about to lose the battle of Camden) and Gates rejected him and his men. Determined to fight, Marion took his little brigade into the swamps and began the career of gadfly. Armed with homemade weapons and a detailed knowledge of the swamps, the band was able to elude capture time after time as it harried the baffled British. Marion became known as "The Swamp Fox," and his leadership played a large part in the eventual defeat of the enemy.

It is a sad commentary on the gratitude of democracies that when the ruined and weary leader returned to his devastated plantation after the war and the Senate ordered a medal for him, the medal was never struck; and that when he was given the command of Fort Johnson, objectors brought about the reduction of his meager salary. Fortunately, Marion married a wealthy widow and had eleven years of peace and happiness until his death in 1795. He was better treated at that than was Moultrie, who, on account of expenditures he had incurred in the prosecution of the war, was put into the old jail on Magazine Street.

The British continued on their way. Thirty officers who had been paroled were arrested for having "fermented the late Rebellion," and were threatened with prison at St. Augustine. After thinking it over, all gave a new parole except Christopher Gadsden, who, whatever may have been his faults, was a man with a backbone. He could be petty about his commission and could fall out with Henry Laurens when the latter, mistaking a jealous gesture for true intention, accepted the resignation he proffered because Moultrie had been given precedence; but when it came to facing up he was unmatched. Alone of the thirty officers, he told the British that as they had cheated him this time, he would never trust them again. Even the confinement in a dungeon had no effect on the fifty-nine-year-old patriot, who went unbowed to San Marcos and learned Hebrew during his stay of almost a year. It is sad to note that Mr. Gadsden, so fiery in his earlier years, became rather querulous in his old age; one of the last things we hear about him is his complaint that Henry Laurens' new house shut off his view of St. Philip's steeple. But there had been much bad blood between the two.

In line with their policy, the British sequestered the property and concerns of those who refused to swear allegiance to the Crown. Negroes were shipped away to the West Indies, and an attempt was made to lure civil leaders and officers to these islands. One of these so approached was Moultrie. His answer is worth noting. It was that "not for the fee simple of Jamaica" would he accept such an offer, and he added to his correspondent: "Think better of me." Attempts at corruption were extended even to society, for it was felt that with the leaders out of the way (several more had seen sent to St. Augustine) the inhabitants might be softened up by a bit of pleasure. The rebel ladies, however, stood firm and refused to have any truck with the conquerors.

But the British still hoped. They bullied women and the weak, quartered horses in the Old White Meeting House, and abused the properties they had seized for residence. Their behavior reached its culmination in a deed of unforgivable and unforgettable infamy.

Among the paroled officers in South Carolina was a colonel of militia named Isaac Hayne, who, having given his word not to fight, went quietly to his home in St. Paul's parish to attend to his affairs. Hayne was popular and influential in his own locality, and the British, aware that the patriots were anxious to have him again, recalled his parole and insisted that he swear allegiance to the Crown. This Hayne refused to do. At any rate, it seemed most unlikely that he would break his parole. His wife was desperately ill, one of his children had just died of smallpox, and the others were down with it. It was a time when any man would have asked for nothing but to be left alone; but at this juncture the British summoned Hayne to Charlestown and told him that if he wished to go free he must declare himself a British subject. They assured him, however, that this would not mean that he would be obliged to bear arms against his fellow Americans. The harassed militia officer, fearing for the safety of his family if he were kept in the filthy prison under the old Exchange (which was then the post office) signed the required declaration but informed his friend Dr. Ramsay, the historian, that he had done so under duress; then he returned home.

Hayne's wife died, but his misery did not keep the British from harassing him. Once more he was threatened with imprisonment if he did not join the British forces. Hayne was angry at this treachery, and evidently considering that his moral obligation in the matter was ended, he assumed the leadership of a company of his neighbors and began to fight. Moreover, by a bold stroke he captured General Williamson, a renegade who is thought to have been in the service of both the Americans and the British. A troop under the command of "Mad Archy" Campbell gave chase, and Hayne's horse, which had been too long idle, was winded, stumbled, and fell. The pursuers recovered Williamson and took Hayne to Charlestown, where he was confined in the cells under the post office before being tried for treason. Swiftly convicted by a partial and unfair court-martial, he was sentenced to be hanged as a spy.

Even the Tories interceded for him, and the ladies of the city signed a petition to Lord Rawdon. But the British were being hard pressed by the militia fighters and evidently wanted to make an example. Furthermore, they had a debt of revenge to pay. It is said that across every petition for Hayne's pardon Rawdon scrawled the name of Major André. Hayne's sister-in-law, with his children, went to the Brewton House, where Rawdon had his headquarters, and there in the drawing room begged on her knees for pity. And old William Bull, as has been mentioned, had himself taken in a litter before Rawdon to enter his plea. Even the British officers objected to Hayne's being hanged as a spy. But Rawdon yielded only to the extent that he allowed Hayne time to make his last farewells to his children.

The condemned man appears to have shown some human emotion when he finally approached the scaffold outside the city walls and realized just what sort of death his was to be. But he behaved like a man to the end, even to signaling the executioner with his own hand.

His march to the scaffold gave rise to Charleston's most famous ghost story: it was said that his sister-in-law, from a window, saw him pass through the street on his way to death. She called to him to come back, and heard him answer that he would if he could. And always after that, if anyone stood in that window after dark, he would hear the sound of foot-steps ascending the stair.

It shows how long Hayne's death was remembered in Charlestown. His execution, in the light of the deeds committed in our time by Hitler and his fellow-perverts, may seem almost trifling; but it was a brutal and stupid piece of cruelty, and besides, the worst possible policy. A large number of partisan officers had done just what Hayne had done, and from now on they fought with the added desperation of men who knew that to be captured meant that they would have the noose around their own necks. Hatred against the British boiled to a new pitch. General Greene, then threatening Charlestown, announced that he meant to hang the first British officer he captured.

From that time on, although the British were to remain well over a year in Charlestown, their star was obviously on the wane. There was great suffering and poverty in the town, where business had come to a complete halt; and British perse-

cution continued in the form of deportation of the wives of
paroled and imprisoned American officers, but the British fortunes were doomed. It was only two months and fifteen days
from the date of Hayne's execution to the surrender of Cornwallis at Yorktown.

The war dragged on in South Carolina. By January of the
next year the British had been driven away except for Charlestown, but their vessels continued to harry the coast. The
Tories, too, were still a danger. An act of confiscation was
passed against them, although there were members of the legislature who opposed retaliation; and when, in 1783, the war
came to a definite end, even more opposed this legislation.

As the Tories had, in numerous instances, profited by the
misfortunes of their fellow-citizens, a modern reader gets
the impression that the South Carolinians were very lenient
indeed in their post-war attitude toward their disaffected neighbors. The state had suffered greatly. But even after peace was
signed, the British retained millions of pounds' worth of loot.

Probably the feeling of good riddance was stronger than
anything else. But since there was considerable ill-feeling, meas-
ures were taken to see that no rioting occurred when the
British marched out. They took with them everything they
could lay hands on, including St. Michael's bells and thousands
of Negro slaves, and as the troops passed through the city on
their way to the wharves, the Americans marched in several
hundred discreet yards behind the departing enemy, to enjoy
their triumph. The event was marred by Greene's refusal to
permit the shabby militia or partisans to share the triumphant
entry of the regulars. General Moultrie, who was to know the
meaning of ingratitude, wrote angrily of this in his journal.
"They were not too ragged to fight," he observed, "only too
ragged for show!"

But if Moultrie's nose was out of joint, everybody else was
happy (except the Loyalists, who crouched behind their doors

and wondered what was going to happen to them). Nothing much did happen. The troops marched past and the governor saluted and the soldiers saluted in return, and one can imagine the burghers and the children hurrahing—or did they huzzay in those days?

Leaving the historians to settle the rights and wrongs of it all, we can accept the *fait accompli*. An era had ended. According to Frederick P. Bowes, in *The Culture of Early Charleston,* the end of the political association with Great Britain put a period to the golden age of Charleston's culture. It is his conviction that, deprived of this stimulus, that culture ebbed. But the city was not dead yet.

CHAPTER SIX

Republican City

Perhaps the breaking of the cord that bound it to England and English cultural forces had ended Charlestown's golden age of cultivation, but the city was entering on a period of nearly eighty years of growth, excitement, and social brilliance and gayety which ended only with the Civil War.

With the evacuation of the British, Charlestown, for the second time—the first occasion having been after the great fire of 1740—set itself to the task of recovery. The invaders were gone, except for a handful of Hessians who had decided to remain and become citizens. Their going had left the city in ruins and they had wrecked the plantations on which the city's life to a great extent depended. Most of the houses in Charlestown had suffered from enemy fire, those in the old section South of Broad Street from the ships' guns and those in the northern half from the land batteries of the besiegers. On the plantations, many of the great houses had been burned, the land left a waste, stock and goods pillaged. It has been estimated that perhaps twenty-five thousand slaves had been stolen by the British. The paper money in circulation was quite worthless; the financial situation of city and state was a mare's nest of complications. In a word, poverty was South Carolina's reward for the part she had taken in the war, just

79

as it was to be eighty-odd years later when the state was the ringleader in secession.

For a time, too, the city was troubled by the unruliness of Greene's soldiers, who felt, naturally enough, that the fat of the land, or such fat as there was, should be theirs by right of having fought for it.

Immediately after the ending of the war, Charlestown became Charleston, incorporating itself as a city under new government and officially changing its name to the present form. When South Carolina ratified the Constitution of the United States in 1788, a new state constitution was adopted. This made Columbia the new capital. However, although the new constitution abolished primogeniture and disestablished the Episcopal Church, it retained the old system of voting by which the Low Country kept its domination, and Charleston was still to all intents and purposes the capital city, and continued to be that until after the Civil War. In 1792 a financial arrangement was made by which the state, like the other twelve, was reimbursed for the expenses it had incurred during the Revolution. If the property of the Tories had been kept, the state would have been considerably richer; but a vast sum (for those days) was returned by the treasury to those from whom it had been confiscated.

Charleston had a great deal of bounce in those days. Although, as we shall see, the city was by no means restored to normal, it was again flourishing at the time of George Washington's visit in 1791. The population in 1790 had risen to over sixteen thousand; to be exact, it consisted of 8,089 whites and 8,270 Negroes. And at least all the whites must have turned out to put on a show for the welcoming of the hero.

The Father of his Country was on his Southern tour. On his way to the South Carolina metropolis he alighted at Colonel Alston's plantation where he spent the night. Next day he went on to Georgetown; then he was breakfasted at Hampton on

SOME QUEEN STREET HOUSES BEFORE RECENT ALTERATIONS.
ST. PHILIP'S SPIRE IN THE BACKGROUND

ST. JAMES, GOOSE CREEK

the Santee, the portico of which had just been completed, and where his hostess was Eliza Lucas Pinckney. He then set out for Charleston in a carriage, via Haddrell's Point, just west of Mount Pleasant.

At that spot he was waited upon by a committee of welcome—and from here on the entire performance begins to have a familiar ring. When the president embarked to cross over to the city he was escorted by a miscellaneous collection of boats, large and small, in which sat ladies and gentlemen anxious to do him honor. From the steps of the Exchange he saluted the citizens.

His lodging in Charleston was at the house of Thomas Heyward on Church Street, that Heyward-Washington House which every visitor goes to see, and he was escorted there through streets which had been watered to lay the dust. From the balcony of a house near Tradd Street, according to a tradition, he spoke to the enthusiastic crowd. He received visitors by the hundreds and probably his back, from all the bowing, suffered the equivalent of that lameness of the hand and arm which is one of the occupational hazards of being chief executive. That, however, is a purely unhistorical supposition. There were breakfasts and dinners and balls, a concert, and a state dinner at the Exchange, where the most beautiful of Charleston's ladies sat opposite him and the wittiest sat at his left—the right being the place of the governor's lady. One wonders just how the wittiest woman enjoyed the distinction. Perhaps she never heard why she was chosen for her particular place; or perhaps she was a bluestocking and would have preferred to be chosen as the wittiest instead of the prettiest.

At the concert and ball, which was a gala affair, the ladies wore bandeaux bearing the president's portrait and a motto of welcome. These, of course, were immortal souvenirs of his visit, as was the great square pew in St. Michael's where he worshipped on Sunday afternoon, after having attended services at St. Philip's in the morning. He dined with the army officers, the witty General Moultrie presiding, and then at five the next morning left the worshipping city and proceeded to Savannah—with which visit we have no concern, though it was very likely as exciting—or as trying—to President Washington.

Gone but not forgotten: "Every relic of his presence," says Mrs. Ravenel, "has been cherished by an adoring people." Probably if all the plates Washington was said to have eaten from were stacked up they would fill a freight car. But worship even of souvenirs of Washington wears off somewhat in time— and the Heyward-Washington House in which he stayed had a bakery on the ground floor in our time.

Now let us turn briefly to the actual conditions in the city. According to Charles Fraser, the artist who wrote *Reminiscences of Charleston,* the post-war aspect of the city as he remembers it—and he was old enough to remember Washington's visit—was "miserable and impoverished." He speaks, also, of the few "miserable Indians" who came into the town as of yore. His unintentionally regretful statement that "there were fewer hangings" (in 1854) than in his early days suggests that crime was fairly plentiful. In June, 1788 there were a number of these executions—the murderers of one Wightman, whose death gave the town its first detective story, and some pirates and mutineers. Fraser also remembers when a boy could swim through the floodgate next to the Daniel Ravenel house, which now abuts the City Hall Park.

It was the era of Jacobinism, particularly among the young men. Some extremists even addressed one another as "citizen" and some wore cockades. In the year 1793 the anniversary of the fall of the Bastille was celebrated with a great civic pageant. St. Michael's bells, recovered from England, chimed amid the rejoicing, and the artillery fired a salute. Citizen

Genêt, too, was enthusiastically welcomed. Not all the citizens were as enthusiastic as one M. Dubard, a hairdresser, who had gone to France particularly to witness the guillotining of aristocrats (which might later have given considerable pleasure to a lot of Charlestonians). Dubard, according to Fraser, found "the guillotining of Marie Antoinette the height of his enjoyment" and long entertained his clients with his account of this historic decapitation. Fraser also tells us that the fashion of wigs, which he deplores along with bustles, arose from the use made of the hair of beautiful Frenchwomen whose heads were cut off. The same chronicler says that when the Pitt Statue was being moved in 1794, the falling off of the head was described by some fanciful partisans as "ominous for the aristocrats."

As late as 1796 John Rutledge cooked his goose with the Senate by attacking the Jay Treaty as too favorable to England, whereupon the Senate retaliated by refusing to ratify his appointment as justice of the Supreme Court. But before the century was out war with France was uppermost in every mind. The city that had welcomed Genêt now built and fortified Castle Pinckney, appropriately named after Charles Cotesworth Pinckney, who had defied the Directory. Mechanics constructed a fort on the East Battery with funds of their own contribution and the townsfolk raised the money to build a frigate in the city's shipyards. Such is the course of history.

And even while the enthusiasts had been crying up the French Revolution and denouncing the upper classes, they had welcomed the refugees from Santo Domingo, some five hundred of whom, in 1792, arrived in the city after fleeing the rebellion in the island. The Santo Domingans, added to the Huguenots, could not but have deepened the French tinge of the town's culture, and, one suspects, added a last polishing to its manners, which Mr. Fraser says were "licentious." They became the teachers, the dancing masters, and on a lower

social plane the *pâtissiers* and candy-makers and launderers of
the town. They were instrumental in establishing St. Mary's
Church, the first Catholic church in the English colonies (or
former colonies). One of them, Madame Talvande, kept the
Ashley Hall of her time, an academy for young ladies, in
what is now called the Simonton House on Legaré Street.
It is said that the high wall, now famous for the Sword Gates,
was built by this lady to keep her young and pretty charges
from being ogled and courted by the young dandies of the
town.

The Santo Domingans are still sadly neglected by the historians of Charleston. It appears that, coming after the
Huguenots, their comparative importance was reduced. The
little burying ground of St. Mary's is a key to part of their history, the files of the *Gazette* contain their announcements and
advertisements, and a few of them are mentioned by E. Milby
Burton, curator of the Charleston Museum, in his book on
South Carolina's silversmiths. Mr. John Bennett has collected
some of the legends of the half-castes, particularly the one
about the beautiful Madame Margot. One Charleston woman
has made a study of them, the results of which may some
day find their way into print, and remedy this neglect.

The refugees, warmly welcomed and aided with money as
well as kindness, settled down in Charleston, which is the
important thing. Their center was in Archdale Street, now
called officially Charles Street in the hope of changing its
reputation by changing its name, and I have heard that one
young lady of the group, in fulfillment of a vow, walked up
and down that street in sackcloth and ashes and carrying two
lighted tapers. They must have been a charming lot.

They were the last of the exotic groups to come into the
Charleston melting pot, and they virtually close the story of
immigration *en masse* save for the Irish who arrived in the
nineteenth century. With them—unless we stop to consider the

formidable proportion of Negroes—we close the story of the exotic influences upon Charleston's name, architecture, food, and manners.

The Negroes were, of course, never officially "assimilated." The first ones had come to the colony in the first ships, and as more and more were brought in and multiplied, they developed a powerful ascendancy over the customs and speech of the Low Country which will probably never be obliterated. Perhaps Charleston would not have been Charleston without them. They were the workmen, the intimate servants, the nurses. From the Negroes of Angola (or so it is thought by some investigators) a generally tractable type favored by the planters of rice, comes the strange and fascinating dialect called *Gullah* which has marked the speech of Charleston to an appreciable degree, just as their presence and that of their fellows has marked the customs and economics of the entire South, possibly beyond alteration.

Things were happening to Charleston, and the South, thick and fast at this time. In 1793 Eli Whitney had perfected the cotton gin, and cotton began its climb to the top position among the crops of the region, though rice continued to be a large source of the Low Country's income. And of course cotton fastened the grip of slavery upon the South as it had never been fastened before.

The city was moving toward its social apogee. With the coming of the Santo Domingans, the theater had reopened in 1793. Racing was a greater craze than ever. Before the end of the century, Charleston was the chief port of entry; over a hundred vessels of varying types came to its docks in January of 1797. "All the retail business of the state was centered in Charleston," says Fraser. There were great "department" stores, in which everything could be purchased, but no specialty stores except two jewelers' establishments and one bookstore.

As the century bowed itself out without another war—but

not without another fire—Charleston was able to point to a
population of nine thousand, six hundred and thirty whites
and—mark the figure—ten thousand, eight hundred and forty-
three blacks. The beauty of the town was such as to bring
enthusiastic praise from such travelers as the Duc de la
Rochefoucauld-Liancourt, and it was beginning to enjoy prestige as a center of American culture second to none. The gay
life made it a delight to residents and visitors.

Lawyers, according to Liancourt, earned immense fees;
Messrs. Pinckney, Rutledge, Pringle and Holmes between
eighteen and twenty-three thousand dollars a year, and eight
or ten others from ten to twelve thousand. Merchants were
prosperous; one of the princes of this class was John Geyer,
who entertained so lavishly that a saying in the town was
"Who is dining with Geyer today?" The factors, who took
the business worries off the minds of the planters, were wealthy,
and lined East Bay with their offices. The merchants were not
in the best society, however, and they had clubs of their own,
among them the "Ugly Club" whose president was chosen
because he was more ill-favored than any of his associates.

The planters constituted the ruling caste, and we shall describe their way of life a little in order to show their part in
the development of Charleston's architectural peculiarities at
this, the great period of the construction of the town's dwellings—the majority of the most notable were built between
1812 and the Civil War.

The residence of the planters in the city depended upon important seasonal causes. The scourge of the great rice plantations was malaria. Possibly in earlier days it was confused
with yellow fever which, as has been said, the city took in
part payment for its shipping trade with the West Indies.
At any rate, more attention was now paid to malaria, or
the incidence was greater; and although the true cause of it
was not to be known for many years, every planter knew that

he must get away from the swampy rice lands before the tenth of May. The Negro field hands, who were immune, remained all the year; but a plentiful supply of house servants accompanied the family to town for the stay during the summer months. This accounts for the many rear-wing additions to large Charleston houses and for those subsidiary dwellings in the backyards which are now stylish apartments. A well-to-do family of the upper class would have a coachman and grooms, a butler and footman, a housekeeper and assistants, a maid for each small child, a lady's maid for each lady, a cook with an apprentice and a kitchen-boy, laundresses as needed; and for good measure each gentleman of the family had a man-servant. Without expressing any approval of the institution which made these retinues possible, a twentieth-century house-holder of these post-war days, when cooks and maids come unwillingly and stand not upon the order of their going, can hardly repress a sigh for those good old times.

Naturally, entertainment was on a scale adjusted to these mobs of servants, justifying the city's reputation for gayety and hospitality. But social merriment in the great houses was not the only life the city afforded. There was a vigorous country trade, with great wagons rolling on upper King Street. If the factors failed to relieve the business worries of the planters, there was a horde of lawyers to settle the difficulties that resulted; the great shops stood in Broad, Tradd and Elliott Streets. And to cap this picture of a rich and luxurious community, there were in the year 1812 in the city of Charleston, according to Mr. E. Milby Burton's compilation, no fewer than seventy silversmiths.

The War of 1812, which ignored Charleston as far as hostilities were concerned, provided a formidable commercial setback to the planters of rice and cotton, during which profiteers made fortunes out of their stocks of goods; but by 1815 the city was throwing off this handicap and regaining its wealth.

The town had a sensation in 1820, when the proprietors of what was called the Four Mile House, just north of the city, were hanged for the murder of a number of people who had been waylaid, and a certain Mr. Deliesselines was brutally murdered in the same year while searching for runaway slaves.

But more was to come. The number of blacks was growing rapidly; where in 1800 it had been a bare majority, by 1830 it was to outnumber the whites 17,461 to 12,828.

In the year 1822 a plot for a Negro insurrection had the town by the ears. Its story goes back before the ending of the Revolution, to the year 1781, when the officers of a slave ship were struck by the beauty and intelligence of a Negro boy of fourteen. They made a protégé of the youngster during the voyage, dressing him up in the fine clothes his handsome appearance seemed to call for—but when the ship appeared at Cap Français, Santo Domingo, he was sold like the rest. Later Captain Vesey, the master and his owner, was informed that the young Télémaque had been rejected by his purchaser as unsound and epileptic, and although he had sold the youth in entire good faith, he was obliged to refund the purchase price and take him back. For twenty years Télémaque was a faithful servant. Then, in the East Bay Street lottery, he won fifteen hundred dollars, purchased his freedom, and set up in business for himself as a carpenter.

He had taken the name of his owner, of course, and was now known as Denmark Vesey. His striking appearance and his domineering manner made him a great swaggerer before his own people, and he was the possessor of numerous wives, which probably added to his prestige. As he had traveled several times to the North, it is possible that he had been influenced by the abolitionists. He became the leader of a plot to revolt, in which he was assisted by one Gullah Jack, a "necromancer" who was greatly feared by the Negroes. The plot appears to have had all the ingredients of a Southern woman's nightmare; even wigs were provided to make the Negroes of light color look like white men, and plans were carefully laid for the murder of prominent white men and the seizure of property. The twelfth of June was the night set for the general insurrection, and it might have occurred but for the fact that two conservative and level-headed Negroes acted as informers. On the night of the scheduled rising, the known leaders in the conspiracy were arrested and, it must be noted, given a trial by due process of law. Fifty-four were convicted; many others were freed as being mere simple-minded and sheepish followers. Of the convicted men, twenty-nine were deported and thirty-five were hanged.

The affair resulted in a more stringent regulation of the Negro population of Charleston, with a volunteer guard to patrol the streets at night and an interdiction of the return of free Negroes who had traveled to the North and were therefore presumably corrupted and dangerous. There were embarrassments when travelers from the North had their black servants along, and the questions of the deckhands on ships had to be met; but there was no open clash of sovereignties.

Obviously the proposed uprising, coming so soon after the extension of slavery to the Louisiana Purchase had been hotly debated, had an evil effect upon Southern thinking. There had been many abolition societies in the South; the time was now approaching when the application of the term to any man would constitute an insult.

Three years later Charleston had excitement of a vastly different sort, when it received the venerable Marquis de Lafayette to its bosom.

Charleston had a particular interest in the old French nobleman who as a young man had done so much for the colonists in the struggle with England. Besides gratitude, which is not always very long-lived, the city remembered that Lafayette had first set foot on American soil in the Low Country and Charleston had paid court to him then. Another circumstance was that his host's little boy Francis Kinloch Huger had sat on his knee. And this was to engender another tie.

When young Huger was traveling in Europe as a youth of twenty-one, his boyhood hero was in prison at Olmütz in Austria. Huger came into contact with a student named Justus Erich Bollman, and the two of them concocted a hair-brained scheme for the freeing of Lafayette. The plan, which involved the furnishing of a carriage and horses and the bribing of guards to free the Frenchman, miscarried and Huger landed in prison as a result of it. He stayed there eight months, uncertain even of his life, and was finally freed only upon the intervention of the British ambassador. It is incidentally interesting that Bollman later came to the United States and became the agent of Aaron Burr.

It was only appropriate that Lafayette on the way to Charleston should be accompanied by Francis Huger. Congress had made a gift of land and the sum of two hundred thousand dollars to Lafayette, and the old man, aware that his would-be rescuer's affairs were not in the most flourishing condition, very generously offered to share this official gift with him. Naturally, of course, this was gratefully refused.

Lafayette's reception in Charleston began well outside the city lines, where he was met by cavalry. When he reached the boundary, the Washington Light Infantry and the Fusiliers Françaises followed his carriage and then the procession was lengthened by soldiers, the Society of the Cincinnati, school children, clergymen, former Revolutionary officers, all of them fifty years older now. When the hero met the two Pinckney brothers, he embraced them French fashion, with a kiss on the cheeks, which made the school children roar with laughter. Then proceeding to the City Hall, he stood on the steps and showed himself to the crowd.

Entertainments followed one after the other, visits, and as a climax the ball at the theater on Broad and New streets where eighteen hundred people were gathered, all dressed in their finest. The old soldier sat it out for an hour and a half and survived. He appears to have been more openly pleased at the treatment accorded him than was the less volatile Washington, but he was probably glad to get away at the end of the week.

Lafayette's visit puts a period to what, with a bit of stretching, might be called the post-Revolutionary phase of Charleston. From 1830 to 1850 the city's white population rose from twelve thousand odd to twenty thousand; in the decade following the rise was much slower. Improved methods of irrigating the rice fields brought a marked increase in this crop; cotton was making men more and more wealthy; and the leisurely ante-bellum culture of the Low Country was in those thirty years to enjoy its full fruition. Those were the times of Mr. Poinsett, the world-traveler and ambassador to Mexico, and his famous breakfasts, admission to which was on the score of wit and ready conversation; of Judge King's dinners; of the charm and humor of Mr. Petigru, the city's great man of law; and of the great races, so much a civic event that, according to Fraser, the schools were dismissed on racing day. The great Greek revival houses and temples were springing up, and Charleston was a byword for elegance and gayety.

Of course, there was a darker side of the picture. Travelers of the 1830's and '40's mention the shabbiness of the city as a whole; Sir Charles Lyell, one of that group of great scientists who lectured in Charleston (others being Agassiz and Maury) was very frank about the city's stench. Obviously everyone was not prosperous, but, after all, Utopia has never existed anywhere. And Charleston was on the make.

In 1830 the first steam railroad puffed out of the city, drawn by the locomotive "Best Friend," which was later melted to make cannon for the Confederacy, and of which there is a model in the Charleston Museum. There were then great dreams of a railroad to "the West," and a line was finally pushed to the Mississippi (amid great rejoicing and ceremony) in which the facilitated passage, years later, of Union soldiers under the command of Sherman was to make the enterprise an undreamed-of curse to the state.

There was a bad rent in the political fabric, too. The question of states' rights, long agitated, came to a head over the new tariffs. Nullification, the new doctrine of a state's privilege of choosing whether to obey or disobey a Federal amendment, split families and broke friendships. In 1830 Robert Young Hayne, of Charleston, stood up to the great Daniel Webster and held him to a draw. In 1832, when the new tariffs had been promulgated, sentiment for Nullification reached such a pitch in South Carolina that the state passed the Ordinance of Nullification. President Jackson, a South Carolinian by birth, partly because of his autocratic tendencies and partly, also, because of the friction between the Jackson and Calhoun groups which had come to a head over the slight to Mrs. Jackson and to Mrs. Eaton, the wife of one of his cabinet members, was in no mood for trifling. He threatened the use of troops to enforce South Carolina's payment of the tariff. Hayne, then governor, defied him; Poinsett, although a Charlestonian, in his capacity of Secretary of War, advised Jackson to send a fleet and troops, and Jackson did so. Almost anything could have happened, but fortunately cooler heads succeeded in averting trouble, and Clay's compromise, satisfying to both sides, brought peace "in our time," as Mr. Chamberlain said many years later of the Munich Agreement.

A ball was held in Charleston for the departing fleet, and civil war was postponed for twenty-eight years.

Here an ominous note creeps into the record. The Federal government began, in 1839, the construction of Fort Sumter, which was still uncompleted in 1860. Another war, however, was to intervene before the omen was fulfilled. The young men marched off to glory against Mexico and not a few distinguished themselves. In 1849 the present limits of the city were established. And in 1850 John C. Calhoun, the champion of the South, drew his last breath.

Mr. Calhoun was a South Carolinian, but not a Charlestonian. However, the plea of the city that the state's favorite son be buried there was granted—and, although Mr. Calhoun had aided in the establishment of a Unitarian church in Washington, it was considered fitting that he should be buried in the churchyard of St. Philip's.

And since this was one of Charleston's biggest public events, the following account, taken from the *Charleston Yearbook* for 1883, seems not disproportionately long:

The funeral obsequies of Senator John C. Calhoun were conducted in this city with imposing magnificence and impressive solemnity on the twenty-fifth and twenty-sixth of April, 1850. The remains arrived from Washington, where Mr. Calhoun died on the thirty-first of March, 1850, escorted by a committee from the United States Senate and House of Representatives, the Sergeant-at-Arms of the Senate, a committee of citizens from Wilmington, N. C., a committee of twenty-five from South Carolina, and a subcommittee of arrangements. Upon arrival, the remains were placed upon a funeral car, drawn by six horses, caparisoned in mourning trappings which trailed the ground, and was escorted, to the sound of muffled drums, to the Citadel Square. Here the body was formally surrendered by the Senate Committee to the chief executive of the State, Governor Whitemarsh B. Seabrook, and by him in turn to the mayor of the city, Hon. T. L. Hutchinson. A funeral cortege was then formed, and proceeded down King Street to Hasell, through Hasell to Meeting, around White Point [i.e., the Battery] up the Bay to Broad Street, thence to the City Hall. Here the body was received by the

Mayor and Aldermen, and deposited within a magnificent catafalque, where it lay in state until the next day, under charge of a guard of honor, composed of two hundred citizens. Thousands repaired to the hall to pay their last respects to the illustrious dead. The next day, 26th April, at early dawn, the bells of the city resumed their toll, business remained suspended, and a civic procession was formed. The remains were removed from the catafalque to St. Philip's Church, which was draped in deepest mourning. An anthem was sung by a full choir, the funeral services read by Bishop Gadsden, and a funeral discourse pronounced by Rev. James W. Miles. The body was then borne by the guard of honor to the Western cemetery of the church and deposited within a structure of masonry, raised above the ground and lined with cedar wood.

Every organized association voluntarily paraded—the civic authorities, the military, the firemen, the Masonic and Odd-Fellows lodges, the benevolent societies—everything that could add to the mournful pageantry of grief had, by its presence, outwardly manifested the inward sorrow of the community.

The funeral cortege was the largest gathering of citizens ever seen in Charleston, occupying over two hours in passing any one point.

And, adds the *Yearbook's* account, "the great 'defender of the Constitution' on this occasion received such offices of respect and veneration as had never before been witnessed in our State."

With a combined white and black population of forty-three thousand, Charleston, rich and powerful, was nearing catastrophe. But naturally there was no hint of this in the lives of its citizens. Racing, the Cecilia Society, the state dinners, shooting, riding, and the making of more money occupied the wealthy and fortunate; and they had ten years in which to enjoy their blessings.

CHAPTER SEVEN

Fall

No doubt a close socio-political history of Charleston could trace, in the years immediately preceding the Civil War, indications that the city's civilization was already betraying signs of having reached a kind of Spenglerian saturation point. It is notable that after the great fire of 1838, the comments of visitors on the appearance of the city become increasingly acid. Rice, cotton, and shipping were, it is true, bringing greater prosperity than ever before—to some—but there were bad slums and a down-at-heel look to contrast with the great temple-like houses and churches of the Greek revival, which added grandeur (and a faint note of pretentiousness) to the city's strongly Georgian and Adam architecture. Well-to-do gentlemen met at literary clubs and listened to lectures and discussions by some of the best men of the time, rather like the ladies impaled on Edith Wharton's pointed phrase, who "pursued culture, in bands, as if they were afraid of meeting it alone." On the other hand, the ruffianly *code duello* had reached a point of refinement which constituted its *reductio ad absurdum*—that is, provided there is anything absurd in murder. Perhaps the long lingering of this custom points to some fiery recklessness in the Southern blood which could be blamed for the Civil War—although that excessive simplification is emphatically not intended as an explanation of the conflict.

Gallantry and *noblesse oblige* were still strongly in evidence. When Major Anderson and his men were uneasily holding Fort Sumter, for example, they were permitted to come to the city for supplies, and the respect accorded the Unionist Petigru at the height of the war is a tribute to Charleston itself. However, the old spirit of tolerance had died out. The Grimké sisters, who were abolitionists, had long been forbidden to return to the city to visit their relatives; the sale of abolitionist literature was forbidden; and the word abolitionist, if we are to take DuBose Heyward's novel *Peter Ashley* seriously as a picture of Civil War days, was enough to provoke a duel when used as an epithet.

Of course the war was fought over the question of states' rights and the doctrine of secession; but the quarrel over states' rights reached a head in questions affecting the limitation or broadening of slavery.

Who knows, however, that the secession movement might not have died a happy and peaceful death had it not been for one man? We must avoid oversimplification but just as Christopher Gadsden had been "The Firebrand of the Revolution," so Robert Barnwell Rhett was "The Father of Secession."

Rhett was not a Charlestonian, and he does not represent in most minds the true type of the Southern aristocrat. However, it is too easy to sneer at him. He was born of good family— the name Rhett, which he took instead of the less aristocratic Smith he was born to, was his by right of descent; he was a brilliant politician, and it must not be forgotten that he enjoyed the respect and friendship of such men as James Louis Petigru. His rise to political power was rapid; at one time South Carolina was known as "Rhettsylvania"! He was even strong enough to defy Calhoun and survive.

But, whether we are to exalt or depress the role of indi-

MARKET STREET AND THE MARKET HALL

THE MANIGAULT HOUSE

viduals in history, Rhett openly worked for secession with might and main. Events played into his hands; the heroics of the abolitionists and John Brown's raid added force to the movement for secession. Perhaps, if these things had not happened, wiser counsels would have prevailed. At any rate, feeling had attained to such a pitch that when the Democratic convention met in Charleston in April, 1860, it was split over the extreme position that a slave owner could take slaves into territories if he so desired. When it became apparent that this plank was not going to get into the platform, the cotton states withdrew from the convention.

There were two conventions at Baltimore that year, and two Democratic nominations for president; the Northern Democrats named Stephen A. Douglas as their man, and the Southerners John C. Breckinridge of Kentucky. When the election approached, South Carolina openly threatened to secede from the Union in the event of the election of an anti-slavery president; and when the election of Lincoln became a fact as well as a foregone conclusion, the state was as good as her word.

A convention was called at Columbia and the delegates met there on the 17th of December. After a committee had been named to draw up an Ordinance of Secession, the convention removed to Charleston, for an outbreak of smallpox in the capital was rivalling, so to speak, the epidemic of secessionism.

At the portentous final session held in St. Andrew's Hall, the delegates voted unanimously to adopt the Ordinance and it was solemnly signed by all of them on the very table that had been used for the ratification of the Constitution of the United States in 1788. When the news was given out, the crowds, wearing palmetto cockades, cheered themselves hoarse; bands played; artillery salutes were fired; bells were rung. The *Mercury,* which Rhett had bought and put under the editorship of his son, had an extra out within fifteen minutes, a broadside which told the citizens, in immense letters, that "the Union is DISSOLVED!" A *Te Deum* was sung at the Cathedral of St. John and St. Finbar, and all the churches rejoiced; pitch was burned in the streets.

When the uproar was at its height, that unbending Unionist, Mr. Petigru, asked if there was a fire. When he was told that there wasn't, but that secession was being celebrated, he replied stubbornly: "I tell you there is a fire. They have set a burning torch to the temple of constitutional liberty, and please God, we shall have no more peace forever." It is fairly certain that he was the only person of consequence in Charleston who felt that way, and he wrote to his sister of his sadness in feeling so alone. (Even the Northern-born Lutheran minister, the Rev. Mr. John Bachman, Audubon's collaborator, author of *The Unity of the Human Race,* and a former Unionist, had opened the Secession Convention with a prayer.) Later, when Mr. Petigru was in his pew in St. Michael's and a prayer was offered for the President of the Confederacy, he arose and left the church.

Things went forward. A commission was dispatched to Washington to negotiate the surrender of Forts Sumter, Johnson, Moultrie, and Castle Pinckney. But the long delay must have been trying to the hotheads.

One of the very first moves came on the day after Christmas. At that time Major Robert Anderson of the United States Army, in command of the garrison at Fort Moultrie, decided that Fort Sumter, then undergoing repairs, was a safer place, and on the night of the 26th of December he spiked the guns of Moultrie and removed his men to Sumter. Whereupon the *Courier* declared:

... Major Robert Anderson, of the United States Army, has achieved the unenviable distinction of opening civil war between American citizens by an act of gross breach of faith. He has, under counsels of panic,

deserted his post at Fort Moultrie, and, under false pretexts, has transferred his garrison, and military stores and supplies, to Fort Sumter.

Rhett's *Mercury* was of the opinion that "the holding of
Fort Sumter by United States troops was an invasion of South
Carolina."

Both opinions are a little like an Episcopalian bishop's
statement, apropos of a project for the union of Protestant
and Catholic churches, that the Church of Rome had undergone great changes since it separated from the rest of Chris-
tendom.

Anderson refused to return to Fort Moultrie, and state
troops then took over Fort Johnson, where Anderson had sent
his men's wives and children; Fort Moultrie, and Castle
Pinckney.

To prevent reinforcements being sent to Fort Sumter, a procedure the United States Government was deliberating, a battery was built on Cummings Point and called Battery Gregg.
In January the *Star of the West*, with provisions and two
hundred men, tried to reach Sumter. The new battery fired
across her bows, and when she attempted to keep on, put another shot through her rigging. The *Star of the West* prudently retreated, and the Confederates began work on the
circle of forest and batteries around Fort Sumter.

Next day, which was January 10th, the *Mercury* screamed:

Yesterday, the ninth of January, will be remembered in history.
Powder has been burnt over the decree of our State, timber has been
crashed, perhaps blood spilled. The expulsion of the *Star of the West*
from Charleston Harbor yesterday morning was the opening of the ball
of Revolution. We are proud that our harbor has been so honored. We
are proud that the State of South Carolina, so long, so bitterly, and so
contemptuously reviled and scoffed at, above all others, should thus
proudly have thrown back the scoff of her enemies. Intrenched upon
her soil, she has spoken from the mouth of her cannon, and not from the
mouths of scurrilous demagogues, fanatics and scribblers. Contemned,
the sanctity of her waters violated with hostile purpose of re-enforcing

enemies in our harbor, she has not hesitated to *strike the first blow,* full in the face of her insulter. Let the United States Government bear, or return at its good-will, the blow still tingling about its ears—the fruit of its own bandit temerity. We would not exchange or recall that blow for millions! It has wiped out half a century of scorn and outrage. . . . Upon each acre of the peaceful soil of the South armed men will spring up . . . and it will be found that every word of our insolent foe has been, indeed, a dragon's tooth sown for their destruction. And though grisly and traitorous ruffians may cry on the dogs of war, and treacherous politicians may lend their aid in deceptions, South Carolina will stand under her own Palmetto tree, unterrified by the snarling growls or assaults of the one, undeceived or deterred by the wily machinations of the other. And if that red seal of blood be still lacking for the parchment of our liberties, and blood they want—blood they shall have—and blood enough to stamp it all in red. For, by the God of our Fathers, the soil of South Carolina shall be free!

This baying, and more of the like, did not win for the older Rhett any position in the Confederate government. Charleston was passed over.

Charleston had race week to get out of the way, and according to the lively scenes in Mr. Heyward's novel, the *Peter Ashley* previously referred to, the threat of war did very little to deflect the minds of the citizens and their servants from the important differences of opinion that were being solved on the race track.

President Davis sent the dashing Louisiana Catholic, Pierre Gustave Toutant de Beauregard, to assume command of Charleston Harbor. The Great Creole arrived early in March, the day after the inauguration of Lincoln, and saw to it that the fortifications around Fort Sumter were pressed forward.

At first Anderson and his men had been permitted to obtain food and supplies in Charleston under an escort, but in April Beauregard put a stop to this, and Anderson notified the War Department that he could not hold out without supplies beyond the fifteenth of the month. Beauregard, after inquiring of the Confederate government, was told that Sumter must be taken. A Federal relief expedition was assembling outside the harbor when, on April 12th at dawn, Beauregard notified Anderson that, unless he surrendered within an hour, the fort would be fired upon.

From the housetops, at half-past four in the morning, the expectant citizens of Charleston saw a flash from Fort Johnson, on the tip of James Island. The batteries and Fort Moultrie joined in the firing, and suffered little damage from Sumter's response. For thirty hours the bombardment continued. Finally a picturesque busybody named Wigfall, a fire-eating senator from Texas, had himself rowed over to the fort under a flag of truce and without Beauregard's knowledge discussed terms with Anderson. Although the parley had been unauthorized, Beauregard accepted Anderson's capitulation under the proposed terms, and Major Anderson and his men evacuated the fort with the honors of war. For the beginning of a fierce war, this was a singularly bloodless battle, for not a single man had been killed on either side. "Never," says Robert Selph Henry, "was a costly victory so easily won."

Lincoln called for volunteers, four more states joined the Confederacy, and it was war.

As in the Revolution, Charleston, after an impressive debut, was safe from war for a time; and almost as if following the same pattern, there was a devastating fire which a strong wind carried from the east waterfront to the Ashley River, burning up, among many buildings, St. Andrew's Hall on Broad Street (where secession had been ratified), and the Catholic Cathedral of St. John and St. Finbar, and making thousands homeless. Charleston's able-bodied men, of course, were active; the city furnished about 6,000 fighting men, a terrific drain upon the population not quite four times that number. It underwent a blockade, too; and on Columbus Day, 1861, the *Gordon* left a Charleston dock with Messrs. Mason and Slidell aboard; thus Charleston had a part, at least, in the Trent Case.

We have mentioned the neglect of Charleston's men in the formation of the new government. There was one important, and from a certain point of view fateful, exception. This was Gustavus Memminger, whom Davis appointed to be Secretary of the Treasury.

Memminger, the son of German immigrants, had been orphaned at an early age, and had been taken from the Orphan House by Governor Bennett, the rice-mill owner and builder. He became a successful lawyer; his most brilliant success was won in a suit to enforce specie payments by the Bank of South Carolina; and he wrote the majority report for the South Carolina Convention, "so much of which," according to Burton J. Hendrick, "was copied in the Ordinance of Secession that he is sometimes called the father of that historic document."

There have undoubtedly been odd selections, in the course of American history, for appointive (to say nothing of elective) office. But on the face of it Memminger seems to have been one of the oddest. He was a man of scholarly tastes, indifferently regarded even in his home city, where he was known chiefly as an amateur theologian. Rhett and others ridiculed his piety, his humble birth, and his other characteristics, which might have made no great difference. However, Memminger was fundamentally miscast. He was a hard-money man in what was to be a paper-money treasury.

He is most conspicuously identified with the great cotton fiasco. Certain elements in the Confederacy had evolved a plan of selling the region's cotton surplus to England for gold credit; another school of economists, if that term may be used, believed that the creation of a "cotton famine" would force England and France to support the Confederacy. Memminger sided with the latter. Cotton in warehouses was set afire and the crop was neglected. It was all, of course, a ghastly mistake. Great Britain, as it turned out, had a huge supply of cotton, and the creation of an artificial famine ran the price up and enabled merchants to make a huge profit. No unemployment, supposed to be a sure forerunner of popular insistence upon supporting the South, resulted, for the increased demand took up the slack.

And, of course, neither Memminger nor anyone else could have managed the Confederate financial problem. It was already too late when the Charleston banker, George A. Trenholm, was called in to do what he could.

Meanwhile Fort Sumter was rebuilt, although General Pemberton, the Yankee turned Southerner, wanted it abandoned. A Federal attempt to enter the harbor had been made just before the second anniversary of the firing on Fort Sumter, when Admiral Dupont led a squadron of ten ironclads into the harbor mouth. The guns of Forts Sumter and Moultrie promptly shot them right out again, with the exception of the *Keokuk,* which sank off Morris Island. Two of her guns were recovered for the Confederacy by a heroic exploit; one was mounted on Fort Sumter and the other on Battery Bee, on Sullivan's Island.

And little Castle Pinckney was a prison for the Federal men captured at the First Battle of Bull Run. There they were guarded by the young boys of the Charleston Zouaves. Charleston was making uniforms, coping as best it could with the ever-increasing shortages of food and goods and men. Then, right after Dupont's unsuccessful invasion, the war came home to the city.

Posterity is indebted to a daring and original Charleston man for actual views of this phase of the war. This was the photographer George S. Cook, the Mathew B. Brady of Charleston, who had photographic materials (another thing in which the agrarian South was wholly lacking) smuggled to

him from the enemy state of New York. Cook, with the clumsy
equipment of that time, photographed Fort Sumter under
fire, and actually obtained a successful picture of a bursting
shell in the very center of the fort. Many of his photographs
were lost or were destroyed by owners anxious to rid themselves of all reminders of the tragic war years, but the interested reader can see a number of them in Miller's *Photographic
History of the Civil War;* and if he is inclined to doubt reports of what the war did to Charleston, they ought to convince him.

In the summer of 1863, Union troops gained a foothold
on Morris Island and besieged Battery Wagner. On August
12th the great Parrott rifles there began to get the range of
Fort Sumter, and from the 17th to the 24th fired steadily upon
the fort until it was virtually demolished. Then the bombardment was renewed, but the fort, although a wreck, still held
on. Two other bombardments, from May, 1864, until September of that year, failed to take Fort Sumter, which was bol-
stered up by bags of sand sent from the city, particularly from
Charlotte Street, which has in consequence never recovered
its original level.

During this campaign, an improved rifle called the "Swamp
Angel," the Big Bertha of those days, had been mounted by
the Federal forces in the marshes between James and Morris
Islands. From five miles away it flung its first shell into
Charleston. Beauregard, again in command, protested, and
asked that the fire be held until the women and children could
be got out of the city. His request was granted, and then the
Swamp Angel resumed fire. One of the shells struck St.
Michael's; but, after it had fired thirty-six rounds, the great
gun blew up. There were, however, plenty of others, and from
August 22, 1863, to February 18, 1865, the city was under
a continual siege. It was thoroughly smashed, though very
few of the citizens were killed.

During the very last months of the war, Federal prisoners, in addition to those in Castle Pinckney, were kept in the Roper Hospital (then on Queen Street) and in one of the large private houses in the southeast end of the town. They were under Federal fire, naturally, and the Union forces retaliated by placing Confederate prisoners in a stockade on Morris Island. Fortunately, nothing came of these reprisals which were due to the bitterness of feeling that had grown as the war dragged on.

More remarkable than the trifling loss of life incurred during this lengthy siege was the fact that the city withstood the long pounding without yielding, and that Fort Sumter, although a mere heap of rubble, was never taken or forced to surrender. The defense of the harbor and city was described by Beauregard as a feat of war unsurpassed in ancient or modern times. A full account of it was written by Major (later the Reverend Mr.) John Johnson. Now long out of print, it is still considered a classic of its kind.

There were some interesting side stories concerned with this long siege. One was the exploit of the *Little David,* a semi-submersible. With funds contributed by Theodore D. Stoney of Charleston, Dr. St. Julien Ravenel, later the discoverer of the deposits of phosphate rock near the city, designed and constructed the fifty-foot torpedo boat. Lying so low in the water as to be virtually invisible, the *David* went up to the U.S.S. *New Ironsides* and discharged a torpedo under her waterline, putting her out of commission, and then got safely back to her anchorage. Some months later came the *Hundley,* a "fishboat" from Alabama. She was so dangerous to handle that Beauregard, after a score of men had been killed trying to navigate her, ordered the end of further experiments. But there is always some young daredevil who wants to make the impossible his duty and to attain glory. This time it was a lieutenant named Dixon, from the same state as the *Hundley.*

He persuaded the Great Creole that improper handling was the reason for the disasters, and got permission to try again. It was more or less a case of "Mother, may I go out to swim," for Beauregard had agreed to this test only on condition that the craft be kept from submerging.

The *Hundley,* accordingly, was armed with a spar torpedo, and under cover of night she got to within a hundred yards of the man-of-war *Housatonic* and let fly. The *Housatonic,* struck amidships, sank almost immediately, but in such shallow water that her complement, with the exception of five men who had been killed by the explosion of the torpedo, escaped with their lives by scrambling up into the rigging.

The *Hundley,* however, had disappeared completely. After the war had ended, divers, working on the *Housatonic* in the effort to clear the harbor channel, found the fishboat jammed into the rent the explosion had torn in the side of the man-of-war, and all her brave crew within her.

The end came for Charleston when Sherman was advancing, and the city had either to yield or be caught between land and sea. Already, the south end of the city was a thing of yawning walls, shattered windows, and lifeless streets. General Hardee moved out of the city's fortifications on February 17, 1865, and Fort Sumter was abandoned, her commander taking the shell-torn flag along in the boats.

Charleston was spared the torch of Sherman, who, as has been said, took the city by turning his back on it, but she was not to be spared one more wartime calamity. Hardee gave orders for the destruction of the Ashley River bridge and for the burning of all cotton stored in the city. It is generally believed that boys at play found a store of powder and in the process of throwing handfuls of it on the burning cotton to aid the good work, started a powder train which led to the Northeastern Railway Depot, where the explosive was stored. This blew up, and the result, in addition to the loss of 150 lives, was the destruction of several blocks of houses and other buildings.

There is an old joke to the effect that if the South had not seceded, South Carolina would have seceded from the South, Charleston from South Carolina, and South of Broad Street from Charleston. Something of that spirit came over the state during the war, for South Carolina stoutly resisted conscription (of which, to do her justice, she had little need) and the impressment of slaves into the armed services. She lost heavily in men and in wealth, and a special vindictiveness was visited upon her, and particularly upon Charleston, by the victors.

But that was to come later, after the ceremonies of occupation, and after the Reverend Henry Ward Beecher had proclaimed, in battered Fort Sumter, that the Union had been preserved. The day was April 14th, and that evening Abraham Lincoln was assassinated.

CHAPTER EIGHT
And Decline

Only photographs can adequately reveal what the Civil War had done to the physical side of Charleston. But the impressions of an outsider convey some notion of the state to which the town had been reduced.

Benson J. Lossing, in his rather spiteful *Pictorial History of the Civil War in the United States* (1866), after gloating over Charleston's plight, adds a letter written just after Federal troops had taken possession. Says the anonymous writer:

The wharves looked as if they had been deserted for half a century— broken down, dilapidated, grass and moss peeping up between the pavements . . . the warehouses near the river; the streets as we enter them; the houses and the stores and the public buildings—we look at them and hold our breaths in utter amazement. . . . No imagination can conceive of the utter wrecks, the universal ruin, the stupendous desolation.

Having got himself wound up, our unknown writer, who must have had literary ambitions or have learned his style from the editorials of the *Mercury*, fairly lets himself go. He continues:

Ruin—ruin—ruin—above and below . . . staring at us from every paneless window; looking out at us from every shell-torn wall; glaring at us from every battered door and pillar and veranda; crouching beneath our feet on every sidewalk. Not Pompeii, nor Herculaneum, nor

Thebes, nor the Nile have ruins so complete, so saddening, so plaintively eloquent, for they speak to us of an age not ours and long ago dead, with whose people and life and ideas we have no sympathy whatever. But here, on these shattered wrecks of houses—built in our own style, many of them doing credit to the architecture of our epoch—we read names familiar to us all; telling us of trades and professions and commercial institutions which every modern city reckons up by the hundreds; yet dead, dead, dead; as silent as the graves of the Pharaohs—

Et cetera.

That, in a somewhat purple light, was the condition of the city to which came the scalawags and carpetbaggers. In 1868, when Union military rule ended in the state, the plunderers assumed control, and as Robert Goodwyn Rhett succinctly expresses it, "every appropriation soon carried enough to pay for the passage of the bill authorizing it," and such organizations as the Sinking Fund Commission plundered wholesale.

Mr. Howard Fast has painted, in *Freedom Road,* a picture favorable to the Negro legislators of South Carolina which suggests not too subtly that they were on the way to a true democracy.

But that is by the way. South Carolina actually had an appalling travesty of government until, in the year 1876, General Wade Hampton was elected governor of South Carolina on a Democratic ticket, almost as remarkable a feat as if, in the time of the late Hitler, a communist had got himself voted into the office of Chancellor of the Reich. There was a majority of 26,000 Negroes of voting age over whites in the state, and every particle of election machinery was in the hands of Republicans.

Hampton, born in Charleston in the famous Rhett House on Hasell Street, was a wealthy planter of strong Unionist sympathies who nevertheless put himself at the service of his state and became commander-in-chief of Lee's cavalry. His long experience in the management of Negroes, and their trust in him, enabled him to do the impossible—aided, of

course, by a little strong-arm work and by the "rifle clubs" that
were organized in the state. There was a tussle over the
election, and two governments pretended to the overlordship
of the state. When President Hayes withdrew United States
troops from South Carolina, Hampton and his Democrats
took over.

On October 2, 1878, Charleston had what the *News and
Courier* described as its greatest day. That was the occasion
of the city's welcome to its native son and deliverer, Hampton.
On this fall day the town really cut loose. There were parades;
floats, wagons, and men on foot participated. Houses were
decorated with evergreens, bunting, and banners, and flags of
all sorts, even German and French ones, waved over the
streets. The procession moved through Calhoun Street to
King, and then at Hasell turned east to Meeting and took its
way down that thoroughfare to the Battery, where the speech-
making was to take place. The general tendency of the oratory
was to accentuate the fact that South Carolina's civilization
had been saved.

The industries of the city and vicinity were again set in motion; and as some of the cannier wealthy men of the state had
managed to transfer money to Europe during the war, evidently without considering the Confederacy's urgent need of
it, there was capital handy to promote commerce. Rice and
cotton resumed their importance. And meanwhile there had
been a discovery which led to great hopes for a new industry.

The earlier discovery of marls in the marshy lands west of
the Ashley River—close to the road which leads to Magnolia
Gardens—had uncovered what was known as the "Charleston
Fish Basin." Critics of the city will tell you that Charleston
has for a long time been full of fossils, but the remains of
ancient life found by the marl diggers were fossils of the scientifically recognized sort. Here, in the words of a contemporary
report, were found "whole acres richly studded with fossils ...

bones of the mammoth, mastodon, megatherium, mylodon, magalonyx, phocodon . . . sauri; also the teeth and bones of the shark, and numerous other fishes in great variety . . . pottery, (and) stone hatchets like those found in Abbeville, France." Most of the fossils were of the post-Pliocene age. Interest in these led to the discovery by Dr. St. Julien Ravenel and others of extensive deposits of phosphate rock, and for a comparatively short time the industry flourished. But, alas for Charleston! better deposits were later found elsewhere.

The South Carolina Institute had promoted a fair in 1870, but the city's prosperity had not seemed to expand greatly after any of these affairs. And, when Mayor Courtenay, in 1879, took over the reins of the city after the long era of misrule, the city was several million dollars in debt, chiefly as the result of railroad investments in the course of its struggle to attain adequate freight services. Restrictions were placed around the incurring of further debts, and the spirit of optimism seems to have been high at the time of the Centennial of Incorporation in 1883.

This took place on August 13, 1883. The day was begun with a salute of one hundred guns. A parade was very sensibly dispensed with on account of the terrific heat. In the afternoon there were speeches, and busts of Robert Young Hayne and James L. Petigru were unveiled and portraits of local heroes dedicated. A poem to Hayne by his nephew, the poet Paul Hamilton Hayne, was read, also his "Centennial Ode." Then activities were adjourned until evening, when a display of fireworks over the Rutledge Street Pond was scheduled.

Half-past eight was the time set, but by five o'clock many small boys were on hand. Over a hundred small boats, most of them strung with lanterns, covered what was described as "the rippling bosom of that now beautiful sheet of water." By the appointed hour there were fifteen thousand people, Negro and white, waiting; and this does not count those who watched from windows and roofs. It must have been quite a display of pyrotechnical ingenuity. To begin with there were striped balloons with explosive charges, followed by large colored rockets—"what the programme calls 'peacock's plumes,' 'silver streamers,' 'golden clouds,' 'eagle's claws,' . . . but which, in reality, looked like a huge chandelier," said the contemporary account in the *Yearbook*. Colored fires burned on the pond, and there were fiery porpoises to delight the children. Then came the "Sunburst," "The Peruvian Glory," "The Casket of Jewels," "The Jewelled Cross of Malta." Then " Charlestown 1670" was flung across the sky, succeeded by the legend "Fort Moultrie, June 28, 1776." After that came "1783—Charleston City—1883." This was anticlimaxed by a "gigantic aerial bouquet" during which the crowd, like all crowds, began to drift away.

And, proving that Charleston had learned its lesson from the many fires in its past, a fire engine remained on duty until eleven o'clock. A modern touch was afforded by the electrical illumination of King Street from Calhoun to Broad, making it, says the *Yearbook,* "as bright as day," and giving "a fair idea of the comfort which pedestrians will enjoy when the public thoroughfares of the city are lighted with electric lights." This vision was rather a long time in being fulfilled, for I remember in my own childhood the lamplighter going around with his taper to light the lamps one by one—although there were carbon arc lamps at intersections. And the comfort of pedestrians everywhere ended forever with the motor car.

But Charleston's valiant struggle to get on its feet was rudely interrupted. In 1885 a terrific cyclone strewed the city upon itself, and less than a year later an epoch-making earthquake toppled buildings as if they had been made of sugar.

On top of this came the political and economic widening of the rift between the Up Country and the Low Country, culminating in the election of "Pitchfork Ben" Tillman as gov-

OLD QUEEN STREET. FOREGROUND SHOWS NORTH SIDE OF
HUGUENOT CHURCH AND ITS NORTH CHURCHYARD

THE CITY HALL AND THE COURT HOUSE

ST. JOHN'S LUTHERAN CHURCH AND SUNDAY SCHOOL
SEEN FROM CLIFFORD STREET

WASHINGTON SQUARE, SHOWING THE PITT STATUE AND
THE FIREPROOF BUILDING

ernor, the defiance by Charleston merchants of the dispensary law and the rebellion of the courts, which threw out cases in-volving the illegal sale of liquor, and, though this was slower in coming to pass, the gradual absorption of cotton shipping by upstate centers, while Charleston, grievously handicapped by discriminatory freight rates, took a back seat. And much of the city's best commercial promise, in the form of its young and progressive men, began to move away to other fields.

The city did not permit itself to be entirely relegated to the position of a monument. It replaced its horse cars by a trolley system, for example, as early as 1897, and in 1900, as a sign of its compliance with modern attitudes, passed an ordi-nance which forbade spitting.

In 1899 Mayor Smyth, learning that the navy was dissatis-fied with the Navy Yard at Port Royal, moved to transfer it to Charleston. With the aid of Charleston's old enemy, Sena-tor Tillman, who promised to back Charleston in the event of Port Royal's losing the yard, he interested the government in his city. The location of the yard at Charleston was recom-mended, but the battle was stiff for a while. Every attempt was made to discredit Charleston as a site; in 1901, during a hear-ing, the salubrity of the neighborhood north of Charleston came into question. Mayor Smyth was among those testifying; he asserted that his daughters lived in that vicinity and that one of them was five feet nine and one-quarter inches tall and weighed one hundred and sixty pounds and that, in short, she was as healthy a young woman as anyone was likely to find. No doubt this testimony made Charleston wince.

The Honorable Hilary A. Herbert, former Secretary of the Navy, who had been retained by Port Royal to carry on the fight, tried desperately to show Charleston's unfitness to receive the political plum, and brought out at the hearing that the city's death rate was appalling—it was, as a matter of fact, being exceeded only by the death rates of Alexandria, Cairo,

Havana, Madras, Madrid, Naples, Rio, and Valparaiso, none of which were at that time exactly health resorts. It was pointed out that even Rome, Pontine Marshes and all, was healthier than Charleston. It was also brought out that the privies of Charleston were a distinct health menace. However, physicians testified that the high death rate was due to the preponderance in the population of the Negro poor, and also to the fact that Charleston's free hospitals were the only refuge for many of them in the surrounding countryside, who died in the city and pushed up the averages. It was also shown that Charleston's financial condition was dubious; whereas the laws required that the debt should not exceed 8 per cent of the assessed value of city property, it was approximately 25 per cent of that value.

Furthermore, there were those in the city who opposed what they called the bringing in of an undesirable element; nevertheless, Charleston got its Navy Yard. It still has it, bigger than ever during the war years, although the exodus of the wartime workers has begun.

With the opening of the twentieth century, it was decided to have an exposition to attract notice and capital from the outside world. Charleston strained itself to the utmost to launch the Charleston and West Indian Exposition. A public-minded citizen, Captain F. W. Wagener, gave money and a large tract of land on the northwest end of the city. A corporation was set up, and capital was solicited. The exposition was rather a grand affair. There was a lake, an Administration Building, a "Cotton Palace," a Negro building; all in all, it was a "fairyland of palaces and towers and gardens, which are springing up there like magic under the touch of twentieth century wizards," as an illustrated guidebook to the city, prepared in advance of the occasion, somewhat floridly expresses it. There was a grand avenue of streets and cities, an electrical palace, a machinery building. There were committees and committees, and presumably everybody was happy and edified. However, as the guidebook rather plaintively admits, "we have here many enterprising business men and financiers, but then, again, we have many who are detrimental to the city and will not invest their money, but hoard it up and thereby are an injury to the advancement of the city's interests." This is paradoxical, for at that time, to judge from the accounts in the same guidebook, Charleston was bursting with the most honest, far-seeing, up-to-date, and public-spirited merchants and professional men imaginable. But what city, in an advertising campaign of this sort, has ever been anything but replete with sterling men of business?

A later comment in the *Yearbook*, which says, "The most remarkable and gratifying feature about the exposition enterprise was that it represented the spirit and power of the people of this community when they pull together," is quite explicit about the lack of financial support. It goes on to say, "It is true that a number of persons in the community of large means did not take an active part in the enterprise, and that some of the people who were most capable of large subscriptions, made the smallest contribution."

Nor was this all. The cotton mills up-state were cool and refused to contribute, and Congress defeated the bill introduced by Senator Tillman to appropriate $250,000 to back the exposition.

Meanwhile the exposition was opened, Chauncey Depew being the speaker, and President Roosevelt was present on Appomattox Day (April 9th) which might have been considered an inauspicious date.

The exposition's financial troubles came to a head when it was still in progress. A firm which had contributed work on the buildings obtained an injunction; this virtually destroyed the credit of the exposition company and led to rumors of the closing of the entire affair, which of course kept an unknown number of visitors from ever entering the city. Cold weather, too, harassed the undertaking.

Nevertheless, the exposition was not a total loss. It brought many visitors and much cash to Charleston, and profitable employment to numerous people. When, after its closing, the company was found to be badly in the red, newspapers and influential men in various parts of the country denounced the stinginess of Congress, and that august body finally appropriated $160,000 to aid in the payment of claims. Not everybody had been pleased, naturally. For one thing, the show failed to impress the colored folk. The Negro group of statuary, for instance—"one of the most artistic"—had been designed to stand in front of the Negro building, but "this attention was bitterly resented by the Negroes of the community, who threatened to destroy the group." Even when the wife of a colored clergyman who was active in the preparation was given the title of "Mrs." in the exposition's official publication!

What industries the fair actually brought to Charleston is a question that might be hard to settle. The United Fruit Company was encouraged to open a branch office; the American Cigar Factory located in the city, and the Oyster Canning Establishment came down from Baltimore.

After the First World War, Charleston was prosperous enough to replace the "new" bridge over the Ashley River with a modern span, but a professional report of 1924 shows discouraging conditions. In the twenties the Tourist Era really began. It was then that Northern millionaires, in the cutting phrase of Jonathan Daniels, became "the real cash crop of Charleston." The great Grace Memorial Bridge was set over the Cooper River; two large new hotels appeared. While the Santee-Cooper power project was still being developed, against the wishes of many, the Second World War began.

Charleston boomed. Real estate values soared; the influx of war workers taxed the accommodations and stores of the city to the utmost. New developments were built north of the city, and war money made it more prosperous than it had been since the years before the Civil War.

Progressive citizens are still making sturdy efforts to promote and encourage industry, but what the future of Charleston will be when the boom dies down, no one can say. That it will be more comfortable cannot be denied. But now, having sketched its history, let's take a look at Carolopolis.

CHAPTER NINE

Church and State

The late DuBose Heyward, Charleston's outstanding modern literary figure, characterized his birthplace in *Porgy* as "an ancient, beautiful city that time had forgotten before it destroyed," and to the melancholy magnificence of that phrase one can best pay tribute by saying that it has the ring of inevitability.

What the receding tide of history has left, besides the pleasant, outwardly calm daily life attuned to the climate and to the temperament of the inhabitants, is a group, roughly about seventy-five, of landmarks of major historical and artistic importance, and several hundred houses which range between interesting and delightful. To describe them all in any detail would obviously be impossible. A sketch of the essential ones is the limit of what a non-specialized work can provide.

The city's most famous feature, certainly, is St. Michael's Church, which architecturally and historically may be said to dominate Charleston. Many noted Americans have worshipped there. Many of the city's great men are buried in its crypts and churchyard. St. Michael's bells have marked the hours for generations of Charlestonians, have warned of fire and flood and storm; their chime, now gone faintly edgy, is in the blood of every native of whatever faith.

The church stands in gleaming whiteness on the southeast corner of Broad and Meeting Streets. Its portico faces, on the south, the lamentable Post Office, an excrescence built with Federal funds at the end of the last century. The old Guard House, which the Post Office replaced, was architecturally in keeping with the other elements in the square, which, besides the church, are the Court House on the northwest corner and the fine City Hall on the northeast.

The site of St. Michael's was that of the first church built in the new town, a small wooden affair erected in 1680 and called St. Philip's. This the town outgrew in the 1720's, and a second St. Philip's was erected on Church Street where the present one stands. It is possible that, before the erection of any church, the spot was used as a burial ground, for during repairs of the south stairway in the last century a coffin was found with the date 1678 outlined on it in brass studs.

In 1751, when the new St. Philip's had also become too small for the number of worshippers, the Assembly authorized the building of a new church on the old site of St. Philip's, and ground was cleared. In 1752 Governor James Glen laid the cornerstone. Construction was at first fairly rapid, but although in the summer of 1753 the cedar for the pews was being solicited, the pews were not allotted until 1760 and the church was not opened for worship until 1761.

The new church was modeled on St. Martin's-in-the-Fields, London. The name of the actual architect is in doubt. Samuel Cardy, the builder, who received eight thousand pounds in Carolina currency for its construction, sometimes referred to himself as an architect, a word of no very exact meaning in the city at that time. There is some possibility that the Mr. Gibson, whose designs the *Gazette* described as those to be followed, was actually James Gibbs, the Londoner who had designed St. Martin's-in-the-Fields, and whose *Book of Archi-*

tecture, according to Miss Beatrice Ravenel, "was a godsend to colonial builders."

St. Michael's, as any illustration will immediately make clear, is exceedingly satisfactory to the eye. It has a single central portico and Palladian windows, and in a manner characteristic of Charleston architecture it combines symmetry and a pleasantly sturdy air. For those who relish statistics, it is 130 feet in length and 60 in breadth. The steeple was originally 187 feet above ground level, but the earthquake of 1886, which caused the entire building to settle, reduced the spire's height by seven or eight inches. A four-sided clock is on the central octagonal course of the steeple. It was installed, with the famous bells from London, in 1764, but was without a minute hand until 1849. When the British fleet appeared in 1776, the steeple was painted black in a vain attempt to lower it visibility.

The interior is somewhat disappointing after the classical simplicity and grace of the outside. There are some rather bad stained glass windows, any further addition to which has happily been banned, and the 1803 chandelier and Tiffany decorations on the chancel leave something to be desired. The galleries are handsome and the vestibule impressive. There is a charming old baptismal font, the cover of which is raised by means of a weighted cord. The altar dates from 1892. A large square double pew is pointed out to visitors as the one in which George Washington worshiped in 1791 and General Lee eighty years later. When one has seen this pew and examined the tablets, the over-all effect of the interior, if he is like one returning native, is to make him long to go outside and to see the sunny churchyard and the magnificent spire.

St. Michael's has always been more than a church. Ever since the early nineteenth century its prestige has exceeded that of even St. Philip's, and membership in either is of considerable social significance, though not in the modern literary sense. But that is not what is meant. St. Michael's tower has been used as an observation post in the Revolution, as a fire signal station, as a signal station in the Civil War, and it housed an air-raid siren in the Second World War. The church and its bells are an institution.

The bells have a history of their own. The British commander, when he evacuated the city in 1783, claimed them as a legitimate prize of war and they were carried off to England. A Charleston merchant bought them, not without an eye to gain from the transaction, and they were shipped back. A crowd of the townspeople escorted them from the ships amid general rejoicing and rehung them. In 1838, the year of the fire, it was found necessary to ship two of the bells back to England for recasting, and their repose was again interrupted in 1862, when they were sent to Columbia for possible use in founding cannon. They escaped this fate, but when Sherman set Columbia afire they were partly melted and had to be sent again to England. Recast by the direct successors of the original founders, they once more chimed over the city in 1867 under the long practiced hand of Washington McLean Gadsden, who had been ringing them since 1837 and who continued to officiate in the belfry until 1898. They have warned of storms and have keyed rejoicing as well as played hymns and marked the hours.

The entry to St. Michael's churchyard is distinguished by the magnificent wrought iron gates, the masterpieces of the ironsmith Iusti, whose name appears on the lintel. The motif is that of an urn, and the tracery is so delicately managed and so graceful that you would think, from a photograph, that surely some other material than iron had been used. Even in Charleston, where superb ironwork is virtually taken for granted, these gates and their scrollwork are outstanding. In fact, they have been called, I do not know by whom, the most nearly perfect gates in America.

Inside the typically Charlestonian brick wall is a churchyard whose air is neither gloomy nor imposing, but mellow. It is all that a churchyard should be, and its quiet dignity is unruffled even by a few freaks—and what churchyard is free of these? Didn't Benjamin Jowett, who, as the squib avers, knew everything that was worth knowing, say "Nowhere probably is there more true feeling, and nowhere worse taste, than in a churchyard"?

St. Michael's and its churchyard are the last resting place of John Rutledge, first governor and great statesman; Charles Cotesworth Pinckney; the artist Charles Fraser, one of Charleston's great men; Robert Young Hayne, who took on Daniel Webster, and his relative, the poet Paul Hamilton Hayne; and also the philanthropist Alexander Shirras, who endowed, among other things, the dispensary which perpetuates his name, and James Louis Petigru. Bishop Dehon, one of the first Episcopal bishops, is buried beneath the floor of the transept. The inscription on the tablet to him is a curiosity in an age determined to forget the classical languages—ending with two lines from Horace:

> *Quis desiderio sit pudor aut modus*
> *Tam chari capitis?*

There is another Latin inscription, this time a complete epitaph, in the churchyard, commemorating an entire family of children. How every old churchyard does remind one of the appalling child mortality of the past! And a New Yorker, not to be outdone in classical inscriptions by citizens of the citadel of culture whither his feet had strayed, is mourned thus:

> *Heu! quanto minus est cum reliquis versari quam tui meminisse!*

A stone to the memory of Ann Bright, d. 1829, quotes Gray's "Elegy." Another commemorates a pious child of eleven whose last edifying words were "Train up a child in the way he should go."

One hopes that it was not any reproach to Charleston's aloofness that occasioned the statement on the gravestone of George Augustus Clough that he died in 1832, aged twenty-two, of "stranger's fever." The first eight lines of his epitaph were written by his brother Arthur Hugh Clough, Winston Churchill's favorite poet, and the last four by Charles Clough, this family having been among Charleston's better-known birds of passage.

A tombstone much sought by visitors is fashioned of the head of a bedstead. It was erected by her husband to the memory of Mary Ann Lytens, who departed this life September 9, 1770. The bedstead, being appropriately of the funereal cypress, has lasted so well that the inscription can still be read, although it was necessary to put a wire screen over it as a guard against souvenir hunters. Another tombstone commemorates Capt. Manuel Antonio, d. 1786, with the fittingly nautical quatrain:

> Although I here at anchor be
> With many of our fleet;
> We must set sail one day again,
> Our Saviour, Christ, to meet.

—which does seem a little matey for St. Michael's, but then there are always contradictions about any old institution. Did not the church accept the altar service proffered by Governor Boone, who was ostracized by Charleston society for too openly featuring his mistress, Mrs. Worthington?

We have left for last the greatest inscription of them all, famous the world over and perhaps unexcelled by any other. The inscription, in one humble opinion, is one of those things that rank in simplicity and grandeur with such passages as Macbeth's soliloquy. And as its subject was a great person, his biography will be briefly related here.

The most memorable thing about James Louis Petigru is that his character, rather than his deeds, made him a great man.

Although this pre-eminent jurist was for a long period Charleston's outstanding citizen, both professionally and socially, he was not a native. His birthplace was Abbeville. His father was of Irish descent, his mother the daughter of a French Huguenot minister named Gibert. The family name actually was Pettigrew; perhaps it was some youthful vanity, such as causes adolescents to sign themselves "Henri" and "Alys" which caused the son to change the name to the more French-looking Petigru. Perhaps he preferred being thought of as French to being identified as Irish.

The Pettigrews had a good many children, and, as most parents will immediately understand, not very much money to spend. Furthermore, the older Pettigrew was bookish in his tastes, and as a natural corollary not particularly acquisitive in his habits. Mrs. Pettigrew was a busy housewife, and the children, male and female, had to help. Young Louis seems to have made up for the time lost in doing home chores by reading, like the poet Southey, while walking.

In 1809, when he was twenty, Petigru was graduated from South Carolina College with highest honors. He had earned his way by teaching at the academy in Columbia and, it is to be feared, by frugality in the matter of food, and that at the very age when a boy's appetite is at its most enviable. Invitations to dinner helped, as they have helped many another struggling youngster; and it is almost tragic that he sometimes had to refuse because of the state of his wardrobe. This poverty did not harden Petigru. He was noted for his generosity.

He took a teaching job near Beaufort while he read law in the office of a local lawyer and learned enough to be admitted to the bar in 1812. After several years of discouragement, during which he constantly added to his knowledge, he was elected solicitor for the Beaufort district. Three years after that he became the partner, by invitation of James Hamilton, Jr., and began his lifelong residence in Charleston. For over forty years he was the acknowledged head of the profession in the state; some say the greatest legal mind ever produced in it. He had some small political success, but his enormous practice chiefly occupied him. A good deal of this practice was without remuneration, for he never would accept a fee, it is said, from a friend, or from anyone who could not spare the money to pay him—and that applied to black or white.

He was the social lion of Charleston and a striking figure. He was strongly built. His portrait shows a heavy chin which gives a strong hint of his Irish ancestry. His eyes were dark and impressive, and his voice was considered magnificent and his wit incomparable.

His letters to his daughter show one side of his character, kindly, just and affectionate; and his iron principle is evident from the fact that when his fortune was completely lost in an unfortunate venture, he refused to consider bankruptcy as the way out, and repaid every cent of his debts when he was able.

At all times a strong Unionist, he fought Nullification. His violent disapproval of secession never swerved in the least. During the early days of the Secession Convention, he was in Columbia, and as he was passing the Baptist church where the convention was held, a stranger asked him where was the insane asylum. Pointing to the church, Petrigru said drily, "There it is."

He was the only Union man of his importance in Charleston. His son fought in the Confederate army and his other children, with the exception of one daughter, sided with the South, as was natural. He was old and his isolation saddened him; we have already quoted his remark about the Ordinance of Secession and cited his remarks to his sister about his lone stand. The esteem in which he was generally held was such that, even after the beginning of the war which he refused to support, he continued his task of codifying the laws of the state. Meanwhile, since he had been district attorney when Fillmore was president, some expected him to turn over information about Northern business to the authorities, but the old lion refused.

He did not live to see the end of the war whose dire results he had predicted. His death in 1863, at the age of seventy-four, was an occasion of public sorrow, and that is a tribute to Charleston as well as to him. Feeling was mountains high in those days, yet the Bar Association met and paid him an extended tribute, and what is more, had it printed for the record, and the order was given for the hanging of his portrait in the Court of Appeals.

His Unionist daughter, Carolina Carson, was evidently made of the same solid materials as her distinguished father. She wished to erect a fitting stone to his memory, and she earned the money for it by painting and, when she was too ill to paint, by selling stockings which she had knitted. Various men of letters aided her in polishing and perfecting his epitaph until it had attained its noble simplicity, which proves the case for collaboration. The inscription has been quoted time after time. Here it is again:

> Future Times will hardly know
> How great a Life this simple stone commemorates:
> The tradition of his Eloquence,
> His Wisdom and Wit may fade;
> But he lived for ends more durable than Fame.
> His Eloquence was the Protection of the Poor and Wronged
> His learning illuminated the principles of law.
> In the Admiration of his Peers.
> In the respect of his People
> In the Affection of his Family
> His was the highest Place;

The just Meed
of his Kindness and Forbearance
his Dignity and Simplicity
His brilliant Genius and his unwearied Industry.
Unawed by Opinion
Unseduced by Flattery
Undismayed by Disaster
He confronted Life with antique Courage
And death with Christian Hope.
In the great Civil War
He withstood his People for his Country:
But his people did Homage to the Man
Who held his conscience higher than their Praise;
And his Country
Heaped honours upon the grave of the Patriot,
To Whom, living,
His own righteous self-Respect sufficed
Alike for Motive and Reward.

No wonder Woodrow Wilson, in the depths of despair, asked for a copy of those words. They would buck anybody up. Along with Booker Washington's autobiography they ought to be compulsory reading for every literate American.

Very characteristic of Charleston is the Georgian City Hall, both in its style and in the fact that it is adapted to its present uses, having originally been built in 1800 for the Bank of the United States. (Many of Charleston's buildings serve a purpose different from that for which they were designed.) The City Hall faces the north side of St. Michael's. A family tradition attributes its design to Gabriel Manigault, the wealthy planter and the city's most famous amateur architect, but there is no definite proof of this. For that matter, credit for the actual erection of the building has not been indubitably assigned.

Architectural connoisseurs may differ about the building, artistically and historically, but it has grace and charm and, like St. Michael's, combines these with a sturdy yet aristocratic air. The double curving stairway is handsome. The large circular windows of the basement floor, with a radiating design in the iron grilles, and the somewhat squat basement door with the goddess of victory on the pediment are beautifully proportioned to the building and to the parapet. If the marble trim was, as is believed, brought ready-cut from Philadelphia, where it had been designed for a house which was never built, the adaptation was skilful. The exterior of the building has been covered with stucco, which has been criticized as adding a smoothness and plainness which are detrimental to the general impression.

The ornate ceiling of the lobby is understandable when it is considered that this was originally a bank and did not become the City Hall until 1819. The interior is scarcely exciting otherwise, but there is a very interesting small museum on the second floor. Here the *pièce de résistance* is the famous Trumbull painting of Washington, which caused the painter acute agony when an official decided that the original, commissioned to commemorate the visit of the Father of his Country in 1791, was too severe in aspect. Trumbull knew Washington well, having been his aide-de-camp, and persuaded him to undertake another sitting, and here is the second portrait. Much bigger than life, it is a striking work in brown and golden yellow, with the storm clouds beloved of the period rolling in the background. Civic pride inflates its financial value (oh yes, they do think of such things in Charleston, every now and then) to the tremendous figure of a million dollars.

Other portraits include one of Andrew Jackson by Vanderlyn, one of Beauregard, the defender of the city, and a man, if his portrait is not too flattering, to set feminine hearts beating a little faster; one of John C. Calhoun by Healy, and one of President Monroe by Samuel Finley Breese Morse, otherwise inventor of the telegraph, who painted for some

MUNICIPAL YACHT BASIN

LEGARÉ STREET HOUSES AND GATES

years in Charleston. Here also is Zachary Taylor's portrait
by Beard, and miniatures of Lafayette and Moultrie by Charles
Fraser. Historical relics include battle flags, General Beauregard's sword which he willed to the city, and the autographed
letter of Queen Victoria expressing her imperial sympathy at
the time of the earthquake.

The Court House, diagonally across from St. Michael's,
while not one of the treasures of the city's architecture, is
interesting for its age. It was first used in 1792. The architect
was another amateur, William Drayton, jurist and owner of
Magnolia Plantation. He died before the building was completed, and he probably would not recognize it now, for it
has undergone frequent alteration, and was considerably extended in 1941 by the addition of a wing. In contrast to St.
Michael's and the City Hall, it is merely imposing in a plain
and matter-of-fact way but does not violate its setting.

A novelty of its time was the old Office of Mesne and Con-
veyance, never called anything but the Fireproof Building,
which stands on Meeting Street at Chalmers, just back of the
City Hall. It was erected in 1822 by Robert Mills, Charleston's
first professional architect, and was designed for the safe-
keeping of records, come hell or high water. Mills' experiment
now houses the county offices and the South Carolina Historical
Society. It is a solid edifice, square except for the porticoes
front and rear, and unless viewed from the proper angle gives
the effect of dumpiness and complacency. Its design was func-
tional; Mills designed it to withstand fire and withstand fire
it did. The steep curving staircase is another of Mills' signatures.

Miss Ravenel considers it "sternly beautiful, perhaps the
most beautiful of Mills' numerous buildings," but there is always a dissenting voice. Here is what one writer thought of
it; his account is taken from a guide book to the fair given in
1870 under the auspices of the South Carolina Institute:

The Fireproof Building is a curiously ugly and ill-contrived affair at the corner of Meeting and Chalmers streets, and within the enclosure of the City Park. It has iron shutters to the windows and stone floors to the rooms, and being intended as a receptacle for important records, it seems to have been built with a view to make it look as much as possible like a huge "Herring's Safe," though it was, doubtless, built before those wonderful and sure protections against fire were discovered. It is only two stories high, is as broad as it is long, has two entries through the middle, steps before, steps behind, and, in short, is about as eccentric a freak of architecture as you will see or hear of anywhere between this and the Middle Ages.

And this right after the fire of 1861, too! It seems to have been written by a man whose feet hurt.

For my part, I would give the palm for general homeliness to the old Market Hall at the foot of Market Street, also on Meeting. The Post Office is bad enough, but the market has some claim to notice, being the work of E. B. White, who left many a mark on Charleston. In the form of a temple with a double flight of stone steps, it has four Doric columns and a good deal of thick and graceless ironwork. It seems to be one story too high, the result of its being built over the long stallway of the market itself. Built in 1838, it was long the center of the city's private victualling; the stalls go through to the waterfront. The market was toppled by the hurricane of 1938, exactly a hundred years after it was built, and has since been restored and painted a sickly color. The setting is poor, too; if you retreat to King Street, a block away, the proportions are more restful.

The neighborhood of the market was once infamous as the hangout of the buzzards, the official scavengers of Charleston, and of which the same anonymous author who attacked the Fireproof Building wrote, after dipping his pen in rather weak acid:

The Charleston Eagle—this melancholy bird, vulgarly called a buzzard, is one of the peculiar institutions of our beloved metropolis, that deserves a passing notice at our hands. The headquarters of the eagle are in Market Street, the neighborhood of the butchers' temple, and there, of a fine morning, he may be seen in all his glory, flying, flapping, hopping, standing, fighting, stealing, walking, sailing, running. The eagle is a sombre bird, dark of hue, gloomy in countenance, and remarkably taciturn—that flies without a song and eats without a quack. So far this eagle is respectable—gravity is dignity, silence is wisdom. But, alas! for his respectability, the Charleston Eagle is a glutton. The race to which he belongs are winged hyenas, they scent corpses from afar; but our bird has become, by habit and education, simply a glutton, gorging himself on refuse meat which is not yet putrid. He might prefer his food a little more game, if allowed to indulge in the natural idiosyncrasies of his appetite, but he meets with much competition in the eating business, and must swallow his food quickly or not at all. Where his respectability ends, however, his utility begins, and in this he resembles many an unfeathered biped who makes his living by doing the dirty work of life. Our eagle might flap his sombre wings and shake his melancholy head with the unction of a parson and the dignity of a judge, and yet be a lawful target for every wandering brickbat, mischievous arrow, or idle ball; but fortunately for his comfort and his safety he can eat dirt, for which quality he was promoted by our sage forefathers to the position of scavenger, and presented with the freedom of the city, and with a perpetual insurance on his life. He too belongs to the privileged class that has not been abolished by the rump Congress, and like other aristocrats, he sometimes puts on airs and abuses his franchise. He has been known to steal meat from a market basket, and to make frequent raids upon the butchers' stalls, and yet these trespasses were committed with impunity, the law protecting his life by a penalty of five dollars. When carried away by the passion of gluttony, his breaches of the peace are frequent, and in fact so notorious, that they have been celebrated by an old poet in the following verses:

> A noble sight it is to see
> The buzzards in their glory
> Fall out about an old beef knee
> And fight till they are gory.

It must be admitted that this suffers from a too Ciceronian fluency, but more guide books should be written from this gentleman's viewpoint. Not only did he describe the Fireproof

Building in those unflattering words we have quoted, but he referred to his description of a sight-seeing tour as "a day among the ruins." The absence of the cooing note is thoroughly commendable.

The Market Hall now houses a museum of the Daughters of the Confederacy which shows various relics and impedimenta of the Civil War, such as the cannon founded from the metal of that first locomotive, the "Best Friend"; and the stalls are still operated downstairs.

But now, like the buzzards we have read of, let's swoop back to the neighborhood of the City Hall.

If you enter City Hall Park, officially Washington Square, by the Broad Street gate, the first thing you will see is the bust of Henry Timrod (Dimroth), the poet, who starved desperately in the Civil War at Charleston and wrote himself rather thin in the process. He was the author of such lyrics as "At Magnolia Cemetery," which begins

> Sleep sweetly in your humble graves,
> Sleep, martyrs of a fallen cause;
> Though yet no marble column craves
> The pilgrim here to pause.

and ends

> Stoop, angels, hither from the skies!
> There is no holier spot of ground
> Than where defeated valor lies,
> By mourning beauty crowned!

When I last saw the bust of the poet, some irreverent hand had scrawled in chalk underneath the dates in such a way as to make it read "Henry Timrod left Sing Sing in ———" It must have been some foreigner.

The park is bordered on the east by a quaint and beautiful old brick wall with rounded arches and pillars, all of brick, and over the wall you may see the sweeping piazzas of the

Daniel Ravenel House, built in 1800 or a year or two earlier, a typical single house of the time with a particularly interesting façade. The park's chief treasure is the famous statue of William Pitt (in a rather absurd toga) which the citizens ordered in a fit of enthusiasm over the repeal of the Stamp Act, and installed in the center of the intersection of Broad and Meeting streets after a celebration at which, according to report, forty-five toasts were drunk. As the colored preacher observed when telling his flock about King Solomon's matrimonial arrangements, men were men in those days. But, as Emerson said, "Every hero becomes a bore at last," and when enthusiasm had waned, Mr. Pitt was found guilty of obstructing traffic and was moved to the grounds of the Orphan House on Calhoun Street, where, according to Mrs. Ravenel, the children thought the statue represented George Washington, and one of them described him as "just getting out of bed." Mr. Pitt lost an arm in the British siege, and this has never been replaced. The other arm has gone the way of Venus's, too. The head was knocked off when the statue was moved in 1794 and was replaced. Then, after the ill-starred Pitt had stood for many years in the orphanage grounds and endured so many misidentifications, the Carolina Art Association had it placed in its present very fitting situation. The earthquake knocked it down and the brief but effective tornado of 1938 once more sent the head rolling. But the statue has some sort of British persistence about it and it endures in spite of everything. It has a very fair claim to being the oldest portrait statue in America. The inscription says, in part, "Time shall sooner destroy this mark of their esteem than erase from their [i.e., the Charlestonians'] minds their just sense of his patriotic virtues," so, considering all he has been through in effigy, it seems probable that the Earl of Chatham is going to enjoy something close to immortality in that city of long memories.

The tall granite shaft on Mr. Pitt's right honors those

heroes of the Civil War, the Washington Light Infantry, and there is also a memorial to General Beauregard. Not an exciting park, this is a very pretty and a very pleasant one, and it used to be the daily haunt of the Dahs, or children's nurses, and their more or less obedient charges.

Turning back into Broad Street, we pass, a couple of doors away, the old Carolina Hotel, later the Home for the Mothers, Widows and Daughters of Confederate Veterans, and now a low-priced apartment house for ladies. No one will disturb you if you care to walk through the front door and into the interesting courtyard and garden; the hall and the grounds, like so many places in Charleston, have the air of being deserted.

The office buildings on this east end of Broad Street are particularly interesting; there are enough varieties of gable and cornice and roof arrangement to keep the knowing observer busy for a long time. Among them is the home of the Chamber of Commerce, formerly the Charleston Library and before that a bank, which dates, with alterations, from 1783 and stands on the site of the old Swallow Tavern. Opposite is a fine old pre-Revolutionary building, not very tastefully modernized, and now the offices of an insurance company. On the corner of Elliott Street is the stately South Carolina National Bank (1817), which has an elaborate directors' room of later date. And number one Broad Street, built in the mid-nineteenth century, is the Carolina Savings Bank but thoroughly un-Carolinian in origin, for it strongly suggests Italian influence.

At the head of Broad Street, on East Bay, is the Old Exchange and Customs House. Its site has always been dominant. Originally the Court of Guard, where Bonnet and his pirates were kept, stood here. The present building was begun in 1767 by the Saxon contractors Peter and John Horlbeck and was completed in 1771. The style of architecture and a good deal of the original material were English; the building is now considerably simpler in detail than when it was first built, but looks solidly eighteenth century. There used to be a portico facing the river, and the ornamental pillars disappeared with the earthquake. Other storms and unperceptive remodeling are responsible for the other changes in the aspect of the still imposing structure. The building is one of the most versatile in Charleston in point of use. The first Revolutionary Congress met there, it was the scene of Charleston's Tea Party, and the British used the cellars as a prison for "rebels," among them the martyr Hayne. George Washington greeted the citizens from the steps on his visit in 1791, and a great ball in his honor was held within. Slaves were sold in the vicinity of this temple of freedom. The first floor of the Exchange later was used as a post office; at present it is the home of the museum of the Daughters of the American Revolution, but was during the Second World War the headquarters of the U.S. Coast Guard.

Flanking the Exchange on East Bay is a tiny building, once the Old French Coffee Shop and now a liquor store—a strong reminder of West Indian influence, with a tiled roof—and three other quaint buildings, one with a bay and a little square glass-enclosed cupola which is duplicated on another. All these are post-Revolutionary.

But let's return to churches and public buildings. Returning to Broad Street, we go down to Church and catch the first sight of St. Philip's Church as a whole, and a noble sight it is. St. Philip's was the first congregation in Charleston. The first St. Philip's Church in Charles Town stood where St. Michael's is now, it will be remembered, and was transferred to its present site in 1723—at least, that was the year in which the new church was first opened for services. St. Philip's of today is the third structure used by the congregation. The first was abandoned as too small and furthermore unsafe.

The second, admired as an extremely rich and handsome place of worship, lasted a hundred and twelve years. The steeple, by no means a spire like the one of today, caught fire in the conflagration of 1800, but was saved from the fire by a Negro sailor who had the presence of mind and courage to clamber up to the top of the bell tower and tear off the burning shingles. He received the gift of his freedom as a reward, but fame has been rather unkind to him, from the standpoint of accuracy; for the popular ballad celebrating his bravery credits him with saving St. Michael's.

No one of equal nerve and resourcefulness was present when, thirty-five years later, the second St. Philip's perished without a soul to save it. The congregation immediately voted a new edifice, which was at first intended to duplicate the burned church, but which was built with changes in its height and interior. Thirteen years after the laying of the corner-stone, E. B. White added the portico and the steeple, and adapted them without violence to the design. The resultant aspect of the building is classical without being Greek revival; the spire is lofty but solid, and although it has several courses more than St. Michael's and a more pronounced flèche, it has a more sober air, possibly because St. Michael's is such a gleaming white while St. Philip's has a weathered appearance. The chimes, melted down in the Civil War, have never been replaced.

White added three porticoes to the church, the central one facing west. As the west churchyard is across the street, the passer-by can get a much better view of the façade than he can of St. Michael's, which is rather crowded by the Post Office.

There is something very mellow and yet dignified about St. Philip's interior. The nave rises to a dome and is upheld by Corinthian pillars which intersect the front rails of the galleries. The effect, if a trifle ornate, is sunny and cheerful.

We need not take too seriously the rather ambitious sobriquet of "the Westminster Abbey of the South" which is sometimes applied to St. Philip's, but its vaults and churchyards do contain the bones of many illustrious South Carolinians. First among them is John Caldwell Calhoun, spokesman par excellence of the Old South. Here lies also Edward Rutledge, signer of the Declaration of Independence, and one of the state's great governors. His tombstone greatly outdoes the modest one that marks the grave of his brother John in St. Michael's. Somewhere in the churchyard Christopher Gadsden is finally at peace—he demanded that his grave be unmarked. Rawlins Lowndes, the statesman, is buried there, and the valiant Colonel Rhett of pirate fame, and we must mention one of the rectors, that versatile cleric, John Johnson, who fought in the Civil War, served God as one of His ministers, and wrote that classic of military literature, *The Defense of Charleston Harbor*. The tablet to his memory in the south aisle of the church is charming. It states that "his book is not marred by one braggart word or vindictive epithet," which, considering the provocation, shows that he was truly the pattern of a Christian gentleman. St. Philip's itself was badly damaged by several shells sent in by the Union artillery.

As for oddities among the epitaphs, one seems to outshine all the rest. It is that of Nicholas John Wightman, killed by robbers in 1786. The inscription informs us that "Divine Providence ordained it so, that a single button, belonging to the coat of the murderer, served with other proof to discover and convict him." One recalls O. Henry's "A Municipal Report," and remembering that he once worked as a drug clerk in Charleston, naturally speculates on the possibility of his having got the idea from this gravestone.

At the north end of the east churchyard is the tiny old Parish House. Passing south again, and admiring the sunny, airy and reposeful beauty of this burying ground, one can stop for a look at the building which is called the "Pirate House" because of a legend, and which is pre-Revolutionary at least. Built of coquina stone slabs, the so-called Pirate House has a "fire mark" tablet sunk into the stone and bearing the date 1782. It has been restored and is now an antique shop with a coffee house.

Just a few doors south of St. Philip's is the French Protestant Huguenot Church, the only one in America. The building is one of the Gothic experiments of E. B. White and replaces an earlier structure, burned in one of those fires that have done so much to change the face of Charleston. The church is one of the oldest-looking, except for its style, in the entire city, for it has a proper moldiness. It is notable for its ritual and its psalm book and its memorials to those of Huguenot descent—taxed a fixed amount for the maintenance of the church funds. In the graveyard, close to the fence, is a small obelisk twisted a trifle off the center of its base, and a testimony to the freakish behavior of the 1886 earthquake. The church itself was badly battered by that malignant one-minute cyclone of 1938.

Directly across the street from the Huguenot Church is the restored Dock Street Theatre, superimposed on the remains of the old Planters Hotel, one of the famous hostelries of the South and the scene of many a merrymaking, but permitted in our time to fall into decay. The Dock Street Theatre began its career in 1736 with a performance of Farquhar's "The Recruiting Officer"; it was in those days on Queen Street, the Dock Street that was. The old hotel is a handsome building, with ornate ironwork balconies and a romantic air, but it owes its restoration to the twentieth-century New Deal, for the WPA financed the work in connection with a project of the Carolina Art Association. The building now contains offices, a handsome modern theatre which cleverly hints at the old style, and a lounge which preserves the atmosphere of the hotel. To this already combined restoration there is a third element in the form of elegant Adam stucco work rescued from the Ratcliffe House, a residence of the early nineteenth century. As do so many Charleston interiors, this one gives the visitor a sense of having suddenly gone backward in time.

The Dock Street Theatre was the occasion of a minor Civil War. A dissident group of players seceded to form their own theater not far away in a coach house. They call themselves The Footlighters.

The Dock Street Theatre was re-opened in 1935, just ninety-nine years after the inauguration of the original house, and with the same play. It operates now on a subscription basis, giving plays of the modern theater several times a year. The evening I attended, the vehicle of the local (and imported) talent was the gangster comedy "Whistling in the Dark," played to the hilt by a company which included, as the chief gangster, the manager of a coffee shop in one of the local hotels, who was as sardonic as could be wished. The ingénue was a girl with a Southern accent of that lachrymose type so trying to the ears of anyone born in Charleston, but the stupid trigger-man righted the balance by playing the part with a local accent of the most powerful sort in place of the appropriate Brooklynese. He certainly was an amateur in the strict sense, for he was an employee of the school board, but I thought he was good. The attitude of the natives in the audience was frankly one of amusement at the first entrances of familiar faces in theatrical disguise, but the players did not seem to mind in the least. It was my impression that one white-haired lady in the audience started a trifle at some of the language, but she stuck it out to the end. When I saw the rival group, a short time afterward, perform *Romeo and Juliet,* I wondered what she would have thought.

I was asked to attend the Shakespeare revival by a delightful lady who was one of the workers in the organization

and who told me that she herself had engineered the sewing
of the curtain. Some time before the performance, I said to
one of the Athenians of Charleston that I imagined some
bowdlerizing would have to be done. He made no very com-
mittal response. As it turned out, the bawdy passages were
played for all they were worth, but no one turned a hair.
The production was a good one, too, with a pretty and girlish
Juliet and a personable cast. Navy discipline had removed
the regular Tybalt from the cast at the last moment, and the
director was obliged to substitute for him. He was sufficiently
sinister, and there was a vivacious and effective Mercutio.
Probably none of them were up to the standards set by Joseph
Jefferson's actors, who played under his direction for a time
in the nineteenth century, or those of M. Placide and his
pantomimists of an earlier day, but a good time was had by
all. It was refreshing, too, to see a Juliet of such youth and a
Romeo with hair of his own and a waistline.

Church Street, being one of the eight original streets of
the city, is naturally full of associations. The old dwellings
have remained here largely intact, and between the Dock Street
Theatre and the Heyward-Washington House the stroller
can see a round dozen houses of pre- and post-Revolutionary
origin and can revel in tiled roofs, doorways, gables and
cornices to his heart's content.

The Heyward-Washington House, built about 1750, is
chiefly famous as the residence of George Washington on his
visit. It is a fine example of the Georgian double house, simple,
foursquare and dignified without, and carelessly elegant within.
The center hallway divides the lower floor into four rooms,
and the same plan is carried out upstairs, insuring plenty of
air and light. You would not be surprised to see a duplicate
of the house in a picture of London. Not so very long ago
this house had a bakery on the ground floor, despite its historical associations, but the Charleston Museum and the

Society for the Preservation of Old Dwellings acquired it and restored it as a public trust. A small fee is exacted for a conducted trip through the house, which is rich in furniture of its period, including a vast secretary in the library. Some exquisite china of the time is shown, including Wedgwood cream ware, and there is an ancient kitchen with appropriate implements. Under the direction of Miss Emma Richardson, assistant to the director of the museum, the formal garden was restored from an old "plat" or plan to include only such flowers and herbs as could have been known in the thirteen states at the time of General Washington's stay.

Immediately north of the Heyward House is the old tenement, now composed of shops and apartments, which was known in the long years of its disrepute as "Cabbage Row" or "Catfish Row," and which is essentially the scene of DuBose Heyward's *Porgy,* although, with a poet's licence, Mr. Heyward, for the purposes of his novel, moved the house to a spot on East Bay. A little down the street, on the other side, is the odd little tile-roofed house in which Mr. Heyward lived —not, however, when he wrote *Porgy,* for that was accomplished in the bracing air of Peterborough, New Hampshire, at the MacDowell Colony. Just next door to that is an equally striking house, likewise post-Revolutionary, with a balcony from which some believe Washington addressed his admirers. It could have happened, anyway. Across the street is a square-set brick dwelling, dating from shortly after the war of 1812, which has an antique shop on the ground floor. There are plenty of antique shops in the vicinity, and I do not wish to libel any one of them when I say that it is popularly believed that most of the antiques come from England. The stable and coach house, once an adjunct of this dwelling but built before it, are now the dining room of the Brewton Inn, named from the proximity of the Robert Brewton house, which dates from about 1730. Next door to this is the Jacob

Motte house, built by that merchant in 1745, and then we come to the First Baptist Church, another of Robert Mills' buildings, and a stately house of worship of which the architect was proud.

Although the average reader does not hear a great deal about him, Mills was a very distinguished son of Charleston. His father, a prosperous tailor, was able to have him educated at the College of Charleston. Mills is generally thought to have been the first American who actually planned the career of architect. He came under the influence of Jefferson and of Latrobe and was precociously successful; at twenty-three he designed the Circular Congregational Church on Meeting Street, long considered one of the most individual churches in the city and unhappily destroyed by the fire of 1861. The modern Romanesque structure dates from 1891.

Mills' career was long, varied, and took him to many places. He contributed additions to Independence Hall in Philadelphia and to other buildings in the North; his Memorial Church in Richmond, built in memory of several hundred people who had been burned in a theatre fire, is said to have inspired the fireproof idea which he carried out in the Charleston building of that description. He was the architect of the Treasury, the Patent Office, the Washington and Bunker Hill monuments, and in his years of service as commissioner on the South Carolina Board of Public Works he was responsible for numerous locks, court houses, jails, and customs houses.

He might very well have said of South Carolina, as Wren did of London, *"si monumentum requiris, circumspice."* In addition to the Fireproof Building, a wing of the County Jail, the old Marine Hospital in Franklin Street and nine powder magazines on the north end of the city which is called Charleston Neck, he designed the Lancaster Court House, the Presbyterian Church in Camden, the State Hospital for the Insane at Columbia. He wrote *Statistics of South Carolina,* a guide to Washington, and *The American Pharos, or Lighthouse Guide.* Add to this that he was interested in all sorts of odds-and-ends and the person of average energy is puzzled to know how he found time and strength to design his innumerable buildings.

The old Marine Hospital has been made part of a housing project which is known as Mills Manor, and which occupies the space formerly filled by the old Medical College, a building which was a terror to the Negroes, one of whose worst fears was that of being dissected after death. Generations of roistering medical students were trained here; but the building was long deserted. Behind its shattered and grimy windows stood bottles holding such grisly objects as fetuses. They made it perfectly fascinating to strolling small boys.

Around the corner from the medical school site is the former jail, also once a terror to the colored folk, who, their experience of white justice having led them to expect the worst, quailed as one when the siren of the "Black Maria" wailed through the streets. This is a strongly constructed old Gothic clink to which Mills added an annex, and it was in this jail that General Moultrie was imprisoned for his patriotic incurrence of debt. Close by the Reverend William Jenkins, a Negro, established his orphanage for waifs and strays of his race, where, as one writer expressed it with rather callous humor, he labored to keep his charges from reaching the near-by jailhouse. Jenkins Orphanage became famous through its brass band, composed (the word is used unadvisedly of such a band) of boys of various sizes and rather likely, as the playing was done by ear, to combine tonalities as boldly as any Bartók or Schoenberg. Nevertheless, its playing was fascinating; the boys traveled all over Europe, even, collecting money for the orphanage where Mr. Jenkins had his boys taught trades. A few years ago I heard shrill voices on New

York's Chambers Street, and looking out of a window saw some tiny colored girls who were singing hymns; and on their uniform was lettered "Jenkins Orphanage." The band was part of the cast of the original production of *Porgy,* and their brief moment on the stage made me actually homesick for a bit.

But let us get on with those public buildings, of which there are many, before turning to some of the magnificent dwellings that enshrine so much of Charleston's picturesque yesterday.

THE GIBBES HOUSE ON SOUTH BATTERY

THE DANIEL BLAKE TENEMENTS ON COURTHOUSE SQUARE,
PRE-REVOLUTIONARY

CHAPTER TEN

Other Churches

There are several churches in Charleston which have never had the pinnacles their architects intended them to have. High up Meeting Street, for instance, there is the Second Presbyterian Church, a vast edifice endowed by the prosperous Scots with the money they had coined out of the wagon trade. When the War of 1812 cut off their sources of income and money became very dear in Charleston, there were no funds available for the steeple, and so there has never been any steeple.

St. Paul's, Radcliffeborough, which was erected on the site given by Mrs. Radcliffe and was sometimes called "The Planters' Church," because the money to build it was furnished by wealthy planters who had their city homes in that uptown neighborhood, also felt the pinch of hard times. It, too, had to forego a steeple, and not until years later was a gesture made in that upward direction in the form of a thoroughly inappropriate crenellated Gothic tower. The huge church, colonial in influence, is rather magnificent in spite of this grotesque addition.

A third unspired (I did not say uninspired) church is the Catholic Cathedral of St. John the Baptist, which stands on Broad and Legaré streets and has interesting associations.

145

The earlier church on this site, the Cathedral of St. John and St. Finbar, was built in the early 1850's by Patrick Charles Keeley, who must have held the record for churchbuilding, having erected more than seven hundred. St. John and St. Finbar's was built of red freestone and had a steeple one hundred and twenty-one feet high. It was destroyed by the fire of 1861. John Bennett, in *The Doctor to the Dead,* retells an interesting old legend about the Wandering Jew which relates him to the destruction of the cathedral.

For years the ruins gathered moss and went on crumbling, while the little Pro-cathedral on Queen Street, just back of the church, served the needs of the congregation. Then, in 1888, through the benevolence of a wealthy member of the parish, plans were made to build a new cathedral which was virtually to duplicate the old one. Keeley, then an old man of seventy-one, examined the wreck of the old cathedral, and the man who had built the earlier structure began the building of the new one—quite a remarkable juxtaposition, when it is considered that nearly forty years had intervened. The new cathedral, which regrettably dropped the name of St. Finbar, that extraordinary Bishop of Cork, at whose death the sun did not set for fifteen days, was not entirely ready until 1907. I have, I do not recall where, seen a postcard picture of it complete with steeple, but this was an exaggeration. The cathedral still lacks the finishing touch of a spire to complete its Neo-Gothic plan.

The interior, entirely conventional, with the choir loft at the back as is still customary in most Catholic churches, was toned down many years ago from its earlier glaring whiteness by a coat of light buff paint. The acoustics were long faulty, with a persistent echo, but perhaps this has been corrected by distribution of loud speakers—for I saw a microphone had been installed on the pulpit, and I could not help wondering, by the way, what some of the old folks would have said to that.

The music of the cathedral was long famous for its excellence under the direction of Madame Barbot, one of the musical leaders of Charleston, at least among the Catholic population. Its bishops and priests enjoy the stateliest rectory in Charleston, the Thomas Pinckney, Jr. house a few doors away. This is a double house with a portico and a double curving flight of stairs and dates from 1790, when it was begun by Ralph Izard. It was not actually completed until 1829. Next door to it is another of the Izard houses, a dainty little Georgian dwelling, built by one of the Izards in 1757. West of the Bishop's House is the great city residence which John Rutledge, as a prosperous young lawyer and planter, built for himself in the year 1760. The façade has been considerably altered by the addition of a balcony of ornamental ironwork which obscures the lordly Georgian lines and by the placing of terra-cotta cornices over the windows. When the house was in the possession of R. Goodwyn Rhett, educator, mayor, banker, and historian of Charleston, it numbered among its distinguished guests President Taft. It is now the home of a physician.

On the King Street corner is one of the very oldest structures in Charleston, a small frame house which was the home of Dr. John Lining, who made the first scientific observations in Charleston, and at the instance of Benjamin Franklin introduced lightning rods to the city. The drugstore on the ground floor is the successor of the second of its kind in America, founded in 1780 and passing through a succession of ownerships until it became firmly rooted in the life of Charleston as Schwettmann's. A gilt mortar hung from its corner; this was called by Negroes "the big yellow bucket." From 1845 to 1870 the proprietor had been William G. Trott, who experienced and withstood the "Mermaid Riot" of 1867. A prolonged rain was ascribed by the Negroes to Dr. Trott's having a mermaid in captivity, and a mob ransacked his store but found no mermaid and went away. The cause of the uproar was a specimen of a sea horse. It all sounds rather like one of the adventures of that sea-going repository of Duggan's Dew of Kirkintilloch, Mr. Glencannon; but as John Bennett tells the story in his collection of legends, it is charming.

In 1921, when the drugstore was remodeled by its present owners, the interior fittings and equipment were removed to the fascinating exhibit in the museum known as "Apothecaries' Hall," the name given to the shop by Dr. De La Motta, who operated it from 1816 to 1845. Dr. Schwettmann the younger's successor, Dr. Huchting, removed the business to a store near-by on King Street, and there the old yellow bucket is kept.

There is another old drugstore away up King Street at Vanderhorst, which has been operated by the same family for many years and has an old-fashioned look not often met with in today's streamlined emporiums of marked-down books, soda and sandwiches, cosmetics and electrical appliances. A drugstore was a drugstore in the days when this shop was outfitted. A good many of the old-fashioned looking shops in Charleston give the impression of having been necessarily kept that way; many that used to be typical of an older period have gone the way of modernity. Really ancient shops are very rare, for Charleston's mercantile center was long ago shifted from its early establishment in Elliott Street, once the headquarters of wholesale establishments. Elliott Street then degenerated to a type of commerce which moved Mrs. Ravenel to say forty years ago that no lady would care to be seen there. It now seems completely respectable.

King Street from Broad to Calhoun has long been the retail center of the city, and here the stroller can see some very interesting old buildings, combined with some nineteenth-century horrors. In general, the street is a shabby one, and the only crowded thoroughfare in Charleston. It is excessively narrow and has been made a one-way street, which is well. There is not much of interest higher up except the post-Civil War Lutheran Church of St. Matthew, the beautiful early nineteenth-century Aiken House, now the office of a railroad company, and the odd little adjacent carriage house of Gothic tendencies. Far up, in an insignificant small wooden house, was born another great native Charlestonian, the first since the Civil War to achieve nationally—and in this case, internationally—important political office. This was the Honorable James F. Byrnes. Charleston, as far as a virtual outsider can determine, is not entirely in accord about Mr. Byrnes, but he is naturally admired by a large section of the people as a distinguished native son.

Now let us turn back to the lower part of King Street. South of Wentworth Street, the first important street below Calhoun, is a short thoroughfare called Hasell Street, extending only east to the river front. (You must call it "hazel" street, by the way.) There are some very interesting houses here; we shall stop for a moment only to consider the fine old Colonel Rhett house, earlier mentioned as the first dwelling built without the city limits and as the birthplace of Wade Hampton, Charleston's (and South Carolina's) liberator, at least from the white standpoint.

On this street is a truly historical church—St. Mary's. The present building dates from 1839 and does not look in any way like the average person's idea of a Catholic Church. Its architect was influenced by the Greek revival, and the church has the classical columns and portico which become almost monotonous in the city's religious edifices. The interior is charming in an intimate way, and the little churchyard is considered a treasure trove for students of the history of those Santo Domingan refugees who arrived in 1793. Here were buried, among others of French descent, the daughters of Admiral de Grasse, commander of the French fleet at Yorktown. The daughters, along with many of their race from the West Indies, sought refuge in Charleston and were housed, for a time, in the fine George Edwards house on Meeting Street.

The Santo Domingans arrived just at the proper time for their liberty of worship. We have already mentioned those two Catholic "conspirators" who were found in the city in 1775 and so roughly expelled. Not until Charles Pinckney insisted upon the deletion of any religious clause from the Constitution of the United States was Catholicism officially freed of all trammels in South Carolina. There is a legend about the coming of Irish Catholics to South Carolina in the middle years of the eighteenth century, but Bishop John England, the first head of South Carolina's hierarchy, scouts this. There is some uncertainty about those Acadian refugees, too. Bishop England gives his opinion that, at the time of the Revolution, "prejudice was so strong that any Catholics in Carolina kept their faith so secret that they were not even known to each other." However, mellower times were ahead. Bishop England continues:

Some time about the year 1786, a vessel bound to South America put into the port of Charleston. There was a priest on board. . . . The few Catholics who now began in the city to be acquainted with each other, and to enjoy the benefit of that toleration which followed the revolutionary struggle, invited him to celebrate Mass, which he did in the house of an Irish Catholic, for a congregation of about twelve persons. . . . The little manifestation of their faith, by the few who attended, induced others, who observed it, to be more confident, and it was soon discovered that the number of Catholics in the city was larger than any of themselves had supposed.

That was a historic Mass—the first in the former British colony.

By 1789 toleration was so firmly established that the purchase of land for St. Mary's Church was undertaken. The actual founding dates to 1800, and this was the mother church of Catholicism in South Carolina. There was for a long time a difficulty in obtaining a permanent priest for the parish, but at last Father Simon Felix Gallagher, a graduate of the University of Paris, undertook the charge.

St. Mary's was the church of the Santo Domingan refugees, and their influence there was strong. Also connected with it is what might be viewed as another instance of the separative tendency in Charleston thought. For there was long a most unfortunate schism over the lay trusteeship of St. Mary's, which was not entirely settled until 1897, when the diocesan powers triumphed.

St. Mary's was burned in the fire of 1838, which is the explanation of the date of 1839 for its rebuilding.

There are two other churches on Hasell Street of the same period and general style of architecture as St. Mary's; the Beth Elohim synagogue (1838) and St. Johannes Lutheran (1842). And an idea of the strength of the Greek revival in Charleston can be obtained by going over to near-by Wentworth Street, where there are two more of these pillared churches, St. Andrew's Lutheran (c. 1840) and the Centenary Methodist (1841), built by a white Baptist congregation but acquired immediately after the Civil War by the African Methodist Episcopal Church.

Charleston's architecture, however, can not be tied to any hard and fast group. There are all kinds—another witness is the Grace Episcopal Church, also on Wentworth Street, built by E. B. White in 1847 and a full-blown example of the Gothic revival, the temporary popularity of which in Charleston has been blamed on Sir Walter Scott. And there are two churches which are difficult for the layman to classify, the aforementioned St. Matthew's on King Street and the Citadel Square

Baptist, on Meeting Street facing the Citadel Green—which, by the way, is Marion Square, only accentuating the fact that changes of nomenclature mean nothing to the natives. Colonial Lake, for example, the little ornamental body of water on Rutledge Street, is "the Pond" to simon-pure Charlestonians, just as the Kress chain store remained "Kirby's" to many people for a long time. I don't know how long it was before Charlestonians generally ceased to refer to Louis Cohen's, a department store now replaced by one of a chain, but I imagine it took a while. For that matter, I shouldn't be surprised to find someone who still called the city Charlestown— or even Charles Town.

Before we close this chapter of churches, there are two charming ones on Calhoun Street. One is the Zion Presbyterian (for Negroes) erected before the Civil War by white Presbyterians' contributions, and quite unlike any church I have ever seen, with a high porch at either side over the doors and shuttered windows. The other is the Old Bethel Methodist Church, a wooden, white-painted temple which goes back to 1800 and is not unlike New England meetinghouses.

There is no lack of houses of worship in Charleston, and the student of American ecclesiastical architecture can have a field day there. The Civic Services Committee, in classifying the buildings of the city, judged thirty-six of the churches to be valuable, notable, or worthy of mention. Virtually every one dates to the years before the Civil War, when the erection of imposing churches and public buildings came to an abrupt end—the Cathedral, the new Citadel, and the new Roper Hospital being isolated exceptions.

CHAPTER ELEVEN

Innovation—and Making Do

Loyal citizens like to point out that Charleston has some notable early developments of a civic kind, dating from the years when its cultural and political energies were more dynamic. The city was by no means backward, among cities of the New World, in providing edification, education, and refuge for the distressed, the orphaned, and the stricken.

There is, for instance, the Library Society, which still carries on in a handsome building on King Street and which is certainly no upstart, for it will be two hundred years old in 1748. It was organized in the year 1748 by a group of literary-minded young men who inserted in the *Gazette* a ringing appeal for the citizenry to partake of the advantages of reading. Legacies and donations brought the society to a rapid prosperity. In 1773 it was able to make its home on Broad Street in the building now occupied by the Chamber of Commerce. In its present comfortable and aristocratic lodging it is the Mecca of local and visiting historians; it has a complete file of the South Carolina *Gazette,* a splendid collection of the writings of Charlestonians, and, as chief librarian, Miss Ellen FitzSimons, whose name fittingly appears in the acknowledgments of many books to whose authors she has furnished encouragement and assistance.

153

Offspring of the Library Society is the museum, the first in the English-speaking part of the New World and said to be the second in the entire Western world. The museum was founded in 1773. The circumstances of its founding were shrouded in uncertainty and conjecture until, fittingly enough, Miss FitzSimons succeeded in obtaining a copy of the society's "Journall" recording the meeting at which the idea of the museum was broached.

As lieutenant-governor, the younger William Bull, then in one of his habitual incumbencies as deputy, was the president of the society, for this was always the privilege of the governor, being withheld from only one such official, Thomas Boone, on account of that frank association with Mrs. Worthington.

After approving the new catalogue of books and fining several members for the non-attendance which, even in those earnest days, afflicted such undertakings, the meeting discussed the purchase of some scientific books, such as Peter Kalm's *Travels,* "Mr. Bufon's [*sic*] *Natural History,*" a history of Kamschatka, and *The Antique Paintings of Herculaneum.* One would give a good deal to know if these included any like the notorious drawings which Signor Mussolini forbade Italian ladies to gaze upon. There is no mention of a history of tittlebats, although the whole affair, at this remove, has a distinctly Pickwickian flavor.

These matters disposed of, "the President proposed that a special committee be appointed for collecting materials for promoting a natural history of this province," and the motion was passed. The committee set to work with such exemplary promptness that it was able to publish a prospectus within a few months. Revolution and all, the new branch of the society was soon functioning quite famously. In 1785 it moved into its first permanent quarters in the Court House. In 1814 the Literary and Philosophical Society of South Carolina took

over the institution and maintained it as the Museum of South
Carolina in a wooden building on Chalmers Street. In 1828
the museum was moved to the new building of the Medical
College on Queen Street and in 1850 to the buildings of
the College of Charleston. At this time it received considerable stimulus from the lectures of Agassiz, who was at the
college, and who pronounced very favorably on the collections.

The museum had a long stay at the college. At the turn
of the century, when the South Carolina Interstate and West
Indian Exposition had put out its lights and departed, it left
the new Thomson Auditorium without employment—the building had been built in 1899 as a memorial to a benefactor of
the city and to house the Confederate Veterans' Convention,
after which it served for the convocation of the National
Education Association in 1900 and formed a part of the
exposition a year later. Arrangements were made to convert
the auditorium into a home for the museum, then straining the
facilities of the college, and in 1907 the collection moved into
its new home and took its present name of The Charleston
Museum. Coming fully of age in 1915, it was incorporated
and began its independent career. It now has city and county
support for educational work and for exhibits relating to
city and state. Contributions finance the other exhibits and
activities.

The museum houses a fine collection of Caroliniana—equipment from old plantations, a series of period rooms, old
ironwork, furniture, a complete room from the Thomas
Pinckney House (although the acquirement of rooms is generally disapproved by the institution); some precious old
silver, Indian relics, clothing worn by men and women who
made Charleston's history; plants, birds, and fishes; an old
horse-drawn fire engine that thrilled at least one visitor who
remembers such fire-fighting apparatus; and, to mention again

one more item in a really fascinating aggregate, Apothecaries'
Hall, an entire old drugstore, about which John Bennett has
written a first-rate monograph. Under the directorship of E.
Milby Burton, the museum, in association with the Society
for the Preservation of Old Dwellings, has acquired, not only
the Heyward-Washington House on Church Street, but also
the exquisite Manigault House on upper Meeting, which has
had a thorough restoration after its rescue from the proposed
status of a filling station.

I remember the museum's little cases of educational exhibits which were sent to schools and from which we learned
to make production maps, sticking little specimens of this and
that over the crayoned outlines of the states and getting our
fingers full of paste in the process. I remember also the stuffed
birds which I tried in vain to draw; and I remember Miss
Laura Bragg, the former curator, who tried to teach us not
to shudder at snakes. Miss Bragg had a pet blacksnake named
Molly which used to twine around her arms and neck to the
delight of small schoolchildren, and she patiently persuaded
us to hold small reptiles in our hands. I am afraid that in
my case her attempts to produce a herpetophile were vain;
I was convinced of this just recently when, on the edge of the
brook which runs through our summer place, I sat on a large
snake and rose with astounding celerity.

Through Miss Bragg's efforts a branch of the museum's
work was enlarged into the Charleston County Free Library,
which occupies a magnificent old house on Rutledge Avenue,
built in the 1850's as the town residence of a cotton planter
and later the home of Mayor Ficken. It is rather sad to see
the rooms of some of these beautiful old homes violated, but
Charleston taste and money no longer run to palatial residences, and the chances are ten to one that if the library hadn't
taken over this house it would have been made into apartments.

Probably there are few libraries in the United States, outside of college campuses, that have such distinguished housing, such a beautiful garden, and such trees, for this house is overhung by lofty magnolias. The library is an active place; on the occasions when I was there it was crowded, and at one of the Monday evening book forums, at which the intelligentsia dissect current literature, the section allotted to the meeting was jammed.

Free schooling was an early institution in the city, dating back to 1698, and Charleston boasts the oldest municipal college in the United States, with a history reaching back all the way to 1785 and an actual existence dating from ten years after that.

The college began its career on lands originally laid aside for a free school. One of its first graduates was the architect Robert Mills; it has since been attended by statesmen and men prominent in the professions. Among its famous students was John C. Frémont, whose career there, however, was somewhat inglorious. Agassiz lectured there, and Stephen Elliott, the financier-botanist. In the second part of the last century the college's facilities were broadened by municipal aid, and in 1918 it was made co-educational. In 1927 A. B. Murray, Charleston's good angel, added a gift of $100,000 to the endowment fund.

The faculty has included some distinguished, if not famous scholars. Nathaniel Wright Stevenson, the historian, was among them; and one of the present staff, J. H. Easterby, has written a history of the institution.

The college buildings have a distinguished paternity. The central part of the main building was designed by Strickland in 1828, and E. B. White added the wings and portico in 1846, getting into difficulties in the process, through no fault of his own, with the board of aldermen. The lodge was added in 1852, and in 1854 the library. The group of buildings with their classical columns have distinction and repose, even through their coating of chalky pinkish red, and the campus is an inviting one.

In 1838, when the college was receiving a boost from the city, the High School was established. This had the odd distinction, later in the century, of being moved into an old mansion on George and Meeting streets, another of those beautiful early nineteenth-century houses which had been the residence of Judge King, a Scots immigrant, famous for his brilliant dinners. Although the house was a superb one, it was a gloomy prison as a school, with old-fashioned Franklin stoves for heat, grimy woodwork, a rowdy tradition of initiation featured by bags of sand and water and an ironclad rule that no boy might come to it wearing socks and live; and a demerit system according to which, if disciplinary infractions had reached a certain level, a boy had to report on Saturday morning and work out an impossible problem in multiplication. It does seem to me that he might have been forced to do something useful instead of thus wasting his time, but there were, even in my time, remnants of ancient educational tradition that would probably make the petted and spoiled students of today shiver.

The principal then was a tall, dynamic, and rather fearful gentleman. Our connection with him was through the class in "mental arithmetic," as distinguished from the written kind. This was an exercise in concentration and the keenest torture I ever suffered. Mr. Whitehead had a sensational method of conducting a class which kept you on your toes for the entire period. He would propound some unlikely problem about the juncture of the hands of a clock, which could easily have been solved for all practical purposes by taking a clock and turning the hands to see when they met. Then, charging down the aisle like an enraged bull elephant, with an outstretched forefinger which looked to the terrified pupils like a good thick policeman's night stick, he would bring it to bear on a quivering thirteen-year-old just as the final thunder of the pronoun "yo—o—o—u" was rattling the windows. I have never had my attention so firmly held at any time since. From various accounts I am inclined to believe that the musicians at a Toscanini rehearsal must feel very much as we did in that mental arithmetic class.

There was one occasion, however, when our principal's charge down the aisle was somewhat spoiled. Some miscreant had been eating an apple and had left the core beside his desk. Mr. Whitehead, beginning his charge, put one foot down on the apple core and performed a swoop down the aisle that would have done credit to Sliding Billy Watson of burlesque fame, fetched up safely with a beautiful recovery, and roared, "Who left that there?" But he couldn't repress a smile. I have only one other memory of him. At the height of the hazing on my first day there, when several boys had been virtually decapitated by sandbags, he put his head out of a window and shouted, "You boys had better be careful, now, or you're going to hurt somebody."

During the recess period we were turned loose into the bare, graceless back yard, where a Negro concessionaire sold cheap candy and homemade groundnut (peanut) cakes, a sad comedown from Judge King's dinners. At this time there was supervised exercise under the direction of an elderly one-legged athlete, "Professor" Valdez, who was usually called "Fess," and who instructed the student body in the proper use of the rope swings and other instruments of physical culture. The Professor was, if I remember correctly, a masseur after school hours.

I wonder how many Americans have gone to school in a mansion built around 1805 and learned physical culture from a one-legged instructor?

The girls' high school was named after Gustavus Memminger, the Confederate Secretary of the Treasury. The orphanage, where he began his career, is, like the college, of ancient lineage as things American go. It was founded after a particularly bad epidemic of yellow fever had made it essential. The building was erected in 1792 on land that had been the site of military defenses, and was made of brick from the old Revolutionary barracks. Thomas Bennett designed the original structure, which was altered to an Italianate style in the 1850's. The chapel, added in 1802, was designed by the amateur Gabriel Manigault, who for the time being abandoned his favorite Adam style in favor of Greek revival. The orphanage ranks as one of the oldest buildings for the purpose in the United States.

Another striking educational building is the old Citadel, former home of the Military College of South Carolina, which in its original form dates from 1829, when it was built by Frederick Wesner as an arsenal. The reader will by this time have concluded that every public building in Charleston has been adapted to some purpose different from that for which it was first meant. He will be in a large measure right. The Citadel served its original purpose for only eleven years and was then invaded by the Military College, which kept it until 1922, when the new and rather grand buildings were erected along the Ashley River, roughly opposite the old settlement at Albemarle Point. The old one is now used as a county center. At first a two-story building with a wooden parapet, the Citadel in time took on two more stories and Gothic turrets. E. B. White had a hand in the Gothic embellishments. The fourth story was added as late as 1910. The quadrangle suggests something out of Rome by the Moors.

That Charlestonians should insist on calling Marion Square the Citadel Green is rather odd, for the green is extremely limited. For many years most of the parade ground has been covered with rough gravel of an orange-brown color. Here

BULL STREET: THE BLACKLOCK HOUSE

OLD BUILDINGS ON EAST BAY WITH THE EXCHANGE
ON THE LEFT

THE COOPER RIVER WATERFRONT AND THE CUSTOMS HOUSE

LOOKING EAST ON CHALMERS STREET FROM MEETING
STREET. NORTH PORTICO OF THE FIREPROOF BUILDING IN
THE FOREGROUND

stands the lofty Calhoun monument, over a well which was said to have medicinal qualities and was very popular. The site was first that of the old Singleton tobacco warehouse. There is a historic relic in the form of a fragment of the original tapia or tappy wall—tapia being ground, burned, and pressed oyster shells—part of the "hornwork" used to fortify the city during the British siege. There are dints in the wall, ascribed to rifle and cannon fire.

In my childhood the Chautauqua tents were spread on the Citadel Green, and the first air show I can recall was held there in 1910. It was thrilling. There was a green silk dirigible, a biplane, a hot air balloon, and a parachute jumper. The colored gentleman who took me to the show was deeply perturbed when the parachutist landed rather heavily, and he could not repress an exclamation which I repeated to the faintly scandalized amusement of my family, but which is not usually printed in a book of this sort.

Returning to the question of adaptation of buildings, curiously enough there are two more important schools in buildings intended to be something else. The Porter Military Academy on Ashley Avenue had as its nucleus the pre-Civil War United States Arsenal; and Ashley Hall, an exclusive girl's school on Rutledge Avenue, is contained in the James Nicholson house, a Southern Greek revival mansion of the 1830's, later the house of the German consul. We may note two things about it here: the extraordinary spiral staircase, from the well of which one can look right up to the skylight, and the fact that Hervey Allen once taught English to the young ladies there.

Not to labor an interesting point, this later use of buildings for another purpose is an interesting thing about Charleston. To sum them up: a library in a magnificent residence, the City Hall in a former bank building, the Chamber of Commerce in the old library building, the museum in an auditorium,

schools in arsenals and elaborate residences. This sort of thing
extends also to business (the adaptations not being always
quite so happy) and has given Charleston such distinctions as
the water works, which are in the fine old Adam dwelling
known as the Middleton-Pinckney House, built in the 1790's;
the electric light company, housed in a residence on Meeting
Street, and the offices of a railroad company in the Aiken
House, while an insurance company functions in a great Gothic
mansion on Wentworth Street. There is almost no end to these
adaptations, and of course they extend to the use of servants'
quarters as separate dwellings, and carriage houses for the
same purpose. One of the grandest and most beautiful houses
in Charleston, the Governor Thomas Bennett house, is owned
by Roper Hospital and is now a doctors' residence.

But this is one of the things that has kept many of these old
buildings. Few people will deny that it is better to remodel
historical and romantic dwellings than to tear them down, if
the remodeling is done with some discretion. The idea of a
bakery in the Heyward-Washington house seems almost sac-
rilegious and that of an oil and gas station in the Manigault
House is repulsive; but all the adaptations are not quite so
bad.

Not all the city's commercial architecture depends for its
beauty upon having been non-commercial in its original form.
The stroller can find all sorts of picturesque structures on East
Bay, for instance, which are still used for their original mer-
cantile purposes, and such ruins as the old railroad gates on
Ann Street and the railroad warehouse built before the Civil
War with its bowed roof and circular window which show
Charleston's determination to combine beauty and utility.

Of Charleston's extensive new buildings, the chief are the
new Roper Hospital on the Ashley River, the vast new Citadel
on the same shore, and the Francis Marion and Fort Sumter
Hotels. The two latter hardly rival in distinction such beautiful

old hostelries as the St. John's Hotel and the Charleston Hotel, but the city has long badly needed modern accommodations and can well be grateful for these. More would help.

Also among the city's grandeurs is the Customs House on the east waterfront, whose classical outline is impressive even though not complete. It was constructed in the 1890's and may be called a typical government building. Certainly it is infinitely preferable to the inappropriate Post Office.

It is a key to Charleston's character that new dwelling houses are generally negligible. Excrescences will hereafter have a hard time making their way into the old part of the city, for a zoning commission and an architectural board have considerable discretion in the protection of the historic area.

CHAPTER TWELVE

Some Famous Houses

W hat is "characteristic" of Charleston's architecture? The massive Georgian Miles Brewton house on King Street, or the Manigault house with its rounded wings and simple lines that bespeak the Adam brothers, or the numerous "single" houses with their long sweeping piazzas, or such little houses with odd tile roofs as the "Pink House" on Chalmers Street and the little dwelling which is associated with DuBose Heyward? You will see examples similar to all. Leaving the settlement of the question to the architectural experts, the layman would undoubtedly plump for the piazzaed single house and I think he would have the support of the cognoscenti. But there are so many individual adaptations and so many actual varieties of architecture in the city that any composite picture in the observer's mind is likely to be shattered in the course of a fairly brief stroll.

It is impossible to get any adequate idea of what the very early houses of Charleston were like as a whole, since the fires that ravaged the city have removed virtually all from the eye of posterity. Possibly those fires were a blessing in disguise, but they must have burned down a good many charming buildings along with the undistinguished ones. Almost no houses in the city exceed two hundred years old, but Colonel Rhett's fine house, which may have been erected as early as 1707, suggests clearly enough that even in the early days Charleston was no frontier town in appearance.

Fires notwithstanding, out of a total of 1,168 buildings considered worthy of comment, the Civic Services Committee listed seventy-one as pre-Revolutionary. The preservation of that number of sightly edifices in a community subject to so many calamities is remarkable enough to need no underlining.

Dominant among the great pre-Revolutionary dwellings is the Miles Brewton mansion on King Street, known nowadays, from its long ownership by the Pringle family, as the Pringle House. Illustrations, by the way, are scarcely just to this eminently dignified residence. The best of them, photographic or otherwise, fail to bring out the proportion of the portico to the body of the house and give the former a slightly pinched look.

Begun in the year 1762 by a wealthy merchant of the city, the house took about seven years to build. The preparation of the hand-sawn lumber, the laying of the foundations and their settling, and the collection of the materials was no small task; and of course the completion of the carving in the interior was a slow process. It is sometimes said that the brick was brought from England; but Edward McCrady, the historian of South Carolina, consulted an expert and found that approximately 4,500 tons of brick would have been required, enough to fill nine of the largest vessels then entering the port or an even greater number if the bricks were brought as ballast. And as lots of brick was made in the vicinity, the evidence would suggest that the brick was local.

As with so many early examples of Charleston building, this one lacks any definite attribution to an architect. One Ezra Waite, a builder, is believed to have been the man; he advertised publicly that he was, and appears to have been indignant at the suggestion that his was not the master hand.

But whoever originated the design, Miles Brewton must have seen, when he looked upon his completed house, that it was good. Recessed from the street, the house is of the familiar double type with a center hallway. It is of English-type brick laid in Flemish bond. The roof was originally of the characteristic tile, which has since been replaced by slate. The portico, supported by four Ionic columns, is divided to form a balcony on the second floor. Once the balcony had a lead-covered floor, but during the Civil War this was given up to the cause. There is a rose window in the gable, and the entablature and cornice surround the entire house. The columns of the portico are of Portland stone and are over twelve feet in height and three feet in diameter. A fine double flight of stairs leads up to the first floor, which is elevated.

Seen from the old garden at the rear, the house is equally impressive. There is a fine Palladian window at the head of the stairway, a double flight of stone steps. On the north end is a flagstone porch, with a set of brick steps leading down to the courtyard and ending in a rounded newel of brick which is characteristically West Indian. Similar steps may be seen on the old Glebe House on the street named from the glebe lands given to St. Philip's Church.

The carriage house and servants' quarters of this old house are as notable as the house itself. They have preserved the tile roofs which originally covered the entire group. The garden, spacious and rambling, is bright and fragrant with such seasonal planting as snowdrops, believed to be direct descendants of those planted by the first owner; Louis Philippe, Devoniensis, and Duchesse de Brabant roses; and a profusion of magnolias, tamarisks, Japanese plums, ferns, and pomegranates.

From the threshold of the ponderous front door the visitor looks along a flagstone-paved hallway fifty-four feet to the rear door. The wide hall has a beam instead of an arch. To the left is the downstairs drawing room, to the right another which was probably the library and study. To the left at the rear is the present dining room—it was the custom when state dinners were give in these old houses for the dinners to be served in the great drawing rooms upstairs. The corresponding space to the right is given over to domestic arrangements. A mahogany and pine stairway leads to the upper floor, where the great drawing room takes up a large portion of the space. Seeing the very limited number of bedrooms, you are surprised until you remember that this was a city house, and that it was meant for family use and was designed to be airy. The quarters in the yard, of course, took care of the numerous servants.

The doors are all of solid mahogany, with richly yet soberly carved doorway and moldings. Each fireplace is different in detail. Only a casual glance is needed to understand how his dwelling cost Miles Brewton 8,000 pounds, an immense sum in those times.

The house, which has passed into the ownership of the Misses Susan and Rebecca Frost, is open to the public at stated hours upon payment of a small fee which is used to defray the expenses of maintenance. Another of the sisters, the late Mary Pringle Frost, wrote a small book of description and family reminiscence, from which the following details of the great Waterford chandelier are derived:

This showpiece is in two tiers, each of which has twelve glass arms, and both tiers are fitted into a crystal-covered glass bowl. The arms are of six-faceted solid cut glass, formed in a double curve with a glass bobêche and a glass windshield fitted into a brass cup. The shields of the lower tier are nine inches high and those of the upper proportionately smaller. The chandelier is five feet in width and hangs six feet from the ceiling; at the very top is a canopy of cut glass eighteen inches in diameter. The effect, in various lights, is extraordinary. The drawing room in which this treasure hangs is of commensurate size, about twenty-eight by twenty, and the ceilings, as they would have to be to accommodate such a chandelier, are over twelve feet from the floor.

Here the original silk hangings are at the windows, and here hang portraits, of Mr. Brewton by Reynolds, and others of the ladies of the family, one, having been stolen, now replaced by a reproduction. The house is literally filled with *objets d'art* (some recently added), including magnificent mirrors, but these must after all be seen. A mere description of them would be secondary to the historic interest of the house.

Miles Brewton was, when he built his house, already an old Charlestonian. His grandfather, described as a goldsmith, was quite possibly a banker as well. He was "powder receiver" for the province in 1717 and served as foreman on the jury that convicted the pirates. His son Robert also served as powder receiver—probably neither one was a smoker—and sat in the Commons as representative of St. Philip's parish. His house is the one previously mentioned, at 71 Church Street, which he built in 1730, a year before his son Miles was born. Miles Brewton became a merchant, and we may judge of the extent of his fortune by the house he began when he was thirty-one. He was conservative in his leanings; in fact, he was among those of the deputation that presented the address of welcome to Lord William Campbell, last Royal governor, upon his arrival in 1775, and the governor and his lady resided in the Brewton home until their own was made ready.

In August, 1775, Brewton and his entire family took ship for Philadelphia. Whether he intended to return after putting his family in a place of safety is a matter for conjecture, for all were lost at sea. The house then passed to Brewton's sister, Rebecca, who had married Jacob Motte. It was her unhappy fortune to act as hostess for Clinton and Rawdon when they made the house their headquarters during the British occupation. A souvenir of their visit may be seen over the fireplace mantel, where some anonymous artist scratched, with the stone of a diamond ring, a not too flattering portrait of Sir Henry Clinton.

Mrs. Motte was a woman of character and decision, as may be judged from her portrait. She must have sized up Rawdon as quite worthy of his reputation, for it is well known that, although she dutifully enacted the part of hostess during his stay, she kept her daughters out of harm's way by shutting them up in the garret under the watchful eye of a faithful old nurse.

When she was widowed in the second year of the British occupation, she retired to her plantation on the Congaree River. The British took possession of that, too. When it appeared that the partisans would have to set it afire in order to dislodge the British, Mrs. Motte was equal to the sacrifice. Indeed, not only did she give her permission, but, it is said, handed the officers a bundle of incendiary Indian arrows with which to do the job. She was an excellent businesswoman, too, and after the war she was able to recoup her fortunes and even to improve the estate. It seems only fitting that the Charleston chapter of the D.A.R. is named after her.

To repeat mention of two incidents in their proper setting, we add that this was the house to which Isaac Hayne's sister-in-law came to plead for his life, and to which William Bull was brought in a litter to ask mercy for the condemned patriot. The house was also the headquarters of the Federal army of occupation at the end of the Civil War.

Through a granddaughter of Rebecca Motte the mansion passed into the ownership of the Pringle family, one daughter of which became the wife of Donald Grant Mitchell, otherwise Ik Marvel, author of *Reveries of a Bachelor*. The present owners are descendants of Rebecca Motte.

Quite different from the Pringle House is the mansion on upper Meeting Street which the museum has restored and which was built by Gabriel Manigault for his brother Joseph.

Charleston, as has been noted, had a number of amateur architects. Probably, in designing their own houses, they adapted the plans in some English and French professionals' books of designs, rather like the books of small houses that you can buy today, except that theirs were not usually small houses. Quite possibly, too, annoying details were left to the experience and judgment of the builder. There is a story that seems to confirm this. One of these amateur house-designers gave his instructions to a builder and then was obliged to be absent a good deal of the time while his house was going up. The builder dogged him for further instructions, and finally, becoming impatient, he told the man to attend to these matters himself. The builder obeyed, and finished the house without a staircase, which was what he had wanted to discuss with the owner. Thus, says the story, the house acquired a flying staircase. The tale ought to be true if it isn't.

The most distinguished of these amateurs, Gabriel Manigault, actually furnished his builder with drawings. He was the descendant of Huguenot immigrants and English stock, a rice planter, active in social life, and, one rather regrets to add, among those who swore allegiance to the king of England in 1780. As the grandson of Samuel Wragg, owner of Wraggborough, and as the son-in-law of Ralph Izard, he was connected with things architectural both by descent and by marriage.

The first known example of his work is the house which (we hope) immortalizes his name. Dating from 1790, it is a fine example of the Adam style, to which Manigault was inclined. The structure is of locally manufactured brick, three stories high, with a two-story piazza in front and a semi-circular porch on the north to balance the curve of the staircase well and the dining room. In our time the house had degenerated into a slum dwelling. The Society for the Preservation of Old Dwellings was able to rescue it, and an arrangement with the

U.S.O., which has been using it as a women's unit, provided rent in advance for a considerable period and thus aided the work of restoration. Under the direction of the well-known Charleston architect, Albert Simons, volunteers worked to restore the house to its original state, scraping off layer after layer of paint in the process and exposing the rich, bold, and varied coloring of the plaster and the beauty of the woodwork and ornamentation. The wallpaper, however, had vanished, and has been replaced with stencilings which carry out the motifs of the decor. It is possible that the Adam brothers sent Manigault the designs for the mantelpieces and moldings, which are delicate and airy. The mantel in the great drawing room features medallions which show the native palmetto trees and the figures of slaves; the ceiling is characterized by cartouches with anthemia. Another notable feature of the house is the flying stairway, which makes its graceful way all unsupported to the third story under an elaborate plaster ceiling. Tourists are thrilled by the "secret" stairway, but Miss Beatrice St. Julien Ravenel, in a revealing article in the *Journal of the American Society of Architectural Historians* (October, 1942) suggests that it was most likely a laundry chute.

This Manigault mansion is the first known example of the Adam style in South Carolina. It is also an example of careful planning and of enduring materials. Miss Ravenel points out that lime in layers was used to prevent deterioration of the brick. The rounded design, which is so arresting, is carried out even to a little gate house of circular form.

The dwelling which Manigault built for himself suffered the fate which his brother's house escaped. It was demolished to make way for a filling station. Antiquarians may take some comfort from the fact that the original materials were partly used for the new structure.

This amateur architect also designed the chapel of the Orphan House, a somewhat thickset experiment favoring the

Greek revival, and, as we have seen, he may have been the architect of the City Hall. His work includes the distinguished South Carolina Society Hall, close to St. Michael's Church, notable for its fine interiors. (The portico of that building, however, was the work of a later time and was added by Frederick Wesner.) His other undertakings, whatever they were, are now impossible to trace.

Another amateur was the famous miniaturist Charles Fraser, who in his middle years designed the cupola of the old Exchange, now removed, and in his old age the tower of St. John's Lutheran. It is Fraser's *Reminiscences of Charleston* which attributes the Court House to still another architect by avocation, Chief Justice Drayton.

Thomas Bennett, the younger, governor of South Carolina at the time of the Denmark Vesey insurrection, was the son, partner, and successor of a busy contractor and builder. The father has to his credit the Orphan House and the imposing rice mill at the foot of Wentworth Street; the son's house on Lucas Street, which he began in 1825, and which stood in lonely grandeur at the edge of marshy land on the river, is perhaps the most serenely beautiful structure of its kind in the entire city. It is a great white-painted single house with sweeping piazzas, twenty-foot ceilings, rooms averaging twenty-two feet square, and a fine flying staircase. Although no longer in private hands, the house has retained its aristocratic exterior intact.

So many of the Charleston houses are connected with persons or events of history that an entire volume would hardly do justice to all the twists and turns of legend and tradition, which is precisely what makes them so fascinating in addition to their beauty. On Meeting Street, for instance, is the lovely old Georgian Huger House, where Royal Governor Lord William Campbell resided for a very brief time and from which he escaped to the *Tamar;* and directly across the street from it is the house in which Lieutenant-Governor Bull lived. A little down the street is the John Edwards house, also pre-Revolutionary, which was the headquarters, during the occupation, of Admiral Arbuthnot, commander of the British fleet, and where later the daughters of Admiral de Grasse found refuge. Notable for its nineteenth-century grace and richness is the Nathaniel Russell House on this street, another of those Adam dwellings, with a beautiful polygonal wing and admirable doorway. The fine old Horry House is pre-Revolutionary and Georgian, although you have to look beneath the piazzas that were added in the nineteenth century and which come out over the sidewalk as a kind of portico. This house is identified with Francis Marion's colleague, Brigadier-General Peter Horry. An amusing story is told of a visitor who was unable to pronounce the name correctly—there are several of these Charleston name stories—and who asked a Negro man if this was the "hoary" house. "No, suh," replied the native, "dis de o-rée house. If you wants the whorey house you better go roun' on B—— Street."

One should know also the George Edwards House on Legaré Street with its marvelous gateway, the Stuart House on Tradd Street which was the home of the Indian agent and from which Marion is said to have escaped, the Blacklock House on Bull Street, the Gibbes House on South Battery.... But the reader would be out of patience before the writer had exhausted his store of adjectives. We shall mention for historical interest Mr. Petigru's law office in St. Michael's Place, built for him in 1848, now painted a poison brown, and call attention to the Daniel Blake Tenements behind the Court House, a building left by its owner to St. Michael's Church with the proviso that it be rented to the respectable poor. It has, among other things, a notable double flight of steps with particularly individual and charming iron railings.

Fortunately there is a voluminous and expert literature on the subject of Charleston's dwellings, which the interested student will find listed at the end of this book, which, hereafter, except for purposes of identification and allusion, will stick to other matters.

CHAPTER THIRTEEN

The Forts and the Harbor

The beautiful harbor of Charleston, which has so far proved impregnable, is still heavily fortified. The chief defense is the oldest of the forts, Fort Moultrie, which is heavily armed today. It is built at the narrowest part of the harbor entrance, where the channel is only about three thousand three hundred yards in width. Before that day in 1776 when it drove away the British fleet, it was known as Fort Sullivan, since it was built on Sullivan's Island, which had been named after one of the first shiploads of settlers, Captain Sullivan. Four years later the little fort played a less glorious part, for it did comparatively little damage to the enemy fleet which sailed through without stopping for a battle, and it does not again emerge into the limelight until that day when Major Anderson, under cover of darkness, spiked its guns and quietly transferred his men to Fort Sumter.

Fort Moultrie is now a bristling harbor defense, but one wonders just what it could do against a modern fleet accompanied by aircraft, to say nothing of that new horror, the atomic bomb.

For the peacetime visitor, it offers few historical sights besides the formidable armament. Chief among these in sentimental interest is the tomb of the Indian Osceola (on which his name is misspelled Oceola).

This Seminole chief was of mixed Indian and white blood. When, in 1835, his Indian wife was reclaimed as a slave by the man who had owned her mother, Osceola protested to the District Indian Agent (one tradition was that he killed him) and was thrown into prison for asserting his rights. When he was finally set free, injustice rankling in his soul, he busied himself with stirring up his people and provoked what was called the Second Seminole War.

Osceola was still too trusting of white men. He was parleying under a flag of truce when he was again seized. For a while he was kept in a dungeon in St. Augustine and then removed to Fort Moultrie. He was promised his freedom if he would persuade his people to migrate west of the Mississippi but this he refused to do, choosing rather to remain in his living tomb in the fort, where he died the year after his capture. Altogether it is not one of the prettier stories of American history, this lonely red man dying in the prime of his young manhood, betrayed and helpless, and probably heartbroken too. It is good that even the poor amends of a tombstone was made to him.

Many years after his death, when the attic of an old house near the city was being cleared, a portrait of the proud Seminole was found, the work of an artistically inclined member of the garrison of Fort Moultrie.

Also to be seen (in peace time) is the underground chamber which Major Anderson made his headquarters before moving to Fort Sumter, and there is a monument to one of the Union ironclads that was sunk during the long siege. The inscription states that the *Patapsco* was sunk by a Confederate submarine but experts apparently agree that more likely she struck a mine. A large portion of her crew went down with her.

Midway between Fort Moultrie and Cummings Point and

FLOWER SELLERS ON THE POST OFFICE STEPS AND
ST. MICHAEL'S PORTICO

LOOKING WEST ACROSS MARION SQUARE TO THE FRANCIS
MARION HOTEL, CALHOUN STATUE, CUPOLA OF THE
ORPHAN HOUSE, AND ST. MATTHEW'S LUTHERAN CHURCH

a little to the west of a line between them, Fort Sumter is built on a sand spit of which one end is covered at high tide. The fort was begun in the year 1839. Ten years were required before the foundations were ready. As the fort now looks from the Battery, from which it can be clearly seen although it is three and one-half miles away, it is a low-lying structure of brownish-red brick, considerably simpler and flatter in outline than in the old pictures made before Confederate and Union guns reduced it to a heap of rubbish.

Fort Sumter today, although as recently as early 1946 it was still partly restricted, is a peaceable enough spot. Going toward it in the trim little yacht which makes guided tours of the harbor from a wharf on the south end of King Street, the visitor is scarcely aware of anything formidable in its appearance. It is exciting to stand in the same place where the shells from Fort Johnson—which looks so close that you feel you could throw a baseball from it to Fort Sumter—fell among the defenders on that April day in 1861. The underground bombproof passages, probably the last word in fortification in that earlier time, are well worth a visit. The guide will point out to you such features as the rifle embrasures made for a last-ditch fight in case the walls were boarded, and the old bullet foundry. There is a memorial to the Confederate heroes of that long and almost unbelievable defense, and also a tablet to the Federal forces commanded by Anderson. One more thread in the intricate network of Charleston's relation to history is the name, among the others, of Captain Abner Doubleday, who years before had instituted the game of baseball and who wrote the history of that thirty hours' ordeal by fire. The flagpole is the gift of a descendant of Major Anderson.

It does not take long to see Fort Sumter, and after all the chief excitement of the visit consists in simply being there, where all that mischief came to a head. You think, too, of the men of the Confederacy who stuck it out for nearly two years, and of Major Huguenin, in command at the end, going through the lonely galleries with his lantern before slipping away with the still unstruck flag in a small boat.

On this harbor trip you will also see Castle Pinckney, that little fortification named in honor of the man who defied the Directory, and erected as a defense against the French in case war broke out. Castle Pinckney stands upon a little bit of land which was originally held by a man named Schultz, who had established squatter rights to the land. It was known as Schultz's Folly—not in derision, however, for the word "folly" in this sense is derived from an old word for a wooded spot. Only after the fort was built was it discovered that Mr. Schultz was technically the possessor of the site, and he got a good round sum for his rights.

During the Civil War, Castle Pinckney served as a prison for Federal prisoners taken at Manassas. Photographs taken of them show their pathetic efforts at gayety—their barracks ornamented with signs reminiscent of their home city, New York, and some of them singing and skylarking under the watchful eyes of the Charleston Zouaves, a group of mere children. It is proposed some day to make Castle Pinckney into a memorial to General Moultrie and the less known General Thompson, whose sharpshooters drove off the forces the British had landed in that first visit of theirs.

When, after the excursion under the towering Grace Memorial Bridge and down past the waterfront, the little yacht ties up at her pier, the visitor has not yet done with the historical aspect of the trip. For this is approximately the very spot from which, in 1878, the sailing ship *Azor* departed.

Most people have forgotten the crusade for Liberia in the nineteenth century, long before the ineffable Marcus Garvey conceived the (to him) profitable notion of sending droves of black colonists back to their "homeland." Overenthusiasm, the simplicity of the would-be colonists, and what appears at this remove to have been greed and unscrupulousness all enter the story.

The *Azor,* at any rate, departed from Charleston, with a full passenger list of Negroes of various ages and both sexes, who were leaving for various reasons the land of their white masters. They told their reasons, not very convincingly, to A. B. Williams, a white newspaperman who reported the trip to the *News and Courier.* He was humane and objective; although he could not fail to see the ridiculousness of some of the things that occurred, he refused to record them in Negro dialect, which he said he considered on the same level as making fun of a deformity, particularly as the dialect was the white man's doing. But he was indignant at the ill-preparation for the voyage—the so-called "doctor," a Negro named Carter, was a fraud—and he was moved to pity by the really horrible sufferings of the people. It was a voyage of failure and misery; many of the emigrants perished on the way. The ship was long becalmed and went off her course, and food and water ran low. Only a remnant reached Africa at last. Williams' account, a brilliant piece of reporting, should be made more available. He tells of the Negro minister's prayer that the white reporter should be prevented from telling lies about the trip. Evidently the prayer was answered, for the report seems more than fair—it is compassionate.

This pier, too, is the spot at which disembarked, in the year 1882, the Princess Mary Louise of England, daughter of Queen Victoria, for a stay in Charleston with which her highness professed herself greatly pleased.

Immediately to the east, in front of the Fort Sumter Hotel, is White Point Gardens, the park enclosed by the two sea walls of the Battery. This was Charleston's earliest playground and one of the prettiest city parks you are likely to find. It is not extensive, but there is a distinguished air about

it and its spreading oaks; the quiet, stately houses on the north
of it and the magnificent harbor view make it a promenade
of the finest sort.

At the northeast end of the gardens is the plaque commemorating the hanging of Stede Bonnet and the other pirates,
who were buried at low watermark. The Battery itself was
then a shell beach. This was followed by a sea wall of palmetto logs; after that hurricane of 1804 it was built up by
dumping ballast rocks from trading vessels. Guns were
mounted here in 1812, from which doubtless arose the name
Battery, and the whole area was strongly fortified during the
Civil War. Now there are cannon, from the primitive products
of the patriots in the Revolution, crude little affairs, to the
great rifles which seemed so formidable in the 1860's, but
which would probably be classed as pop-guns now, and the gun
which was rescued from the *Keokuk*. There are obstruction
torpedoes such as were used in the harbor and a number of
the fat eight-and-one-half-ton mortars that were used by the
Federal forces.

There is a monument to the heroes who ventured forth in
those first torpedo boats, the *Little David* and the *Hundley,*
and the Fort Sumter monument, on which is mounted a naked
warrior with a shield and what looks like the spirit of white
Southern womanhood behind him. She is really the City of
Charleston. She holds a garland of laurel in one hand and
with the other points seaward toward the enemy. The pedestal
is ornamented with designs representing men busily engaged
in repairing the fortifications. There are eleven stars, one for
each of the Confederate states, upon the base, and the entire
monument is surrounded by ever widening circular shallow
steps which personify the seven states of the first Confederacy.
A conventionalized wave encircles the entire pedestal. This
monument is another bequest of Andrew B. Murray, who certainly outdid himself in the display of civic spirit.

Close by is the monument which commemorates the Battle of Fort Moultrie, upon which stands the daring Sergeant Jasper holding the flag he rescued. There is also a memorial to William Gilmore Simms, the novelist and historian.

There was once a floating bathhouse off the Battery, an eyesore and a scandal, which was removed after right thinking citizens had protested.

It is not only historical events which make this harbor fascinating, for the port has commercially a romantic past; ships from all over the world came to deliver their cargoes, and wharves were piled high with cotton and rice for them to take away, and swaggering Negro stevedores, men every inch of them, and clattering drays lined the wharves on the East Bay.

Charleston could still be a great and busy port if the rest of the world were sufficiently interested, but its position as concerns the back country is not advantageous in modern times. Whether the Santee-Cooper project will cause actual deterioration in the form of shoaling remains a matter for time to settle. At least the inflow of fresh water is viewed favorably by waterfront men as the teredos, which eat away dock piling, cannot survive in fresh water.

In May, 1946, twenty-eight vessels entered the port, fifteen being American and thirteen foreign. The net registered tonnage was one hundred and two thousand tons. In the same month twenty-six vessels cleared the port, fifteen of them American and eleven foreign, with a net registered tonnage of ninety-eight thousand tons. There is a large modern port terminal on the Cooper.

The harbor was a busy spot during the war years when it served as an embarkation point, and because of its magnificent Navy Yard, said to be the only first-rate one between Hampton Roads and the West Coast.

Other features of the harbor include the inland waterway and a yacht basin on the Ashley River. No mention of the river front and harbor would be complete without a notice of the famous Mosquito Fleet, the flock of frail swift craft long associated with Charleston which go out in the dawn to fish the plentiful waters and come scudding back with the flood tide to sell their catch. It was always a custom of this fishing fleet to go out and return in a body. The boats are generally small, under thirty feet long, and heavily rigged with oversize jibs and mainsails. Their daring and skilful pilots year in and year out have risked all but the most impossible weather to bring the city its daily ration of sea food. Of recent years an effete modern note has crept in, and many of the boats have been equipped with auxiliary engines. Some of the boats served reconnaissance purposes during the war but their sailing was handicapped by the presence of enemy submarines, one of which was captured outside of the harbor mouth.

In recent years there were a number of hulks still submerged in the harbor. They were said to be blockade runners of 1861-65, and their presence indicates that it was just as difficult to get out of the harbor as to get in.

CHAPTER FOURTEEN

Environs

Just where Charleston begins and ends would be a difficult
question to answer accurately, for the city was the center
of a vigorous and wealthy plantation culture, which was busy
with rice fields before the end of the seventeenth century and
which in actual wealth made the Indian trade look like very
small potatoes. Most of the planters had their city homes in
Charleston where they spent the summer and it is said that
"town" always meant Charleston to a Low Countryman. Of
course, there were variations in the pattern; some of these
planters went to Newport for the summer or to the mountains,
but the pattern standardized by the majority was Charleston
for the summer and the plantations for the fall and early
winter. Then, when Lent put an end to festivity, they went
back to the plantations until late spring brought the danger of
malaria.

The plantations of the Low Country were grouped chiefly
around the three principal rivers—the Santee, a noble and
important stream though little heard of by the average American until the newspapers and magazines publicized the Santee-
Cooper Power development and the not unnatural complaints
of those who objected to the destruction of some of the old
plantations by the lakes which were formed to store the

water power; the Ashley, and the Cooper. The Wando, the lower reaches of the Edisto, the North Edisto, the name of which is something of a puzzle, as it is not north of the Edisto proper, and the Stono also contributed to the arrangement of the plantations community, which may be roughly located as thirty miles along the coast on either side of Charleston and about forty miles north of it, the north end being narrower from east to west.

Plantations of the Carolina Low Country lists and describes about fifty of these Low Country plantations as notable, so it can be seen how extensive the plantation life was. Rice was the chief crop of nearly all, though indigo flourished until the Revolution put an end to the bounty on that product. Cotton was raised on a few estates but was a troublesome crop until Eli Whitney revolutionized the industry. Silk culture was attempted, and Mulberry, which dates from 1714, owes its name to this. Sir Nathaniel Johnson's plantation was called "Silk Hope." But rice was the life of the Low Country.

There is a pretty myth about a certain Landgrave Smith, who received a bag of rice from a ship captain just out from Madagascar and planted the first crop on a lot on the Charleston street now called Longitude Lane. Like many pretty legends, it is untrue. For one thing it has been pointed out that as the marsh that stood on the site of Longitude Lane was salt, the rice could not have been grown there.

The truth is that Henry Woodward, who had so much to do with the early founding of South Carolina, was the enterpriser in the planting of rice. Some years before Woodward's death Captain Thurber, master of a ship which had touched at Madagascar, no doubt for the laudable purpose of transporting slaves, gave Woodward a couple of bags of what is called gold seed rice. Woodward planted this seed and gave the seed crop to various friends to try their luck with. The new crop took so easily to the soil of the Low Country that, by 1690, rice was an important element of trade. By 1700 there were not enough ships in the harbor to take the crop away, and rice was on its way to becoming the chief source of the Low Country's wealth.

This crop was rather primitively handled at first but it grew to be a matter of close and energetic engineering and when the English millwright, Jonathan Lucas, perfected a pounding mill in 1790 it became a vast industry.

The planting of rice on a large scale called for big acreages, creeks that could be damned and released to flood the fields, both of which the Low Country afforded naturally, and Negro workers who were able to withstand the dangers of working in the swampy fields. An intricate system of drainage gates was devised to flood and drain the fields in turn. A large body of help was needed for harvesting and winnowing the grain. Even after the introduction of mills—the great Bennett Rice Mill in Charleston is an example—the rice that was to be used for seed had to be threshed by hand in order to avoid injuring the germ. Negro hands were developed into skilful artisans; a plantation system grew up with characteristics and customs of its own. In 1850 the industry had reached its highest point with the production of one hundred sixty million pounds of rice; the acreage can be roughly estimated by allowing about thirty bushels to the acre. It comes fairly close to one hundred thousand acres.

After 1860 the acreage declined rapidly. Lack of slave labor and the rise of other industries had something to do with this, but the chief cause was the discovery that rice could be grown more cheaply in Louisiana and Texas. By 1900 the rice industry in South Carolina was a mere shadow of what it had once been, and it has been estimated that by 1906 probably not more than five hundred acres were under cultivation. One by one the plantations were deserted and the houses fell into decay. The owners used the acreage for hunting a few weeks of every year and then left the plantations occupied by a skeleton force of Negroes.

Northern millionaires have taken over a number of these old plantations and on some the planting of rice has been restored. However, the Santee-Cooper Power Project which has flooded a number of the old plantation estates has had its part in eradicating traces of the old life. As the cash value of the rice crop in the United States in 1944 was about one hundred five million dollars it can be seen that rice growing is by no means impractical if the cost can be kept down.

When the rice plantation was in its glory, it was what has been described as a great hydraulic undertaking, a perpetual contending with water. The early stages of rice growing are submerged; the water has to be let in, and then, after a suitable interval, drained off and kept out. For this a network of canals, ditches, dams, and gates was necessary, for the water was flooded on and drained off by gravity; and a big troop of hands was necessary for the planting and hoeing and repairs and the gathering of the crop. "Every rice plantation," says David Doar, "was a complete and busy community in itself." There were the overseer and his driver or head man; the trunk-minder, or what might be called the irrigation superintendent, and bird-minders to chase off or shoot the rice birds that would otherwise eat the seed before it had a chance to grow. Carpenters and blacksmiths and bricklayers swelled the number of slaves and there were shepherds and cattlemen and swineherds. Depending upon the size of the plantation, there were quarters of varying extent at some distance from the owner's dwelling, composed usually of two-family frame cabins, unglazed according to Mr. Doar, but very comfortable. There was also a sickhouse presided over by an ancient nurse who had charge of the children while their mothers were busy in the fields. The paternal system also included regular rations, clothing, Christmas handouts, and "worming." Missionaries were brought to preach to the slaves and they were allowed to go to churches where suitable accommodations, usually in the form of a gallery, were made for them.

The center of each of these self-contained industries was the hall or family dwelling which was cared for by the house servants. These traditionally held themselves above the field hands, for there were castes within castes. Anyone who has been thoroughly managed by a good old fashioned Southern Negro housekeeper will understand, without explanation, the dignity and self-respecting pride of the plantation butler who had charge, like his British colleagues, of the pantry, the cellar, the house, the house servants as a whole, and matters of etiquette, protocol, and punctilio. A similar position was that of the coachman who was master of the stables, often extensive, and was greatly looked up to and envied by his inferiors, or of the patron who was master of the boats and barges that were used for traveling to Charleston or to other plantations in the neighborhood. The driver, not to be confused with the coachman, was the Negro boss of the hands and workmen. He was directly under the white overseer and was also a person of consequence. Julia Peterkin has immortalized a relic of this type in her novel *Black April*.

Illustrating the jealousy of prerogative that prevailed among the slaves is an old story about George Washington. The Father of his Country on one occasion rode up to his house and roared to an elderly Negro to take his horse. This happened to be the butler. Sensible of his position, he replied respectfully that he would call a groom, but Washington, not taking the hint, roared at him again to hold the horse and do whatever was necessary. The old man still demurred, whereupon the great man bellowed at him, "Look here, do you know who I am?" "Yes, suh," replied the butler. "You is de man that married Miss Martha."

Southern apologists are sometimes fond of pointing to this distribution of caste as showing that all Negroes were not indiscriminately lumped in their owner's mind as mere property. This attitude seems to proceed from the notion that if you have given a man or a woman some superiority, however insignificant, you have paid proper tribute to his dignity as a human being. Sometimes this line of reasoning is made to redound to the credit of the institution of slavery. Mrs. Ravenel, for example, in her *Life and Letters of Eliza Lucas*, winds up by defending a system that in *six generations* (italics ours) was able to transform a large group of people from savages into men and women who were acquainted with the lessons of Christianity, and who (with possible exceptions) behaved themselves with some regard for law and order. It does not seem to be a very tremendous accomplishment, considering the length of time, to convert savages into reasonably responsible menials.

For that matter it is interesting to see what a late eighteenth-century clergyman thought of the elegant manners of the Negro servants of Charleston. Travelers' tales are always suspect, as in that case of Crèvecoeur's story of the hanging of a Negro's body in a cage for the vultures to tear at. At any rate, Deacon Timothy Boardman, writing in 1788, was horrified by the informal behavior he witnessed. He says: "Yet I have seen a servant of Both Sexes (of course the good man meant of either sex) enter in such dishabitable as to be obliged to Display those Parts which ought to be concealed."

But here is another picture. Miss Mary Pringle Frost, describing a typical Charleston dinner in the old days, says "This dinner would be served by servants who waited with gusto and ceremony; also secretly, at times openly, fully appreciating the wit and good speaking." One can form a picture of Mr. Petigru making one of his famous sallies and of the footman and butler, unable to restrain their mirth, whooping as soon as they could retreat to the pantry.

A good many tales are told of the keen sense of correctness of these old servants and of their somewhat officious willingness to impart it to those unaware of the fine points. A certain visiting dignitary was whisperingly reproved by a butler for wanting rice with his fish. I myself ran afoul of this sense of propriety when, absent-mindedly accepting a drink, I failed to notice the coaster provided with it. The butler, a large and impressive specimen of his profession, murmured politely to me, "That's to set the glass on." No doubt he put me down in his black book, too, as just one of those visitors. But this is not intended as any reflection on the courtliness and genuine amiability of the colored people of Charleston.

Returning from this digression, the life that arose from this rice civilization has been described in varying terms— feudal, romantic, baronial, even unromantic. It has been said that the planters knew too little of business and that they read too much Scott. No doubt one could find proof of every kind of statement. But it is at least undeniable that the legends connected with many of these plantations are romantic, that the people who built them were lovers of good building and beautiful surroundings, and most of us, unless we are determined to follow some sort of party line, will prefer to think that the life lived in them was as spacious and romantic as the buildings and their legends suggest.

Some of these plantations are open to the public for a small fee, and conducted tours are made to them by a sightseeing company. During the tourist season the ladies' auxiliaries of St. Michael's and St. Philip's churches conduct visitors to a number of the plantations by courtesy of the owners. The stranger, of course, will have to be content to see those open to the public, and if he is fortunate may have an introduction or two in his pocket when he visits the Low Country. But

this is not a guidebook—there is no need for more—and the
houses which are open to the public are easily accessible by
the main motor highways. So we shall omit details of routes
and schedules and confine ourselves to some of the salient
facts.

The oldest of all the plantations still standing is Medway,
the date of which, 1686, makes it also the oldest known
building in South Carolina. It is on a little tributary of the
Cooper River, and was built by a Dutchman named Van
Arssens in a typically Dutch style. The house is notable for
its stepped gables, a great double avenue of oaks, and as
having been the model for John Bennett's novel, *The Treasure
of Peyre Gaillard*.

Mulberry, or Mulberry Castle as it is sometimes called
(also Broughton's Fort) is the third oldest of the Low Country plantation houses. It was built in 1714 by Thomas Broughton, a planter and politician. The house is representative of
its Jacobean period, and has four little towers at each corner
in which cannon were mounted during the Yemassee War. Its
builder was involved in one of South Carolina's earliest election squabbles, a forerunner of some of the ballot-counting
brawls of our time.

The quarrel came about in this way. Edward Tynte, appointed governor by the Proprietors in 1709, died after seven
months of office. There were only three of the Council in
the colony at this time, Broughton, Robert Gibbes, and
Fortesque Turberville, the Duke of Beaufort's deputy. They
met on a certain morning to choose a successor but adjourned
without any announcement; but that afternoon it was announced that Gibbes was their choice. That night Turberville
died unexpectedly, and next day Broughton made the claim
that Turberville had voted for him in the morning and then,
when his palm was greased, had turned around and voted for
Gibbes in the afternoon. With Turberville no longer able to

bear witness, Broughton and his supporters marched from Mulberry to the city to depose his rival. There was at that time a drawbridge at Meeting and Broad Streets. Gibbes had it raised to forestall the invaders, but there were Broughton fifth columnists on the inside to seize the gate and permit their partisans to enter. After an exchange of blows (and probably of good lusty Jacobean compliments) a compromise was arrived at and Gibbes was allowed to remain governor until the Proprietors should be heard from.

Fenwick (pronounced Fennick) Hall, on the Stono River on Johns Island, was built in 1730 by John Fenwick, whose work was added to by his son, who extended the house by two octagonal flankers, only one of which stands today. This son was a great lover of horseflesh, and his stud was particularly famous. The story is that one upper window was specially placed so that the guests could look out from it to the race track in front of the house.

There are numerous legends clustering about this house and family. I know only one of them, that this horse-loving Fenwick had imported a thoroughbred and that a young Englishman had brought the animal to the colony. One of the Fenwick girls eloped with the young Englishman, and the father overtook the couple, hanged the presumptuous young man to a tree, and forced his daughter to lash the horse until it dashed from under her husband and left him dangling. The ghost of the hanged man, as a matter of course, haunts the Hall. A photograph of the building before its restoration suggests that it was as likely a place as any for a ghost to haunt. This restoration was the work of the financier, Victor Morawetz, who included in his landscaping a cactus garden for which even the soil was imported. After his death the property was acquired by Claude Blanchard, a Charleston builder, who in a certain measure perpetuates the Fenwick tradition by raising prize cattle.

Stately Hampton, on a tributary of the Santee River which is called Wimbaw Creek, has been brought back to some semblance of its former grandeur by Archibald Rutledge, the poet, who has inherited it and has opened it to the public and written an informal book about it. The house was built in 1735 by the grandson of a Huguenot immigrant. The builder's daughter married one of the Horrys, who after her death, married the daughter of Eliza Lucas Pinckney. The Horrys greatly enlarged the original six-room house. The great portico, with its eight Doric columns, was put on after the Revolution. Albert Simons, the architect and scholar, has traced it to David Garrick's Adam villa at Hampton.

Here George Washington, on his way to Charleston, was entertained, and here he saved the life of a great oak tree which is still there to bear out the story, and which has attained a growth in keeping with the proportions of the great house, which is well over eighty feet in width and thirty in depth, not counting the portico, and has a ballroom forty-two feet long and twenty-eight feet from floor to ceiling.

This oak is not, even at that, the largest of the trees surrounding Hampton, for another considerably outdoes it in the amount of shade it casts. If you want your great-grandchildren to have lots of shade, plant a live oak for them.

Hampton was Francis Marion's headquarters, and here, surprised by the notorious Tarleton, he awoke with such a start that he wrenched off the arm of a chair. Tarleton stole the parish Bible from Hampton and a Baskerville Milton. John Rutledge, when the State of South Carolina was in his carriage, put up here, as did his brother Edward.

Harrietta, on the Santee, another of the plantations which may be seen by the unconnected visitor, is related by marriage to Hampton, for it was built by Mrs. Horry for her daughter in the year 1797. But that daughter never lived in it and it was left unfinished. Later, when it was being prepared for

A FAMOUS CHARLESTON VISTA: LOOKING NORTH ON MEET-
ING STREET TO ST. MICHAEL'S CHURCH, WITH PORTICO
OF SOUTH CAROLINA SOCIETY HALL IN FOREGROUND

THE OLD EXCHANGE AND CUSTOMS HOUSE AT THE EAST
END OF BROAD STREET

that daughter's son, the same thing happened, and none of the Horrys or Rutledges ever made it their home. The accidents of marriage kept the Rutledges at Hampton, and it has been owned by them ever since.

Not far from Magnolia Gardens, on the Ashley river, is the proud Drayton Hall, a great Georgian house built around 1738. In it was born Chief Justice William Henry Drayton, whose uncle William Bull was compelled to unseat him from the Council because of his incendiary speeches in behalf of liberty. Here Cornwallis had his headquarters, and when Negro troops, during the Civil War, burned and destroyed a number of plantations, they left Drayton Hall strictly alone, when its owner at that time, a physician, had the presence of mind to turn it into a pesthouse.

The house was once larger than it is now, for two detached flankers have decayed and left only the foundations. Marble pillars uphold the double portico on the west; the river side has the usual double stairway of these Georgian structures, leading up to a pilastered doorway which is imitated by the three central windows of the second floor. Photographs of the interior show a wonderful richness of detail, and a magnificent double staircase with richly carved banisters and ornamented stair stringer brackets. Certainly it must be the most elegant building that was ever used as a pesthouse.

Ashley Hall, the famous plantation, which was the home of William Bull and in a little building of which the treaty with Attakullahkulla was signed, has no great house for the traveler to gape at, for the last owner, when Federal troops were on the way to possess or destroy it, set fire to it with his own hands. "But what a gesture," as Cyrano de Bergerac remarked in Rostand's play.

The planters, naturally, had their parish churches, a number of which have survived. Most famous of these is St. James', Goose Creek, built by the first Church of England parish

outside of the city. The present structure, the second on the
site, was begun in 1711, but, like St. Michael's, it took a long
time to finish, for it was not dedicated until eight years later.
The Goose Creek planters, being Barbadians, followed a
style familiar to them on their island, so that this little house
of worship is one more suggestion of the West Indies. It has
a jerkined roof, a pilastered door over which is a peculiar
symbol, a pelican feeding her young, which was the device
of the Society for the Propagation of the Gospel, and windows surmounted by plump cherubim. Overhead are the great
live oaks dripping Spanish moss and dappling the sunlight
over the church.

Services are held in St. James' once a year, and when I
visited it the little building was being aired for the next day's
ceremonies. Even the prayer books and hymnals were heaped
on the lawn getting the blessing of the spring sunshine. A
young Negro acted as our guide and seemed to enjoy doing it.

The church is charming, both for its miniature quality and
for the beauty of the interior. The pulpit, directly in the
center, is enclosed by a semicircular rail. On either side are
tablets, one with the Lord's Prayer and the Apostles' Creed,
the other containing verses from the twentieth chapter of
Exodus. The chancel is richly ornamented and is surmounted
by the Royal arms, which saved it from profanation during
the Revolution. The center aisle is of flagstones. On the railing
of the gallery, which was added to the original structure,
hang the hatchments of Ralph Izard, and there is a memorial
to the Reverend Mr. Francis LeJau, the first rector. Mr.
LeJau, coming from the comparative peace of England, must
have been aghast when he realized what his new charge was
like (a ditch was dug around the churchyard to protect the
tombs from wild beasts) but he stayed on for the rest of
his life, eleven years. Arthur Middleton lopped off four acres
from his estate, "The Oaks," for the parsonage.

Wild beasts, Indians, wars, and the earthquake notwithstanding, St. James' still stands. Of late years a neat fence
and gateway have been added; otherwise the little church
is almost exactly in its original state.

In the same year in which the Goose Creek planters began
St. James', the men of St. Andrew's parish began to erect
their church. The original structure was enlarged and made
cruciform. It burned down in the 1750's and was rebuilt in
1764. The general atmosphere is similar to that of St. James',
but less relieved by sunlight and color. There are some imposing neglected-looking tombs, mossy, grass-grown, and
moldering.

A third of these little parish churches is Christ Church,
which is in the parish of that name, east of the city and south
of the Wando River. Contemporary in origin with St. James',
Goose Creek, and St. Andrew's, it was burned in 1724, and,
after rebuilding, was gutted by the British in 1782. Negro
troops of the Union army demolished the interior in 1865.
The church has an attractive bell tower topped by a cross,
and a little outside chimney with the groined chimney pots
typical of the regional architecture.

You might have thought, if you had been alive at the time,
that the Low Country was sufficiently equipped with churches,
but the Puritans did not. A group of these apostles of tolerance moved, pastor and all, to a spot about four miles from
the present Summerville, which is about twenty miles out of
Charleston. Their purpose was "to encourage the promotion
of religion in the Southern plantations." They established a
free school and built a church within their fortified village,
which they called Dorchester. The Church of England, however, soon provided a church of its own, St. George's.

Some twenty years before the Revolution, the Puritan settlers virtually deserted Dorchester, and by the time of that
war the former abode of saints was little more than a ghost

town. The fort built to exclude the Indians was repaired to provide a refuge for the people of Charleston in case the British should seize the town. Marion's bushwhackers and the British alternated in firing at each other from behind it, and then it was left to rot. The fast-crumbling ruins of St. George's tower and the old walls of the fort are still to be seen, but time will probably take care of them, too.

Near Dorchester is Bacon's Bridge, an important crossing during the skirmishes of the Revolution, and within view is a huge oak where, according to legend, Marion's men received a British officer under a flag of truce and gave him a banquet consisting entirely of sweet potatoes. The tale is edifying; the young Englishman was so impressed by the patriotism and determination of men who could fight when they had only potatoes to eat that he gave up his commission and returned to England, ashamed to fight such men. This story is ubiquitous, and various places are identified, if we may use that word, as the scene.

One usually takes in Dorchester as a side trip on a visit to Summerville, that flower-decked village among the pines, which should, like the gardens, be seen in the early spring. The town owes its origin to malaria, for it was a refuge for the planters of rice, but it is now a winter resort for hunters and other sports enthusiasts, as well as a flower showplace. Not far distant are the Mateeba Gardens, which have the distinction of standing on Anthony Ashley Cooper's own Ashley Barony, which the King granted to him, but for which he "paid" the Indians cloth and trinkets. Another estate which goes very far back in the history of the colony is Yeamans Hall, named after that unpopular Barbadian, and now a millionaires' winter colony, in which country homes of the more luxurious sort are strung along winding roads. It is secluded, restricted, and strictly private.

There are two old plantations virtually within Charleston.

Lowndes Grove, on the east bank of the Ashley, is associated with William Lowndes, a brilliant statesman of the early Republican years. It is just outside the city boundary. Another is Belvidere Farm, on the west bank of the Cooper River, and until not so many years ago the home of the Charleston Country Club.

So, as we said before, it is difficult to say where Charleston begins and ends, and the same is true of the Low Country.

CHAPTER FIFTEEN

Representative Men

When Charleston was a great city and a center of politics and culture, it produced out of its civilization a number of really remarkable men. Several have already been described in some detail. Though they will by no means exhaust the list of worthies, certain others are especially deserving of biographical notice if we are to have a reasonably clear picture of the life they represented and influenced. They were men with very human traits; no doubt their lives could be written by a biographer of the Strachey school and made to appear less edifying than in the accepted accounts. But their good qualities far outweighed their bad, and they did important work for the United States, for South Carolina, and for Charleston.

Typical of them, and a typical blend of what was best in American life, was the sturdy, keen-witted, shrewd and kindly Henry Laurens. Moderate, tolerant, occasionally coarse, religious without being narrow—he was shocked by the severity of Calvinist doctrine but he knew the Bible from cover to cover and he revered it—generous and humane, and yet sometimes a bit callous, he seems so real (particularly as shown in David Duncan Wallace's *Life*) that it is impossible not to feel warmly toward him.

He was the son of a Huguenot of good family who, after leaving France, tried England, Ireland and New York in turn before he finally rested from his travels in Charleston. Arriving without fortune, he set up in business as a saddler and became well-to-do.

Henry Laurens was his third child and eldest son. In boyhood he formed a close friendship with Christopher Gadsden, from whom he was afterwards estranged. At twenty he went to England, not to receive the usual "finishing" of a gentleman's son, but to be further trained as a businessman. His cultural education was to be the result of a long, wide, and constant reading. He was unable to write French, he says, although he could evidently speak it sufficiently. But he wrote English with force and precision, if perhaps not altogether with elegance.

Returning to South Carolina at twenty-three, and immediately after his father's death, he took over the flourishing family business. He built up such a fortune in wine, rice, skins, indigo, and slaves that when he was in his early forties he abandoned the mercantile enterprises that had enriched him and concentrated on his plantations. He had already given up the slave trade, to which he was strongly opposed. He kept slaves, of course, and treated them with consideration. And here is one of the indices of the man's character: he did not try to reform others. He simply abandoned a trade to which he was inimical. Similarly, although he disapproved of duelling, he accepted challenges when he could not avoid it and always fired into the air, with the observation on one occasion that although another man might challenge him, he could not make a murderer of him. Gambling was another of his dislikes, but he sometimes took part in games, always cheerfully paying his losses but always refusing his winnings. And he was a temperate man, yet he always drank his bottle of Madeira per day, giving it up only when gout forced him to.

Politically he appears to have preserved a similar reasonableness. He was against taxation without representation, but he felt that any changes in the system should be brought about by peaceful means. When he was in England in the early 1770's, he labored to convince his acquaintances among merchants and statesmen that England was making a bitter mistake in her treatment of the colonies.

As soon as he saw that a crisis was inevitable he took an active part in resisting the Crown. He was elected to the First Provincial Congress and became its president. It was at this time that he incurred the enmity of his boyhood friend, Gadsden. Gadsden, resenting the precedence that had been given to Moultrie, resigned his commission. Obviously he meant it as a gesture, but the straightforward Laurens accepted the resignation, and Gadsden, thus deprived of the opportunity to dramatize his grievance, never forgave him. Laurens, it must be admitted, did not miss many chances to sneer at his old friend.

Laurens was president of the Council of Safety, and, under the first state constitution, vice-president of South Carolina. The story is that he wept when the Declaration of Independence was read, but he did not turn back. He was a member of the Continental Congress in 1777 and served on several important committees, and he succeeded John Hancock as president without a vote being cast against him.

In 1779 he was sent to Holland to borrow ten million dollars and to arrange a treaty. His ship was captured by the British. Laurens took from his bag the rough draft of the proposed treaty and flung it overboard, but a British sailor fished it out of the water. The papers were a great find for the British, who were by no means pained at having this excuse for declaring war on Holland.

Laurens should, obviously, have been treated as a diplomat, but the British, with that callous stupidity often characteristic of them, saw fit to send him to the Tower of London on a charge of high treason. Laurens was now fifty-six, afflicted with gout and otherwise ill, but it is said that he was even denied the attention of a physician until one could be found who was willing to double as an informer.

Through the offices of a woman employee of the Tower who smuggled pencils and paper to him, he wrote letters pleading for the American cause. He had made a friend of Lafayette by taking the wounded Frenchman in his carriage to the hospital at Bethlehem during his stay in Philadelphia, and the Marquis and his wife did all they could to have him released. They accomplished nothing. Laurens was kept very closely guarded, and forbidden any visitors except under rigid and unpleasant conditions.

On top of this, the British had the cheek to charge him rent for his miserable apartment in the Tower. The man who, when the mob had come to search his house for tax stamps, (no madder, of course, than any group of philatelists), had asked them not to trample his garden, now remarked with grim humor that he had always provided food for captive birds. Then he was handed a bill for the services of his two jailers. This the sturdy provincial flatly refused to pay. He stated that if he had enough money to fill the rooms he was kept in he still would refuse, and added a truly eighteenth century witticism. "It's enough," he observed, "to provoke me to change my lodgings."

He addressed a long memorandum of appeal to the House of Commons, in which he pointed out his long record of loyalty to England, his moderation in all actions against the Crown. This infuriated his countrymen. The language of his appeal was the subject of an attack in Congress. James Madison wanted his commission annulled; others accused him of "serving" Great Britain. The appeal is rather hard to explain, and it is still considered a regrettable incident. But Laurens was only human, and could be wrong, as he had been in the controversy over the French commissioners, Lee and Deane.

The British, on the other hand, had been unable to break his obstinate spirit. Besides informing him carefully of every American defeat, they tried to bribe him with his freedom if he would deter his son John from going to ask aid from France. Finally Burke took up his case and Laurens, crippled from gout and his confinement, left the Tower on bail on the last day of 1781. When his case was to be heard in court, he was instructed to sign a paper which began with the words "Our Sovereign Lord, the King." Here his wit and tolerant give-and-take spirit deserted him, and the captive ambassador made a reply which, even one hundred and fifty-odd years later, is thrilling in its stubborn courage: "Not *my* sovereign lord."

He was finally freed in exchange for Cornwallis, surely one instance in which the Americans got the better of a deal. When fit for travel, he was ordered to Paris to join the peace commissioners. Upon his arrival he found that they had virtually completed their negotiations, but he was able to bring about the protection of American fishing rights. He then returned to England and was in effect, though unofficially, the first American ambassador to Great Britain.

Again in America, he retired from public life. He had been badly hurt by the death of his son John, killed in one of the skirmishes that occurred in South Carolina after the surrender at Yorktown. The last eight years of his life were spent at his plantation, Mepkin. He sometimes acted in the capacity of elder statesman, where his experience and wisdom could be valuable.

This singularly level-headed man was not entirely free from the odd prejudices and fears that afflict the most sensible of us.

Years before his own death, his daughter Martha had been pronounced dead after a fever, and premature burial of the child was avoided only because when she was placed by a window the cool air revived signs of life. This had evidently come to be what we would call a phobia with Laurens; and his will directed that he should be cremated. His wishes were carried out, and he became the first person, outside of native Indians, to be cremated in America.

Little remains in Charleston to commemorate Laurens except those relics and mementos in the possession of his descendants. There is an unimportant street bearing his name, but his great city house on the east side of the town with its jerkined roof, the house which cut off Gadsden's view of St. Philip's, has been demolished.

Henry Laurens, though it is said that he never put a man into jail for debt, was nevertheless firm in his business dealings; and it was in the course of one of these that he turned over to the stripling John Rutledge the latter's first case.

Laurens' great house has vanished; Rutledge's still stands and has been described. There are similarities in the course of life of the two men, for both were moderate in politics and both have been criticized for their conduct.

John Rutledge represents well the type of citizen who, in those times of rapid growth, became wealthy and influential. He was of Irish descent, his grandfather having been an innkeeper in County Tyrone. His father, a doctor, came to the colony in 1735 and found fortune very quickly, for he married in 1738 a fourteen-year-old heiress, Sarah Hext. At fifteen she had her first child, John.

Sent to England to study, he was admitted to the bar at twenty-one, after which he came home, for his father had died and the family estate was in a bad way. The boyish son and his thirty-six-year-old mother faced a situation that was diffi-

cult indeed. But John Rutledge was a very mature young
man. It is often said that ours is the day of youth, but one
thinks of Pitt as prime minister at twenty-four and Rutledge
as attorney-general (pro tem, it is true) at twenty-five and
wonders. After Henry Laurens had given the young lawyer
his first case, and a few more had come his way, he was on
the path of success. He was elected to the Commons, too,
and took Gadsden's part in the controversy with Governor
Boone, making a brilliant speech. At twenty-six he was chosen
as one of the delegates to the Stamp Act Congress, and his
eloquence was reported as impressive.

After the repeal of the Stamp Act, Rutledge retired to
handle his bulky law business and to enjoy social life in his
imposing new house—an indication of how rapidly his success
had come. In 1774, with his younger brother Edward, whom
he had aided with sound advice which seems amusing now
coming from a man who was so young, he was a delegate to
the Continental Congress. Rutledge was thirty-five now, a
solid and mature citizen, and hopeful of finding a way to
reconcile the differences between the colonies and England. He
nevertheless was, like Laurens, heart and soul for the cause
of independence once he realized what the outcome was going
to be. Under the new constitution of the state, he was, at
thirty-seven, the first governor of South Carolina, with the
title of *president,* and had already assumed this office when
Fort Moultrie resisted the British fleet. In spite of which his
brother Edward, when he returned with young Edward Lynch
Jr. from signing the Declaration of Independence, was in no
hurry to tell his brother John about it. Even after he had
been head of the state for two years of war, Rutledge resigned
after the drafting and adoption of the new revised constitution, feeling that it made reconciliation impossible. However,
he again assumed the office in 1779 with the title of governor.
He became known as "Dictator" Rutledge, and the saying

was that the government of South Carolina was in his carriage, even to a printing press which he carried around with him, for he had been persuaded to leave the threatened city for the general good. It is now generally agreed that his famous suggestion to neutralize the city for the duration of the war was a good piece of strategy, gaining a delay of forty-eight hours and saving it from Prévost, but it was much criticized in his time.

After the war, Rutledge was influential in bringing about the passage of laws that would not bear too harshly on those who had been loyal to the king, no matter for what motives. He served, quite humbly for a man who had been so powerful, as representative from St. Andrew's parish, was elected to Congress, and went on a mission to the various states to plead for their financial support of the new government.

With Charles Cotesworth Pinckney, his cousin Charles Pinckney, and Pierce Butler, Rutledge was a delegate to the Constitutional Convention. Charles Pinckney has been generally credited with the greatest single contribution to the drafting of the Constitution, but Richard Barry, in *Mr. Rutledge of South Carolina,* has argued very earnestly in favor of Rutledge as the chief begetter.

Rutledge had now reached the height of his fame. South Carolina's first electoral vote under the Constitution of the United States, cast for Washington as president, named Rutledge as vice-president. He was appointed associate justice of the Supreme Court, but resigned to become Chief Justice of South Carolina.

The remainder of his life was tragic. The death of Mrs. Rutledge in 1792 was a blow from which he never recovered. He had begun to exhibit symptoms of mental disturbance, and this hastened his decline. Still, Washington considered him fit for the position of Chief Justice of the Supreme Court. In the meantime Rutledge the moderate had become a rabid

Anglophobe, and was so angry at the favor shown to Great Britain in the Jay Treaty, at the expense of France, that he attacked the treaty in a violent speech before an indignation meeting in St. Michael's Church. The Senate revenged itself by blocking his appointment on the grounds of mental unbalance. Rutledge was never again the same after this rebuff, although he lived five years longer.

Most of his fortune had been lost during the Revolution, and such is the proverbial ingratitude of democracies that his reputation now dwindled too. Although he was one of the great Americans of his time, his modest tombstone in St. Michael's churchyard suggests nothing of this. There is no monument to him in the city, and his fame was eclipsed by that of his brother Edward, a great governor of the State, just as his modest tombstone is overshadowed by the elaborate tribute to Edward in St. Philip's cemetery.

A third Rutledge, Hugh, the youngest of the three brothers, rose to eminence, too, being speaker of the state House of Representatives and afterwards chancellor. Altogether, it is not a bad record for the second generation of one small family in America.

Well, if Rutledge has only a small tombstone, that of Charles Pinckney, like Gadsden's (and Mozart's) is unknown. Which is extraordinary for a native son who so strongly influenced the final form of the Constitution, who held so many offices, and who was the founder of the Democratic party in his state.

Charles Pinckney, not to be confused with his cousin, Charles *Cotesworth* Pinckney—middle names do have some use, now and then, besides that of pleasing relatives—was the son of a wealthy planter who was also a distinguished barrister. The elder Pinckney seems to have had considerable difficulty in making up his mind about his loyalties. At the outbreak of the Revolution he was Tory in his sympathies; then he sided with the patriots and worked hard for the cause, but in 1780 he recanted, and was faithful to the Crown even while his son was in prison in St. Augustine. This is not necessarily so reprehensible as it sounds, and if you read the pronouncements of South Carolina historians you can see how difficult it was for a judicious person to arrive at a just decision.

But there were, after all, other divided families, for instance Dr. Garden and his son. Perhaps if Charles Pinckney had been educated chiefly in England, like so many young men of his time and station, he might have sided with his father, but then it might have made no difference, for a good many of the young firebrands of the Revolution had been to the mother country's universities. Charles Pinckney was a native product, educated in his native city and trained in the law by his father. He was admitted to the bar, but he did not pursue a legal career.

He was only a boy when the Revolution began, but at twenty, when Savannah was besieged, he was fighting as a lieutenant. He was taken prisoner when the British took Charlestown, and it was 1781 before he was released from St. Augustine and returned home. At twenty-seven he was a delegate to the new national Congress, and when the matter of drawing up the Constitution was attacked, he was one of the leaders. It is generally accepted as a fact that thirty-one of the thirty-two points he suggested were embodied in the final document. Once more, who says that our times are the times of youth?

Later, there came a great change over Charles Pinckney. He had been aristocratic in his political outlook and a Hamiltonian in principle. It is little wonder that, like Franklin Roosevelt, he was considered a traitor to his own class, for he now became a violent Jeffersonian. He campaigned for a state system of free public schools; during his first term as governor, Charleston lost (nominally) the place of capital to Columbia; and he was Jefferson's campaign manager at the very time that his cousin, Charles Cotesworth Pinckney, was running for vice-president on the Federalist ticket. As a reward for his services, Jefferson made him minister to Spain, where he had a rough time of it over the Louisiana Purchase. He was finding political activity expensive, too; by this time a good deal of his fortune had vanished. He had the reward of being called "Blackguard Charlie" by his adversaries.

He was elected governor for the fourth time in 1806. Obviously, whatever gnashings of teeth his conduct aroused, he was pleasing the majority of the state voters. In 1808 he supported the amendment which was to give the back country additional representation; two years after that, he came out in favor of manhood (white) suffrage irrespective of land holdings or tax payments. He served as a member of the U.S. House of Representatives from 1819 to 1821 in the sixteenth Congress, and further alienated his fellow Low-Countrymen by his speech against the Missouri Compromise. He refused to stand for re-election, and died three years later at the age of sixty-six.

Pinckney must have been a remarkable personality. He was extremely handsome, had a charming manner, and was well liked by the ladies. Although not a college product, he was able to read six languages, and his library consisted of approximately twenty thousand volumes. His magnificent house in Charleston, filled with valuable works of art, was destroyed, with all its appurtenances, in the fire of 1861, when even the earth beneath it was dug out to strengthen the fortifications on the Battery. And he has no known grave. *Sic transit.* . . .

Add to his distinctions that he was the son-in-law of Henry Laurens and the nephew of Eliza Lucas Pinckney. When you set out to tell about the Pinckneys, you are dealing with an

GEORGE WASHINGTON MAY HAVE SPOKEN FROM THIS BAL-
CONY ON CHURCH STREET. AT THE RIGHT IS THE QUAINT
HOUSE ONCE OCCUPIED BY DUBOSE HEYWARD

GARDENS OF THE CONFEDERATE HOME, BROAD STREET

HASELL STREET. ON THE LEFT IS THE RHETT HOUSE, BIRTH-
PLACE OF WADE HAMPTON, AS IT APPEARED BEFORE RECENT
ALTERATIONS

STALLS IN THE OLD MARKET HALL

organization, as the hackman said when urged to flick the hornet's nest with his whip. Not the least remarkable of the Pinckneys was Eliza.

Eliza Lucas was the daughter of a British official who left her in charge of his Low Country plantation while he was away in the West Indies. She was only a girl at the time, but she took hold of things like one of the apparently impossible heroines of girls' books. She managed the estate, got an education for herself (her letters are delightful), grew silk, was largely responsible for the prosperity of indigo-planting, in which she made the first experiments in South Carolina, and learned to think for herself. In her early twenties she married Chief Justice Pinckney, one of those colonials whose failure to find preferment was one of the grievances of the Americans; his dying wife had recommended the match. The marriage lasted only fourteen years, but it was an extremely happy and prosperous one. The Pinckneys had two sons, Charles Cotesworth and Thomas. Charles evidently brought out some of the germs of the bluestocking latent in his mother, for he afterwards spoke disapprovingly of her efforts to begin his education at a too early age, and remarked that she had very nearly made him into a dullard. This is one of the only instances where her usual good sense appears to have been taking a vacation.

When Chief Justice Pinckney was made an agent of the province in London, the Pinckney family went there en masse. Finding smallpox rampant, Eliza, up-to-date as usual, had her children inoculated. She put them to school, and when they were still quite young returned with the Chief Justice to South Carolina, where he died. Her letter expressing her grief is terribly touching. She outlived her husband a long, long time, and died in Philadelphia during the administration of George Washington, who remembered the lady who had been his hostess at Hampton and requested the honor of being one of her pallbearers.

Charles Cotesworth Pinckney was educated at the prohibitively expensive Westminster School and studied law at Oxford. After he had made a tour in France, where he studied both the natural and military sciences, and a trip to Germany, he returned home at twenty-three to practice law and to aid in the management of his father's property. It was not long before he was acting attorney-general. He was an officer at the battle of Fort Moultrie, served Washington as aide, fought in Florida and at Savannah, and was captured by the British, who held him until 1782. At the Constitutional Convention to which he was a delegate he did not play as important a part as his cousin, but he performed valuable service in helping to prevent the insertion of a religious clause in the Constitution. He also assisted in the drafting of South Carolina's new state constitution.

No public office hunter, he accepted the appointment as minister to France in 1796. France refused to acknowledge him, and he was even threatened by the police. He left and went to Holland, but returned with Marshall and Gerry, and it was on this occasion, when the Directory suggested a bribe, he defied them in words which have become so famous that they have been garbled.

Once more home, he was made a general in preparation for what looked like the inescapable war with France, and his fellow-defenders named Castle Pinckney for him. The war scare having blown over, he was Federalist candidate for vice-president in 1800 and headed the party's ticket in 1804 and 1808. In addition to these honors of frustration, he had many private satisfactions and died full of years and respect.

History has its distortions and no man is exempt from them. Thus the pompous pronouncements Washington is supposed to have made while crossing the Delaware are no more real than Leutze's pretty picture; the great man's chief utterance during the trip was a coarse and explicit order to the obese Knox about trimming the boat. And thus legend has it that Charles Cotesworth Pinckney told the Directory, "Millions for defense, but not one damned penny for tribute," and the epitaph which Charles Fraser wrote for his tablet in St. Michael's softens this for ecclesiastical purposes to "not a cent for tribute." Both are, as always, more lofty and exciting than the truth. What Pinckney really said was, "No, no, not a sixpence." Somehow that has the rhythm of actual Charleston speech. And the point is, after all, that he meant what he said.

Among the orators who, more than any other, have caused acute agony to the American schoolboy, one would add to the names of Cicero and Burke those of Daniel Webster and his opponent in the Great Debate, Robert Young Hayne. Adolescents who have had to study these men with loathing naturally find it difficult to realize that they were very human and very much alive, and naturally they could not be expected to feel the gravity of the question which Webster and Hayne aired at such length. I suppose sectional attitudes determine one's judgment on who was the winner. History has declared Hayne's point of view the losing one, but he certainly did not come off badly in his argument with the most overpowering pleader of the day. He was not exactly a youth at the time, for he was thirty-nine, an age at which in our day people are referred to as "promising young American novelists" or something of the sort, but his precocity was notable. The early achievements of these men certainly make one wonder about the present. Maybe there's more to learn now.

Hayne was born outside Charleston, in the Low Country, but came to the city as a boy of nine and attended grammar school there. That was his only "formal" education. At eighteen he entered the law office of the brilliant Langdon Cheves (pronounced Chiv-vis), the most successful man of law in the city, and passed the bar examination with distinction before he was legally old enough to practice. As soon as he attained the requisite majority he began to practice law in association with Cheves, and when the latter was elected to Congress he left this mere boy in charge of his immense practice. At twenty-two Hayne had made such a name for himself that he was invited to deliver the Fourth of July oration before two important local societies; at twenty-three he was elected to the legislature and was appointed quartermaster-general. At twenty-seven he was Speaker of the House, and the story is that to prepare for the assumption of this office he sat up all one night and memorized a manual of Parliamentary procedure. Next he was attorney-general of the state. Before his thirty-second birthday he was in the United States Senate and remained there for two terms. By this time, of course, the prodigy had grown into the mature legislator.

After Hayne's brilliant debate with Webster, he retired from the Senate in order to make way for Calhoun, who was anxious to take up the cudgels himself. It was Hayne's fortune to be governor of South Carolina at the time of the Nullification squabble and it was he who defied his fellow South Carolinian Andrew Jackson over the issue. It must not be imagined, however, that Hayne was an all-or-nothing fanatic of the type that later got into the saddle. He knew the value of compromise and was active in the attempt to reconcile the nullifiers and non-nullifiers.

Hayne was mayor of Charleston for a term. His last great undertaking was the attempt, as president of a railroad company, to provide South Carolina with a route to the West, but he did not live to see the plan carried out; in fact, he died while the stockholders' meeting was in session to dissolve the project.

Bull, Laurens, Gadsden, the Rutledges, the Pinckneys,

Hayne, and Petigru—it is a pretty good showing for any city within one century, and it does not by any means exhaust the list of representative men. Statesmen of this caliber were not plentiful during the Civil War—in fact, one is strongly inclined to believe that they might not have let it happen—and if we except Wade Hampton and some well-meaning mediocrities, there was an end of the aristocratic tradition in South Carolina government.

CHAPTER SIXTEEN

Birds of Passage

Pirates, Royal governors, and British conquerors were not the only folk who stayed more or less briefly in Charleston. From the earliest times, the city has had a succession of distinguished visitors, semi-permanent residents who remained long enough to play a part in the city's development, or to be associated with its life and history; and those who came, saw, were conquered, and stayed on. And of course there were the carpetbaggers, the Northern educators and missionaries, and their like in the wake of the Civil War. However, their stay must have seemed eternal to the citizens.

There was, for instance, that world-traveler Captain Anson, who looked in on the city in the course of his years of patrol duty along the coast, played that memorable game of cards with Christopher Gadsden's father, and left behind him the name of Ansonborough, Anson Street, and such streets as Centurion and Squirrel, named after two of his ships, but no longer so listed in the maps. And we have told of the memorable visits of Washington and Lafayette. James Monroe was there too; Mrs. Ravenel says it was the only occasion on which the St. Cecilia Society gave a special ball for one person.

Almost a Charlestonian, as another of those typical epitaphs has it, was Washington Allston, the painter, who was

born at what is now Brookgreen Plantation, the model for
the plantation in Julia Peterkin's novels, and who spent some
of his formative years in Charleston, where he first revealed
his talent for painting, which was considered alarming by his
parents. Later in his career he returned. In a weak sense of
the word, he may be considered a citizen of the Athens of the
South. His name, at any rate, serves to swell the list of
Charleston artists.

Another painter who left an impress on Charleston was
Samuel Finley Breese Morse. Most people have forgotten that
he was a painter, since his name is so exclusively famous as
the inventor of the telegraph, but he was an ambitious and
serious artist. In Charleston's rich 1830's he worked for
several years as a favorite portrait painter. Tradition assigns
him a stay on Chalmers Street and suggests that he tinkered
while there with his telegraph. Toward the end of his stay
he was greatly put out by the captiousness of a Mrs. Ball,
whose dissatisfaction with the execution of her portrait made
his life rather difficult for some time. Shortly after this unpleasantness, he decided to return to the North. But artists
were no novelty in Charleston; during its heyday there were
more of them in the city than you could shake a brush at.

The beautiful and charming Theodosia Burr, daughter of
Aaron, was the wife of Joseph Alston, governor of South
Carolina, and lived for a time in Charleston. When her father
returned in disgrace to New York she embarked near Charleston to visit him and was never heard from again. Legend
has it that an old sailor, thirty years later, upon his deathbed
in North Carolina, confessed that he had been one of the
crew of pirates who seized the ship on which Theodosia Burr
had sailed. He stated that all the passengers had been compelled to walk the plank, and pulled out a small portrait of
one of the ladies, which was recognized as that of Theodosia
Burr. I do not believe this story is an article of faith among

Charleston traditionalists, but there it is, whatever it may be worth. At that, it is the only solution of the mystery.

At the time of Dessalines' uprising in Santo Domingo, which was a dozen years after the revolt which drove so many of the islanders to Charleston, a Monsieur Thomas and his wife and eight-year-old daughter were obliged to flee in an open boat. They were picked up by an American vessel and taken to Charleston. M. Thomas, walking along the street, chanced to meet Alexandre Placide, the pantomimist, who was then the manager of a theatre on Broad Street. Placide gave him a job. William Winter, who tells the story, says very discreetly and tactfully that "he never attempted acting," which suggests that he may have taken tickets or acted as doorkeeper. At any rate, his little daughter became a pet of the Placide family and grew up on the stage. She married Thomas Burke, and when in 1826 he died of alcoholism she married the older Joseph Jefferson. Their son, (is it necessary to mention that he was virtually the reincarnation of Rip van Winkle?) in after years played in Charleston on his Southern tour, and it is said that he managed a theatre there for a while. He did not seem sufficiently impressed by this latter experience to mention it in his autobiography, nor does William Winter say anything about it, although both mention his playing in the city.

James Gordon Bennett worked for a while, beginning in 1823, on the *Courier*. Young Ralph Waldo Emerson was briefly present. And Edgar Allan Poe, in his youth, was stationed at Fort Moultrie, where he remained a little over a year and took away with him memories of the scene and a profound misconception of the regional Negro dialect, both of which he used in that curiously dull story, *The Gold Bug*. Fanny Kemble, the actress, was in Charleston en route to her husband's Georgia estate, and wrote in rather uncomplimentary fashion about the appearance of the city. Sir

Charles Lyell, the geologist, and Matthew Fontaine Maury, the geographer, appeared before the literary club of planters and professional men, and Agassiz lectured for some years at the college. Another visitor was that remarkably observant and open-minded traveler, Frederick Law Olmsted, who wrote *A Journey to the Slave States,* and who did not, as Crèvecoeur had done, tell any story about a Negro suspended in a cage for vultures to peck at.

John C. Frémont, "the Pathfinder," studied (rather ingloriously) at the college and was befriended by Joel R. Poinsett, Charleston-born world traveler, collector, benefactor of the museum, and ambassador. On a later visit Charleston presented a sword to Frémont. Jenny Lind came to sing in 1850 and donated five hundred dollars to the Ladies' Benevolent Society. Mrs. Mary Baker Glover Patterson Eddy (at the time Mrs. Glover) spent a couple of years in the city with her husband and aired her opinions on the subject of slavery in the form of letters to the local paper.

Also briefly connected with Charleston was the little Jewish boy from the West Indies, Judah P. Benjamin, who came there with his parents in 1822 and lived at 165 King Street for three years. That was his only prolonged residence in Charleston, but it was just at the time of the great Vesey plot, and Robert Douthat Meade, his biographer, suggests that the affair may have profoundly influenced his thinking. Young Benjamin's stay at Yale was financed by Charleston's Hebrew Orphanage. After an exciting youth he became, as students of the Civil War well know, the Confederacy's attorney-general, secretary of war, and finally secretary of state. He also came close to a duel with Jefferson Davis. The proposal to emancipate the slaves and to arm them to fight for the South came from Benjamin.

When the Confederacy was disintegrating, Benjamin escaped to England, and in his middle age began a new climb to prominence. At his death he was one of the leading figures of the English bar.

A soldier of the immortal Light Brigade remained long enough in the city to be buried in Magnolia Cemetery; his name was John H. L. Fuller. And another Englishman who came there during the Civil War was to provide Charleston with one of its greatest sensations.

He was a young English playwright, Francis Warrington Dawson. Enamored of the Confederate cause, he enlisted in the Southern army and became a captain. After the war he worked on the staff of the *Mercury,* and in 1873, with two partners, bought it and merged it into the *News and Courier.* He was chiefly responsible for the South Carolina statute which outlawed duelling—which some nostalgic commentators still defend—and in recognition of his accomplishment Pope Leo XIII in 1888 made him a Knight of the Order of St. Gregory the Great. The sequel was to prove this ironic.

Captain Dawson lived in 1889 in the house at 99 Bull Street with his wife and children. Mrs. Dawson's young maid, a girl from Geneva named Marie Bardayron, who also was governess of the Dawson children, was causing some uneasiness on Captain Dawson's part, and he was observing her closely. She was found on a street car with Dr. T. B. McDow, a young physician of poor reputation who was married to the daughter of a well-to-do Charleston family.

McDow's house was about a hundred yards away. At 3:45 o'clock on the afternoon of March 12, Captain Dawson went to the doctor's house. Three hours later his body was found, badly beaten and with a bullet wound which, physicians testified, showed that he had been shot from behind. McDow had attempted to conceal the body under the floor of a small closet in his office.

The city was in a turmoil. Some irate citizens were prepared to lynch the killer, who had surrendered, but were dissuaded.

The case came to trial on June 24 before a crowded court-room, among the crowd being several clergymen. There were seven Negroes on the jury, not one of which was challenged by the defense.

McDow pleaded self-defense as his justification. He said that Dawson had struck him with a cane and then twice with his fist. He had told the police, on his way to prison, that he would shoot any man who caned him; and he had added that his profession taught him where to shoot to kill. At the trial he testified that he had fired wildly to protect himself—but there was the testimony of two physicians to the effect that Dawson had been shot from behind. And, besides, there was that matter of McDow's attempt to conceal the body of his victim; and the little Swiss girl made a very good impression. She stated that McDow had made advances to her.

Nevertheless, after a trial lasting three days, and ending with an impassioned plea by Asher D. Cohen, for the defense —he told the jury that McDow was a changed man, and begged them to let him go home and be "baptized by the tears of his little girl into a nobler and better life"—the jury, out for eight hours, returned a verdict of not guilty. It has been assumed that corruption or subordination influenced the verdict, but the New York *Tribune* was of the opinion that the result was due to a brilliant defense and a stupid jury.

Feeling was high. The Reverend Mr. C. C. Pinckney, from his pulpit in Grace Church, denounced the verdict, and Mr. Vedder, from his in the Huguenot Church, reminded his hearers that Charleston was sometimes called "the city of disaster" —and this, he said, was the greatest disaster of all.

McDow, though free, was a ruined man. He resigned as surgeon of the Lafayette Artillery, which was badly shaken by the affair, and was expelled from the Medical Society. Socially ostracized, he died some years later under circumstances suggesting suicide.

Sudden death has visited Charleston fairly often, for that matter. Another newspaper man, Sidney Cohen, an innocent bystander, was killed in an election brawl about thirty years ago; disasters have accounted for numerous others; and in the spring of 1946 a ship, torn from her moorings by a squall, banged against the Cooper River bridge and destroyed a section of it, precipitating a car with several occupants to death in the river far below. There have been several mysterious murders.

One murder, which preceded the Civil War, seems remarkable for the fact that to our Freudian-minded contemporaries there would immediately be the suggestion that there was more in the affair than met the eye. It occurred in a house on Mary and Nassau streets in the year 1858. A grocer's clerk, Henry Linstedt, was found murdered by an unknown hand. The circumstances were odd. The only weapon recovered was a small German pocket pistol, which physicians declared could not have produced the various cuts and injuries to the face of the dead man. Those of sanguinary tastes will be interested to know that a small fragment of the dead man's tongue was found near-by.

Everyone had a theory about the murder, but when Linstedt's employer and bedfellow, John H. Reickles, came to trial, he was acquitted. The testimony has been reprinted complete in a small pamphlet, as written down by Josephus Woodruff, the first "phonographic reporter" in Charleston, who had just recently perfected himself in the art of shorthand by means of a review copy of a Pitman manual which had come into his possession. But there is no suggestion in the proceedings of any perverse motive. There were money dealings, but none sufficient to account for the deed.

There are two great fictional murders related to Charleston, too—the murders of Robbins and Crown, in DuBose Heyward's novel *Porgy*. But that is by the way. And there was that Wightman murder which we have told about in connection with St. Philip's churchyard, which may or may not have given O. Henry an idea, when he was working as a drug clerk in Charleston.

And speaking of authors, Henry James came to Charleston and wrote about it, and William Dean Howells, and Galsworthy, who found Magnolia Gardens topping, and Amy Lowell, who failed to swoon at sight of the azaleas and, so it is said, limited her comment to one word: "Magenta!"

General Lee also came, and sat in the very pew in which George Washington had worshipped, and Theodore Roosevelt, during the exposition. He very nearly duplicated the earthquake, too. Mistaking the import of the good words he had heard about a certain Dr. William D. Crum, he appointed this Negro collector of the port. President Taft was a visitor at the home of the Honorable R. Goodwyn Rhett, the house built by John Rutledge.

And—tell it not in Gath—in an earlier incarnation Father Divine was for a time in the metropolis. He was more modest then, it appears, and was content to call himself "The Son of Righteousness."

Charleston, however, has its own way with celebrities. Once a famous contralto visited the city on tour. Her accompanist was a Charleston-born lady, the daughter of a famous local musician. One local paper, moved no doubt by a justifiable preference for the home angle, reviewed the accompanist but paid very little attention to the singer. (Accompanists as a group will consider this entire justice.) The assisting artist was a young Hungarian lady pianist. Said the review politely of her performance of a Liszt rhapsody: "She played it like a real Hungarian."

There remains that great, generally anonymous mass of birds of passage—the tourists. Of recent years they have come in great flocks to see the footprints of history, as many as

200,000 in a single year. It would be idle to suggest that they
have not influenced Charleston. They are responsible for the
sight-seeing tours, the uprush of antique shops, the Negro
flower sellers on the steps of the Post Office, and very sub-
stantial advances in the cost of board and lodging during the
city's brief springtime. They go to see the sights, and they
want to believe that Washington spoke from the balcony on
Church Street, and that the old fire engine house on Chalmers
was a "slave market." They flock to see the bedstead tomb in
St. Michael's churchyard; some, the natives claim, even ask
for the tomb of Rhett Butler. They buy the guidebooks and
the souvenirs—who but a tripper ever buys a souvenir?—and
they spend a very great deal of money. Before the Second
World War they were the chief industry of the city.

For all that, Charleston does not put on too much of an act
for them. And it doesn't have to.

CHAPTER SEVENTEEN

The Arts

Architecture was certainly the great art of Charleston, but the city has encouraged and produced practitioners of the other fine arts in very respectable number, and has been rich in gifted, if often anonymous craftsmen.

Not much is known of the local cabinetmakers or their work, except, of course, that the magnificent woodwork comes under this head. Among the early burgeonings of craftsmanship in Charleston was the arrival of the silversmiths; the museum displays a tankard made by Luke Stoutenburgh, earliest of the makers whose art has been positively identified, who was working in the colony possibly as early as 1718. But he was not the first; one Solomon Legaré, a Huguenot, was active there in 1696. Eliza C. K. Fludd published in 1876, a biographical notice of Legaré and his family, from which the following amusing passage is quoted by E. Milby Burton in *South Carolina Silversmiths:*

It was customary, at that early day, for families to dine at 12 o'clock noon. The Huguenot Legaré was ever very strict in the observance of regular hours, and to his great annoyance the Reverend Mr. Stobo, then pastor of the church, introduced the practice of preaching sermons of such unusual length, that the church services interfered with family arrangements for the usual dinner hour. Mr. Legaré and the other church officers had several times told Mr. Stobo of this difficulty and requested him to divide his sermon into two parts, for morning and afternoon. But the reverend gentleman believed in having everything done in his own way, regardless of the convenience of the whole congregation, and obstinately persisted in preaching his one long sermon, notwithstanding the remonstrances of the church officers. The other church officers were displeased at Mr. Stobo's conduct in this matter, but submitted to the annoyance for fear of creating a disturbance in the church. But Mr. Legaré told them *he* would not submit to the innovation another Sabbath and would find a way of letting Mr. Stobo know *his* determination in the matter.

Accordingly, the next Sunday, as the town clock struck twelve, Mr. Legaré got up in the midst of the sermon and left the pew, followed by his wife and children and several other members of his family. As they were silently walking down the aisle of the church, Mr. Stobo, after pausing awhile in his discourse, called out to Mr. Legaré in a loud (sic) Scotch accent, 'Aye, aye, a little petcher is soon full.' Upon this irreverent remark from the pulpit the Huguenot's French blood became excited, and turning himself around in the aisle, he still more irreverently retorted, but in a suppressed tone only heard by those near to him, 'And you are an old fool!' Mr. Legaré then quietly went home with his family, where they ate their dinners; after which they all returned with him to the church, marched noiselessly up the aisle, behind him to the pew in front of the pulpit, and listened to the balance of the sermon as gravely as if nothing had occurred to disturb the services of the morning.

This silent reproof had the desired effect; Mr. Stobo yielded the point, and the next Sabbath he preached the first half of his sermon in the morning, closing the service in time to allow the congregation to go home and take their dinner at the usual hour. After which they returned to the afternoon service in proper time and heard him preach the last half of his discourse, and so the difficulty ended.

Nothing, of course, is said of the embarrassment of the children, whose ears must have been pretty pink, or of Mrs. Legaré, who was probably mortified.

This same Mr. Legaré was a man of odd character in most of his dealings. For years he kept on his porch an old chest apparently full of rusty nails and other junk and it was not

ST. MICHAEL'S FROM THE NORTH. ON THE LEFT IS THE
FIREPROOF BUILDING, ON THE RIGHT THE PIAZZAS OF THE
TIMROD INN AND THE FACADE OF THE HIBERNIAN HALL

THE PITT STATUE IN WASHINGTON SQUARE. PERHAPS THE
OLDEST PORTRAIT STATUE IN AMERICA

revealed until years later that this was where he kept a considerable amount of gold and silver and other valuables.

It was natural that silversmiths should be working in Charleston, for the wealthy men of the time had a good deal of plate and a taste for luxury. It is estimated that the British carried away more than a quarter of a million pounds' worth of loot when they evacuated the city and one can only guess how much of that was in the form of graceful silver tankards and teapots, classically simple spoons and massy candlesticks. A group of men who were capable of taking St. Michael's bells with them as legitimate prizes of war were certainly not likely to be deterred by a silver teapot that weighed only a few pounds.

However, Charleston did not by any means give up the making of silver on that account. With the rise of prosperity which reached its climax at the time of the war of 1812, the number of silversmiths rose too; and there were seventy of them, by Mr. Burton's calculation, working in the city in 1812. In 1850 there were only thirty-five and, as Mr. Burton notes, by 1860 mass production had succeeded the work of individual craftsmen.

Some of these craftsmen made fortunes. One of them, Jonathan Sarrazin, bought, in 1774, the Rhett house in Hasell Street. He sold it four years later. And some of them seemed to have been obliged to combine silversmithing with storekeeping and the selling of jewelry. One, John M. Lunquest, who probably suffered from the decline of his trade in Charleston, was making daguerreotypes in the year 1848. He advertised that "from his superior light and chemicals he is enabled to take likenesses in a shorter sitting and in a style superior to any other in this city."

What is left of the production of these craftsmen is generally distinctive. But unfortunately not much is left. Much was probably lost in the city's long series of disastrous fires and, when Columbia was burned, it is likely that vast quantities of silver were melted and ruined, if the metal itself was not completely oxidized. Add to that the wartime looting of the British and the acquisitiveness of Sherman's gentlemen and you have comparatively little to show for all the years of prosperity and production.

Mr. Burton has rescued from *The Southern Historical Society Papers,* published in 1884, the letter of a Boston officer to his wife which is revelatory of the systematic stealing that went on—and the systematic division with officers. "I have," he says, "at least a quart of jewelry for you and the girls and some No. 1 diamond pins and rings among that. General Sherman has gold and silver enough to start a bank. His share in gold watches and chains alone at Columbia was two hundred and seventy-five." Good old Sherman! No wonder the South consigns him to a place where that stolen jewelry would sizzle.

The Senate in 1882 passed a bill to restore some of this property but without being too cynical about it, one may assume that the chances are that the bill accomplished very little. And no doubt a lot that was restored was soon dispersed among many collectors.

Much of the early art of Charleston was of course unconscious. It was the work of men who, commissioned to carve the woodwork of doors and entablatures, worked according to pattern and did their best to achieve grace and symmetry. Some of the most charming productions of the city's art were the work of men classed merely as artisans—the blacksmiths and ironworkers who made the delicate shutter guards, the beautiful locks, the graceful grilles, or who fashioned the iron tradesmen's signs which have now virtually disappeared also—into the hands of collectors, no doubt. If you are fortunate enough to see some of them or the drawings of them in Alston Deas's fascinating book, *The Early Ironwork of Charleston,* you have only to compare them with the neon signs of the present day or with those hopeless primitive monstrosities which still adorn shoemakers' and hat cleaners' shops and wonder about progress.

And what a variety of ironwork there is in the old city! Balconies—some of them authentic and appropriate, others switched around or mere additions—balcony supports, window guards with the characteristic lyre pattern, the passageway grille in Cabbage Row. Iusti's Sword Gates, originally part of the old Guard House but now adorning the Simonton gateway in Legaré Street, are as famous as his gates for St. Michael's churchyard. Fine gates are also to be seen in the Sass House on Legaré Street, in St. Philip's churchyard—but here again there is no end to the list. The City Hall has some striking ironwork; and the stairways of the Gibbes House and the Blacklock House, the gate of the Pettus garden, the gates of St. John's Lutheran, are a proof of the taste and skill that flourished in the great days of building. There are all varieties from the severely and classically simple to the rococo; and for special interest there is a pair of cast-iron gates on Montague Street which has a quaint charm.

The men who filled their houses with graceful furniture and fine silver and china were naturally anxious to possess the work of painters, both to adorn their houses and to do the recording now largely left to the photographer. Henrietta Johnson came to Charleston early in the 18th century. She has left among other work the famous painting of Colonel William Rhett. Jeremiah Theus, several of whose portraits are shown in the Gibbes Art Gallery on Meeting Street, came from Switzerland in 1735 and lived in Charleston the last thirty-nine years of his life. In post-Revolutionary times there were many painters and artists in the city; advertisements of thirty have been traced in the *Gazette*. Malbone spent the first year of the nineteenth century there; and Thomas Sully lived there as a child—he was one of a family of actors—and did some of his early work. Samuel F. B. Morse, as has been mentioned, painted Charlestonians for three years, and Jarvis paid a visit in 1810.

The particular glory among Charleston's native (and resident) artists was Charles Fraser, the celebrated miniaturist, who was born in 1782 and lived until the year preceding the Civil War. Fraser began, at the age of fourteen, a sketchbook, which has been reprinted. He experimented in architecture, as we have seen; but his great mark was made in the exquisite miniatures of which he painted so many. A celebrated one, that of Lafayette, whom Fraser saw on his visit to the city, is in the collection at the City Hall. The Gibbes Art Galleries have dozens of examples of his work and they are all enthralling.

Charleston today has its busy art colony; prominent among the artists are the native-born Elizabeth O'Neill Verner, whose etchings are widely known and who has published two volumes of prints with informal comment on the life of the city; Alfred Hutty, painter and etcher, who has made Charleston his home; Alice R. Huger Smith, whose book *The Dwelling Places of Charleston*, written in collaboration with her brother the late Daniel Huger Smith, did much to arouse interest in the preservation of the old buildings; and John Bennett, the author, who is also a gifted artist, as witness *The Pigtail of Ah Lee Ben Loo*.

And who, with a spark of talent, wouldn't want to be an artist in Charleston?

We do not wish to end this chapter on a note of gloom or to be like the author of an old children's book who observed that churchyards seldom wooed him in vain, but we must not neglect a comment on the cemeteries. Those same gentlemen who wanted to be perpetuated by the art of the brush were also desirous of being ushered out of this world with a bit of a flourish, and Charleston's burial grounds afford some beautiful examples of the stonecutter's art, particularly the older stones with the graceful lettering. Some of the newer ones can be dismissed, of course, with that remark of Jowett's about true feeling and bad taste.

True Charlestonians would consider this account incomplete without mention of the art of living, which they consider they have developed to a high degree of perfection. But we shall let the reader gather that for himself.

CHAPTER EIGHTEEN

Of Men and Books and Some Women

It was all very well for the late Thomas Wolfe to sneer at the culture of Charleston as a static affair which had never really produced anything; but aside from the fact that Charleston has never been particularly beloved by its neighbors in the two Carolinas and that Mr. Wolfe was from North Carolina, his remarks are obviously wide of the facts. A city that produced Gabriel Manigault, Robert Mills, Charles Fraser, and the houses the entire world comes to look at cannot be so lightly dismissed, even by Asheville's most distinguished citizen.

In literature, Charleston has an excellent record. It may not be the "Athens of the South," and it has had no Faulkner, Wolfe or Caldwell (for which perhaps the natives are just as grateful as not) but it has encouraged and produced a creditable body of work. There is no evading the fact that civic pride has occasionally blown up the home product to a size beyond its true value; but historically and esthetically, a good many works of letters by Charlestonians have a definite worth.

The city was from the first receptive to literature. There are lists of books in the homes of well-known citizens which are impressive. Charles Pinckney, who read six languages, had a library of twenty thousand volumes. His aunt, Eliza Lucas, read the classics with understanding and wrote letters which range between girlish charm and the bright and incisive comment of a mature and thoughtful woman. In a later day Charlotte Perkins, wife of Samuel Gilman, also wrote some excellent letters. Gilman, the Unitarian minister who wrote the words of Harvard's Irish song, was also a one-man institution for the freeing of slaves (he had an arrangement by which he allowed them after learning a trade to buy their freedom).

As early as Revolutionary times Charleston had two notable historians, James Hewat and Dr. David Ramsay, who was, it is true, accused of plagiarizing from his predecessor; but that was not an age of copyright laws. One recalls the remark of Handel about a theme he had appropriated, that the fool that wrote it did not know what to do with a good tune, and Dr. Ramsay was probably more preoccupied with getting the facts down than with being original. Ramsay's history had the interesting fate of being banned in Great Britain. It was considered illegal "on account of the long catalogue of British villainies and murders it contains," reported the *Gazette* in 1786.

Of course a literary prophet, even in Charleston, was not always honored in his own country to the extent he deserved. Dr. John Linnaeus E. W. Shecut, in his *Medical and Philosophical Essays* (1819), having listed the excellencies of library societies and local artistic talent, has this to say about support on the home grounds:

Yet, notwithstanding these energetic attempts of numerous individuals to establish the literary character of South Carolina and to prove to the world that her soil is by no means unfavorable to the generation or cultivation of the arts and sciences, and that her sons want the appropriate stimulus to their labors, that of public patronage, to shield them from loss, while endeavoring to raise her literary fame to a level with that of the most favored nations, examples are yet to be seen of the most unpardonable apathy and shameful neglect of her citizens.

After this ninety-word sentence, which hardly stamps Dr. Shecut as a candidate for high honors as a stylist, he continues:

> Dr. Ramsay's *History of the Revolution,* his *History of South Carolina;* and Governor Drayton's *View of South Carolina,* with many other publications that might be named, although works of acknowledged superior merit, have scarce cleared the expenses of the paper, the printing and the binding.
>
> Until the Carolinians are aroused to the formation of a permanent national character and until the utility and vital importance of the arts, sciences and literature, form a predominant feature of that character, these things must and will remain the reproach of South Carolina.

The good doctor adds that his own *Flora Caroliniensis* put him eighteen hundred dollars in debt. If he had seen, as I did in Legerton's Book Store, a first edition of Mrs. Harriet Kershaw Leiding's *Charleston, Historic and Romantic,* priced at sixty dollars, he would probably have fainted.

The first Charleston author to become world famous was the novelist and historian William Gilmore Simms, a voluminous follower of Cooper and Scott who wrote *The Yemassee* and many other works of fiction. The reproach is often made that Charleston did not appreciate Simms, and began to read him only after his fame in the North and elsewhere had redounded to the credit of his native city. It is also pointed out that he was socially unsuccessful until after his second marriage had gained him an entree. Charleston is not easily impressed. But Simms was a good citizen. He espoused slavery and he served as a military engineer during the Civil War.

Paul Hamilton Hayne and Henry Timrod, two entirely respectable minor poets, dominated the Civil War period. Timrod, whose family name was Dimroth, another instance of the integration of varied racial strains in the life of Charleston, was ill and wretchedly poor and his output was spread thin. His verse is rather sweet; it has a faded air, but so has much of the American verse of his period and earlier. He has given his name to the Timrod Inn and his bust is in a prominent spot in the City Hall Park. There is a memorial to Simms, too; it is on the Battery.

"Aunt Fanny," a favorite children's author of the later nineteenth century, was born in Charleston in 1822.

Charleston also produced a classic of military history, the Reverend Mr. John Johnson's *The Defense of Charleston Harbor,* which received that very charming tribute in St. Philip's. The most important productions of the turn of the century were Edward McCrady's standard History of South Carolina and Harriett Rutledge Ravenel's (Mrs. St. Julien Ravenel's) *Charleston: The Place and the People,* which, written in her extreme old age, is a compendium of intimate knowledge of the more decorous doings of the city. Mrs. Ravenel concluded her history with the end of the Civil War, which she saw as ending the old life she had known and enjoyed. This seems regrettable, for she undoubtedly could have written a marvelous story of Reconstruction and the years which ended the nineteenth century. Her book is now forty years old and its style and manner are both somewhat dated, yet it stands very high in the list of books about Charleston. Mrs. Ravenel also wrote *The Life and Letters of Eliza Lucas* and *The Life and Letters of William Lowndes.*

Another local historian was Mrs. Harriet Kershaw Leiding, author of *Historic Houses of South Carolina, Charleston: Historic and Romantic* and various pamphlets.

Technically speaking John Bennett, according to the old joke, would come under the classification of "visitor" for he first came to Charleston as late as 1898, in search of health. He obviously found it, for he is now over eighty although no one would ever guess it. Mr. Bennett, technicalities notwithstanding, is a Charleston author through and through. He had already written *Master Skylark* when he came to the city; devoting himself to a close study of the legends and manners of his adopted home, he produced *The Treasure of Peyre Gaillard* and the delicate and atmospheric *Madame Margot.* Forty years of listening, observing, and recording have gone into *The Doctor to the Dead* which only recently appeared. This is a collection of the tall tales and legends of the city, including some in the Gullah dialect which Mr. Bennett has mastered, and a condensation of *Madame Margot.* His son, John Bennett, 3rd, has written *So Shall They Reap,* a novel of the disaffected upstate poor whites during the Civil War, of which they wanted no part.

Herbert Ravenel Sass, the novelist and naturalist, is a native of Charleston. The list of his writings, fiction and non-fiction, is considerable, and he has been long known as a contributor to magazines. So has Octavus Roy Cohen, another native, creator of the entirely artificial but undeniably amusing Florian Slappey, Lawyer Evans Chew ("my advice to you, brother, is to fill yourself full up of philosophy and bow to the inexorable"), and other colored citizens of Birmingham, and author of the popular mystery play, *The Crimson Alibi,* and of various light novels.

Ludwig Lewisohn spent his boyhood and youth in Charleston and attended the college. He has written interestingly of the city, with a mixture of affection and censure, in *Upstream,* although he refers to the city as "Queenshaven." This delicacy in uttering the name of the city as though it were something ineffable extends also to Owen Wister's *Lady Baltimore,* in which the author of *The Virginian* succumbed wholly to the atmosphere and charm of his setting. He called the city "Kings Port."

Of the three men who founded the Poetry Society of South Carolina, two were not natives of the state—John Bennett and Hervey Allen. The third was DuBose Heyward, native to the core, and beyond reasonable doubt the outstanding figure of Charleston's literary history. Mr. Heyward's first success,

Porgy, was based on the life of a well-known Negro beggar, who pursued his calling (and his benefactors) in a goat cart. It is a distinguished and dramatic short novel, written with passion and art and a color undoubtedly derived from Mr. Heyward's earlier experiments with verse. Unless there is some forgotten or unpublished masterpiece by one of Charleston's writers, this is the top production of the city. It has been dramatized, most successfully, and has also been made into a much-admired folk opera by George Gershwin. Mr. Heyward also wrote an excellent long story of superstition, *The Half Pint Flask.* His other works about Charleston include the historical novel of Civil War times, *Peter Ashley,* and the popular though not very convincing *Mamba's Daughters,* in which, like many Southern authors, he became self-conscious and rather obvious in displaying his points.

His collaborator in the stage version of *Porgy* was his wife, Dorothy, not a native, but a resident. She has written, on her own, various short stories, and a play about the Negro insurrection of 1822 which, as this book is written, is scheduled for Broadway production.

A charter member of the Poetry Society and perhaps its best-known poet, Josephine Pinckney is known for her volume of poems *Sea Drinking Cities,* for the historical novel *Hilton Head,* a tale of Woodward and the early days in South Carolina; and, most of all, for *Three O'Clock Dinner.* This novel of the clash of upper and lower classes in Charleston, notable for its fine re-creation of the physical atmosphere of the city, is also perhaps the first contemporary treatment of the crossing of social barriers in a community which is in everyday intercourse extremely democratic, but which is somewhat choosy about alliances. Miss Pinckney's novel was a book club selection and has been bought by Hollywood. One awaits the film production with curiosity.

The writer is naturally reluctant to include mention of his

own novel, *Pride's Way,* but does so for the sake of the record of books by Charleston-born authors. This novel, which appeared in 1945, was an attempt to portray the middle-class Catholic group of Charleston, rather than the more striking facets of its life, such as Mr. Heyward's Negroes or the upper crust and the untouchables of Miss Pinckney's book. The background, re-created chiefly from memory, is distinguished for one glaring botanical error, the blooming of azaleas in May.

There is still a great deal to be written about the everyday people of Charleston, who have their problems, their folkways, and their by no means negligible wit.

Samuel Gaillard Stoney, the architect and historian, is one of Charleston's brilliant apologists. He has written (in collaboration with Gertrude Matthews Shelby) *Po' Buckra,* a novel of respectable indigence, and *Black Genesis,* a re-telling in Gullah dialect of the Bible stories. Mr. Stoney has also contributed the text of *This is Charleston,* a volume of photographic statistics and that of *Charleston: Azaleas and Old Bricks,* a folio of admirable photographs by Bayard Wooten. He is also the author of *Plantations of the Low Country.* Other fictional works by natives include *Crowded House,* by Katharine Ball Ripley, who also wrote *Sand in My Shoes.*

The most recent production of Charleston's literary group deserves a paragraph to itself. This is a charming specialized work, *Architects of Charleston,* by Beatrice St. Julien Ravenel, poet, journalist, book-reviewer and the granddaughter of Mrs. St. Julien Ravenel. Her book is the result of many years' study and research, and, aside from its documentary value, is readable, witty, and perceptive. It has the additional merit of magnificent photographs by Carl Julien.

R. Goodwyn Rhett, sometime mayor of Charleston, educator, and banker, wrote *Charleston: An Epic of Carolina,* a somewhat pedestrian history which is nevertheless full of facts and valuable for its treatment of financial affairs and of the post-Civil War period. Albert Simons and Samuel Lapham, both architects, have compiled two excellent volumes of photographs and architectural drawings in addition to collaborating on *Plantations of the Low Country*.

Charleston has stimulated the writing of a number of novels by outsiders: Owen Wister's *Lady Baltimore; Balisand,* by Joseph Hergesheimer; *Red Lanterns on St. Michael's,* by Thornwell Jacobs; the opening scenes of Evelyn Scott's *The Wave;* and *Road to Folly,* a detective novel by Leslie Ford. Miss Ford, not being a native, had the ill-luck to choose at random for one of her characters a name which was that of a prominent Charleston citizen, who protested. This is the kind of thing that makes authors turn over in their sleep. The Low Country is also the scene of Francis Griswold's *The Tides of Malvern.*

And we should not forget the Charleston scenery in Margaret Mitchell's *Gone With the Wind,* or the grave of Rhett Butler, which local exaggeration declares is constantly sought in St. Philip's churchyard by impressionable lady tourists.

Not a bad showing, is it?

There must be still a lot of imaginative literature to come out of this old Southern city. The material naturally tempts the historical novelist but perhaps it would be better if the modern scene were adhered to. There are many aspects of life in Charleston which are characteristic, unusual, and dramatic; for instance the story of a typical businessman's life in Charleston, in the face of countless reverses, has never been told. A good-mannered reticence and the natural fear of offending friends and relatives by possible resemblances may stand in the way of freedom in treating such a subject. In a thoroughly inbred community it is difficult to choose a name which won't refer to somebody's family; and after the production of a novel there is, in a city of Charleston's limited size and somewhat provincial outlook, naturally a good deal of identifying, right down to the minor characters who were no more than names to the author himself. In addition, there is a sacrosanct image of Charleston in the attitude of a certain group of its citizens—they resent criticism bitterly and some appear to feel that the city should be the hero and the people the background of anything written about the city. I have been told that they never quite forgave DuBose Heyward for making Porgy the central figure of his novel.

Yet there is every stimulation for the Charleston author. His works are eagerly read nowadays, for the many people who have visited the city are glad to read about it. The Free Library has for some time conducted a weekly book forum in which the work of native authors, naturally, comes in for sympathetic though searching comment, and the newspapers are more than hospitable to any kind of news about him or her.

We have mentioned earlier, among the artists, Elizabeth O'Neill Verner. She has made some very interesting comments on Charleston life in the texts of her books of prints and deserves prominent mention among the literary interpreters of the city.

CHAPTER NINETEEN

How They Do Talk

Mention Charleston to someone who is fairly familiar with the city and the chances are ten to one that he will make some sort of joke about "the Bott'ry." The inhabitants of this Athens of the South are somewhat sensitive on this point; they deny vigorously that they say anything like "bott'ry" when they mean the Battery. However, it is undeniable that their short *a* is a very broad sound, shading over into a close approximation of *ah*. The natives just don't hear it.

Charleston speech is really unusual. For the person whose notion of Southern pronunciation is limited to the nasal grunting and groaning and the caterwauling you hear from inhabitants of some portions of God's country (I refrain from specifying), Charleston speech is likely to be a shock. You won't hear any nasal drawl or any dropped syllables; if you do, it won't be the speech of a native. If you were to hear a Charleston accent and had not been told in advance what it was, the chances are that you wouldn't recognize it as Southern. I know of one lady, who had never been off the eastern seaboard and had not even any Irish ancestry, but who was sometimes taken for an Irishwoman.

No, Charlestonians don't groan and they don't howl. Some element of the original settlers' speech, plus the influence of

239

the Huguenots, the Scotch, the Irish, the Santo Domingans, and certainly not least, that of the Negroes, has given to the people of the Low Country and its metropolis a pronunciation not to be duplicated, as far as I know, on this side of the Atlantic. There are elements of resemblance in the speech of the college-bred West Indian Negro, but only elements. Call it Scotch without the burr and Irish without the harsh corners and still you haven't quite characterized it. Other Southerners have a way (envious, of course) of putting the matter. They say that Charleston people talk as if they had salt in their mouths.

To go into particulars, Charleston speech at its best is clear, rapid, and smooth. It may drop its *g*'s here and there, but usually all the syllables are enunciated. The *r,* of course, is unrolled at the end of words, but so is the *r* of standard English, and you will never hear a Charleston native say "river" with the particularly repulsive second syllable that a Brooklynite brings out. It is a lip-speech; none of the hideous garglings of New York and Philadelphia afflict it, although catarrh is not unknown in the Low Country. In general the consonants are clear—not by the standards of midwestern speech, but fairly crisp.

The vowels of good Charleston pronunciation are pure continental vowels without the diphthongal quality associated with most English. Where the average American, and the Englishman, make diphthongs of long *a* and long *o,* the Charlestonian produces a single sound without any further movement of the lips. He says "day" in a manner which, to foreign ears, sounds rather like "dee"; he says "go" in such a way that it almost sounds like "goo." More peculiarly still, he sometimes makes his short *i* so short that in such words as "fish" and "milk" he appears to have been on the point of saying "fush" and "mulk" and to have changed his mind at the last moment. This may sound grotesque, but good Charlestonese is not grotesque

THE DANIEL RAVENEL HOUSE, A CHARACTERISTIC TOWN
DWELLING, BUILT ABOUT 1800, OVERLOOKING WASHINGTON
SQUARE

THE IZARD HOUSE ON BROAD STREET. TO THE RIGHT, A PRE-
REVOLUTIONARY DWELLING BUILT BY RALPH IZARD; ON
THE LEFT, THE WORK OF A LATER IZARD, IS THE COLONEL
THOMAS PINCKNEY HOUSE, BEGUN 1790

(a native speaking). Of course, to describe vowel sounds and inflections in the silence of print is rather like trying to describe accurately the difference between the tone color of an oboe and a clarinet to a person who has never heard either. So, if you think of the short *a* so pronounced as to make "battery" sound like "bott'ry" you are exaggerating, and no more can be said. Not that *some* Charleston speakers don't make it sound that way, but that is another story. There are degrees of Negroid influence which produce infinite differences of shading. It can generally be said, however, that if you hear somebody say "bettery" or "hend" you just know he isn't a native.

Some of the old-timers used to say "cyart" and "gyarden" and "gyirl" and "cyards" and doubtless a few of the younger generation still do, if English teachers haven't made them self-conscious about the matter. This is simply, I suppose, an exaggeration of the liquid sound of *g* and *c* as in "c(y)arry," "c(y)andy," "g(y)et," characteristic of all educated English that I ever heard. If you say "khabbage" with that guttural sound of the "k" you are a barbarian. So why not "cyart" and "gyarden"? And, anyway, they are not limited to Charleston.

As for the letter *o* as in "got," "pot," and "hot," it must be admitted that the Charlestonian says something very like "gawt" and "pawt" and "hawt," English fashion. Who hasn't heard affected speakers deliberately practice this? Some natives shorten the double *o* as in "book" to make a sound like "buck," but I have heard an Anglo-Indian do so too, and I have certainly heard "roof" and "food" made to rhyme with "good," and you can't hang these distortions on Charleston. And if the Charlestonians want to call it the "Cooper River," pronouncing the *oo* as in "book," well, it's their river, isn't it? Let them call it what they like, and go on, by analogy, calling a chicken house a "coop" with the same shortened sound.

And nobody can deny that they have a very pretty way of saying such words as *"church," "hurt," "pearl,"* or a soft pronunciation of short *e* as in *"bed," "very," "America."* You never hear a Charlestonian, however humble, say "Amurrica" or "vurry" or "bid."

Undeniably there are peculiarities in their way of choosing to pronounce some words. A good many of them say "ex-*qui*site," but you could probably justify that if you traced it back sufficiently far. Their way of saying "dear," "fear," and "ear" has been traced back to Chaucer. "Buoy" is "boo-ey" instead of "boy"; a good deal of attention has been paid to the fact that top-grade Charlestonians pronounce the title, Mrs., "mistress."

They call a pier a wharf, and a stone a rock, and a spot a place. In fact, they rather abuse the word "place." It crops up in every description of Charleston—"the spirit of the place," "one of the characteristics of the place," until it becomes almost unbearable. You'd think they might use "locality" or "vicinity" once in a while for variety's sake, but they very rarely if ever do.

When it comes to "bough" and "house," I concur whole-heartedly with the Charleston vocalization, which, instead of rhyming with the German *frau* and *haus* is midway between that sound and what might be indicated as "boo" and "hoose" but is neither. And if the folk of the Low Country make a long *o* in "glory" and "story" and "store," that sounds better than "glawry" and "stawry" and the like.

Naturally, the people of the old city never say "you all" in the singular. If a native asks "How are you all?" he delicately accents the "all," and he is asking about your family; he would not be so impolite as to ask just about yourself.

Some say "under the doctor," which is just old-fashioned, and "sick" for "ill," and they call white potatoes "Irish pota-toes" and grits "hominy" and lunch "dinner" and dinner "supper."

Their speech, in general, is rich in racial idiom, and this

gives it a liveliness it might not otherwise possess, for it is rather homespun in its choice of words. "Down in the mouth," "don't care a continental," "red cent," (some of the old-timers referred to "a copper"), "poor mouth" (probably Negro), are just a few of the elements in a firm decisive way of looking at things and speaking one's mind. I have known old ladies who couldn't talk without scattering proverbial expressions all over the place. They didn't sound like clichés to me; they were merely characteristic. Still, the vocabulary is simple, as if modern jargon had been excluded.

Once upon a time, if you heard an exotic pronunciation in the streets, you were tempted to turn around slowly in well-bred curiosity. A new boy in school, fresh from the Up Country, was a notable occurrence; and a real live Northerner was a seven days' wonder, at least. But not now. The war, particularly, has brought people to Charleston from all over the United States and from the South in particular; and you are just as likely to hear an Up Country or a Northern accent as a native one. Probably in the course of time this will have such a considerable influence on the speech of Charlestonians themselves that it will make noticeable alterations. That doesn't seem to have happened yet.

It does seem as if the tourists, so numerous in the past twenty years, have made the natives a little self-conscious about their speech. On a tour of Fort Sumter the guide, before beginning his spiel, explained that some of the party might have difficulty in understanding his "lingo." Quite possibly they did; it was good, rich local stuff, with a touch of James Island or Sullivan's Island in it; and it was curious to hear the difference when the second guide took over. He had a drawl and a twang, and you knew he hadn't been born where he could hear St. Michael's.

The Negroes do not seem to appear to have been much influenced. For a long time in the majority, in numbers, they have been the nurses of generations of children, and they have impressed their dialect upon that of the whites. Not everybody seems to notice their oddly flavored way of talking; Mr. William Oliver Stevens, in a generally perceptive book about Charleston and perhaps the first such ever written by a complete outsider, said rather surprisingly that the speech of Charleston Negroes was undistinguished from that of colored people in any other part of the South. The peculiar Gullah coloring, however modified by education, is so strangely unlike any other that I wonder how Mr. Stevens could have come to his conclusion.

Nobody knows exactly the origin of that word "Gullah." There is a supposition that it is a corruption of "Angola," the part of Portuguese Africa from which these people may have come, and some shadow of proof has been adduced in the form of related words of African origin. I should be inclined to hazard that it might just as well be a corruption of "colored," but that is only a wild and very unscholarly guess.

As an adjective applied to language, it may mean the simon-pure Negro dialect of the Lowlands, or it may be used in a derogatory sense to indicate white speech too strongly flavored with Negro inflection and grammar—of which there is aplenty.

In its first meaning, Gullah stands for a really wonderful variety of English, of a soft, almost mushy quality, heavily accented at times, quick, full of elisions and liaisons, without any Southern drawl. The consonants, grammar, and inflections are all *sui generis,* all tortured into a form of English that, to an outsider, is usually incomprehensible.

Gullah is somewhat sullen in its music; it is particularly well adapted to growled rejoinders. It is noticeably more rapid than most Negro dialects; the number of syllables an excited Gullah talker can pour out in a given number of seconds is really remarkable. When you consider the extreme terseness of the dialect, this means that he can express a number of ideas with machine-gun speed. As an example, there is an expression cited by Elizabeth O'Neill Verner: "She tie me fuh loose she." Expressed in conventional English, this may be said to mean, "That woman is trying to implicate me in this affair, so as to shift the responsibility from herself," and if classical Latin could better that I am willing to be shown.

There is an odd and individual use of adjectives as nouns; where we occasionally say "the good" and "the bad," the Gullah Negro extends this to almost any adjective, without the article. "Gawd don't love ugly" means that God doesn't bless or favor people who are mean or disagreeable. Not all the idioms are as easy to understand as that; "He tell me a lot o' who-kill-John" means, for instance, that, in the Gilbertian phrase, the speaker was employing corroborative detail to lend verisimilitude to an otherwise bald and unconvincing (and probably quite untrue) narrative.

The vocabulary is rich and efficient. "Buckra," perhaps the best known of the words, means a white person of some standing; its opposite is "po'buckra." "Stepney," a rarer word, meaning hunger, has been traced back to the name of a notorious British prison. "Swonguh," which rather resembles "swanky" in meaning and spelling, is possibly a corruption, possibly African. "Back a letter" means to address it. "A mice" means a mouse; "a mens" is sometimes used to mean "a man." But there is no French Academy for Gullah; it seems to be subject to no law whatever. And, elusive though it may be, this language has fortunately been preserved, as nearly as possible, in written form. Ambrose Gonzales, in *The Black Border* and his other volumes, has recorded it with almost scientific accuracy.

Gonzales has been eminently successful in capturing the sly turn of mind and phrase of the Gullah folk and their keen sense of the ridiculous. He is, like so many excellent masters of dialect, a rather stiff and awkward narrator, but his sketches are delightful, nevertheless. John Bennett has written down some of the tales; and Julia Peterkin has made the language decipherable by simplifying the phonetics, which, for one unfamiliar with the actual sound, are difficult to follow in Gonzales' versions. And since a good deal of Mrs. Peterkin's narrative is in a modified stream of consciousness, the reader gains considerable insight into the thought processes and attitudes of the people themselves. For anyone who wants to know more of this fascinating subject, Mason D. Crum has written a comprehensive study of the people and the language (*Gullah,* Durham, 1940).

Samuel Gaillard Stoney, who has been cited before as an authority on the subject of Charleston, is a master of the Gullah dialect. I had the good fortune to hear Mr. Stoney, who has recorded the Goose Creek variety of the dialect for the phonograph, conduct a conversation with a girl who was going from door to door selling vegetables and flowers. Part of it was something like this:

"Good mawnin', suh. Does you want fuh buy some bean an' pea?"

"No, sistuh, I thengk you. I got me dinnuh."

"Maybe you like fuh buy some dai-*zee*?"

"No, sistuh. I ain't got no gal fuh buy dai-*zee.* . . . You come roun' yuh 'bout Thursday and gives me anothuh chance and maybe I buy some pea and bean. . . ."

The flower seller was delighted to find a gentleman who could really talk such good language, and she grinned from ear to ear. They have the pleasantest smiles in the world, these Gullah Negroes, and they seem to confer a blessing on you when they grin. And polite! I saw a bowed, elderly Negress waiting for a chance to cross a street at a corner where the traffic was swift and busy. A young Negro took her by the arm, as gallantly as you could wish to see it done, and said

"Now, Aunty, ain' no use to t'row yo'self under de wheels. Dat ain' gointa help."

Every white native is a repository of stories about his colored brethren, as in every city of the South. Much of the humor of the stories derives from the white man's cherished sense of superiority, and is rather patronizing. There is one about the old country Negress who was asked by her master what she thought of the new gas stove. "Boss," she said, "I never see sich a stove. You know when you bring 'em las' Monday? I put a match to 'em and 'e ain' go out yet." Well, that is just the humor of laughing at someone who is ignorant or simple. I am fonder of the story of the mule-driver, who approached his master just after a remarkably bad thunderstorm.

"Cap'n," he began, "you know them two mule, Rock an' Rye, I have out een de fiel', when de storm come up?"

The owner, fearful immediately that his mules had been struck by lightning, asked what happened.

"Well, cap'n, I been plowin' w'en dat first lightnin' come, and I does take de mules out de harness and lead 'em back to de barn."

"Well, that's good," said the owner, relieved.

"Boss, you know dat second clap o' thunder?"

"Yes, the big one. What about it?"

"Well, cap'n, dat big clap o' thunder hit Rock and kill 'em."

The boss swore to relieve his feelings. Finally he said. "Well, I'm glad we saved one of them, anyway."

"Yes, cap'n," said the plowman, "but de funny t'ing 'bout dat clap o' thunder dat kill Rock, 'e kill Rye too."

My mother told of a servant who came to her one day and said that she was going to get married, and would Miss —— please keep her money for her?

"Well, of course, Ellen," said my mother, "but don't you want to give it to your husband?"

"No, muh," replied Ellen. "I ain' gointa trus' my money wid no strange man."

But one suspects that a good deal of the humorous attitude of these people is placative and defensive—making a joke of things so that the white man will ignore them. Not as in the grim stories of Faulkner and Caldwell and Richard Wright; Negroes have not as a rule been treated with physical brutality in Charleston. The city has never known a lynching, and even the plotters of 1822 received a trial before they were punished.

I do not mean that Charleston has solved the Negro problem, or should we call it the white problem? There is a great deal of kindness and sympathy and there are many instances of understanding. Still, there *is* a Jim Crow practice in Charleston, and the lower down you go in the social and intellectual scale, generally speaking, the less concern there is over the Negro's deprivation of his rights and the more contempt you find for him. I met instances of resentment at Negroes' being well dressed, and at the comparatively high wages they are receiving now, compared to the starvation pittances formerly paid to cooks and other servants. Yet the Negro children I saw in school groups were notably better nourished, better cared for, and cleaner than those I saw as a child; and whatever one may think of the local papers' attitude in racial affairs, letters from Negroes protesting against segregation are actually printed. And, though Charleston does not consider this a credit to the National Maritime Union, that organization's office on Church street is one place in Charleston where whites and Negroes openly fraternize.

Of course the little social absurdities of a bi-racial system persist—not using the titles of Mr. and Mrs. to Negroes, not asking chance visitors to be seated except in a very special and understood way. There is even a code of some sort, which, in a city justly noted for its manners, is hard to understand.

For example, there is a scene near the end of DuBose Heyward's novel *Mamba's Daughters* in which a Charleston Negress, now a famous singer, comes back to the city and is met at the station by the young master, St. Julien. St. Julien quite properly picks up her suitcase and carries it. Believe it or not, Charleston was disturbed by that. A relative of mine, who is dead now, and won't mind my relating this, said "That's not Charleston." And I have heard of arguments proffered by people whose gentility and breeding is unquestionable to the effect that St. Julien was not a gentleman, for no gentleman would pick up a "darky" girl's luggage. But that, after all, is comic. Though not to the Negroes. That is the sort of thing, I suppose, that their humor enables them to laugh off. I hope so.

Among themselves, far from indulging in humor which acts as a screen, the Negroes are good at repartee and are great name callers. I once heard of a discussion between two small boys, the mother of one of whom was notably thin. As the other small boy perceived that he was losing the debate, he fell back on the *argumentum ad hominem*. "Go 'long, boy," he sputtered. "Your ma does look like a Johnny Cock Horse." As with Yiddish jokes, this one has to be spoiled a little by explaining. Johnny Cock Horse is the popular name for that strange angular insect, the praying mantis.

And as a final specimen of Gullah, here is a ditty we all knew as children:

> Buh Rabbit, wha' you fuh do dey?
> I does pick oshta fuh young gal.
> Oshta does bite off muh finguh
> An' young gal does tek 'em fuh laugh at.

It means:

> Brer Rabbit, what are you doing?
> I am picking oysters for a young girl.
> The oyster bit off my finger,
> And the young girl thinks that is funny.

Every Charleston child, of course, who has been properly brought up, that is, reared by a Negro nurse, is a master of Gullah. There used to be campaigns in our house to eradicate the tendency; and once, when my younger brother and a friend at school had been unusually annoying in the use of the dialect, the schoolteacher was obliged to write a letter complaining about it. But it was like Sidney Smith's Mrs. Parkington trying to hold back the Atlantic Ocean with her broom. No wonder, the way they are thrown into constant intimate contact with Negroes, that some Charlestonians do grow up to speak just like them. I remember a public-school principal whose speech was, except for some grammatical refinements, indistinguishable from that of any James Island fisherman, and a former chief of police whose English was not much better, if better be the word. That was a good many years ago, but the tendency still persists, and I recently heard specimens of white speech that had little more than the speaker's white features to distinguish them from the deepest and broadest varieties of Negro dialect. And the speakers said "bott'ry," too, and would probably deny it vigorously. So there we are, right back where we started, which is not unusual in amateur linguistics.

CHAPTER TWENTY

Food and Drink

Charlestonians love to eat, and their meals, being based on old-fashioned ways, are plentiful and varied. And Charleston cookery has been applauded by gourmets time out of mind. The city is no place for one on a diet, unless, like Mark Tapley, he wants a chance to come out strong in the face of temptation.

An ancient wheeze holds that the Charlestonians are the Chinese of America because they eat rice and worship their ancestors. Of course it goes only part way, for those who have no particularly brilliant ancestors to worship eat rice too. Everybody eats rice, at least once a day.

This probably gives radical dietitians the horrors, for the Charleston rice, eaten in such quantities, is the polished grain, robbed of all its nutritive mineral-rich coatings, and containing very little else but starch. But the variety of diet crank who insists on eating the shuck along with the corn can shudder if he likes. Charleston will probably go on eating its polished rice until some atomic infernal machine destroys the crop all over the world. And then what would Charleston be like, one wonders.

The growing of rice in the New World originated right in the neighborhood, the grain was long a chief crop, and

Charleston knows how to cook it. You pick any discolored grains out of the amount you have chosen to cook—in older days this was a ritual which allowed Negro cooks to rest their bones while sitting out on the back piazza—wash the talc or other coating off in several waters, pour the moistened grain into salted boiling water and boil for about half an hour. Then the rice is put into a colander or strainer, rinsed with hot water, and put over a kettle (or on the back of the stove) to dry.

The result, ideally, is a snowy mass of distinct grains, each separate from the other but each tender and plump. The half-dried kernels, more like popping corn or dried beans, that are sometimes served in Chinese restaurants, are not rice as Charleston knows it, and neither is the gluey, lumpy mass that often results from unskilful cooking or ignorance of what rice should be.

This snowy dish of simon-pure Charleston rice is the Boston bean of the city. It is served for dinner, barring acts of God, seven times a week. Generally speaking, it is covered with gravy. Informally it may be put into soup or moistened with the soup. Charlestonians find it good in various ways; they require only that it be present at the table. If it tastes to you like so much laundry starch, that is your loss. Connoisseurs are reputed to be able, like winetasters, to distinguish between the various kinds, which ought to prove that rice has a flavor after all.

There are, in addition, all kinds of rice dishes, chiefly in the form of a pilau (which Charleston calls a "pilloo"). As elsewhere the term denotes a flavored or garnished rice, the most ordinary variety being a dish hopped up with tomato sauce and cloves and salt pork. Another pilau is made with chicken giblets and cloves—but there are chicken pilau, okra pilau, shrimp, and squab, and all sorts of fancy varieties. You can even have rice croquettes and some people in Charleston even eat rice pudding. It is traditional that the serving of rice with fish is taboo, probably because of the absence of gravy. But if the rice is really hot there is no better sauce than butter.

Another rice treat, and perhaps the best of them all, is the dish known as Hopping John (and don't ask me why). This is a combination of rice, cow peas, and salt pork or ham, seasoned with a good deal of pepper. The outcome is a walnut brown in color, delicately flavored with the somewhat earthen taste of the cow peas. Possibly the taste has to be acquired but it's worth it.

Second only to rice as a staple is hominy, or what is called in some parts of the South "grits" and in the North "hominy grits." It is usually served for breakfast, although when I was in Charleston in 1946 there was a shortage of it. The essential thing is to have it well done until it is creamy in texture, with the grains well swollen, for this really brings out the flavor. A large lump of butter is placed on the hot hominy and either (a) allowed to melt or (b) stirred in, giving the hominy a rich cream color. The best accompanying food is shrimp, served ice cold. The cold shrimp is taken on the fork, enveloped in the hot, smooth, buttery hominy, preferably from the outside edge (there is a Negro saying "his mouth ain't 'fraid o' nuttin' but hot hominy" which explains this) and then conveyed to the proper spot. Hogshead cheese, eggs, fish, salt roe, steak, chops—anything goes well with hominy; beef à l'Alsacienne (marinated beef served cold) was a favorite with us under the name bouillie-salade.

Breakfast, when I was a boy, used to consist of one such combination, preceded by fruit, and/or radishes, a small dish of oatmeal or other cereal with the usual milk, butter, and sugar, and followed by muffins, hot bread, biscuits, pancakes, or waffles. It usually got us through the day at school until "recess," when we had a sandwich or two and an apple or some cake. On days when we were at home, the eleven o'clock sustainer was often left-over breakfast bread or biscuits or muffins with a liberal addition of molasses.

Dinner in Charleston used to mean the early afternoon meal, anywhere from half-past one to three o'clock, the lateness depending on the social station, customs, or pretentiousness of the family. The official closing of the cotton exchange used to be at two-thirty, which has been assumed to be the reason for the three o'clock dinner custom. It seemed to me that more people were having dinner at night than ever before; Charleston has spread out and not everyone can get home to dinner at midday. Children, naturally, are hungry early and often but it seems to me now that the later you have that dinner the better, for you are not much good for anything the rest of the afternoon with one of those dinners inside and weighing you down. Perhaps Charleston needs, for the sake of energy, to give up that midday meal and substitute crackers and milk. This could be put into effect about as easily as having *Uncle Tom's Cabin* made required reading in the schools.

Every family, of course, has its favorite dinner dishes. One that is especially good with the rice and meat is a baked custard made of boiled sweet potatoes, mashed with milk, cream, eggs, and butter, and flavored with sugar and cinnamon. In my family this was called *gâteau-patate*. There are various chicken and turkey dishes; and the ways of preparing fish are endless.

Charleston, like all seaports, is a great spot for sea food. The local fishermen bring in whiting, porgies, shrimp, and hencrabs. You can buy them at the markets, naturally, but the calls of the vendors used to be a Charleston institution. They varied from simple announcements, such as "Raw swimp!" prolonged and almost like a chant (*cf.* "strawberries" in other cities), to ditties, such as

De porgy walk an' de porgy talk
An' de porgy eat wid a knife and fork—
Por——gee!

and to elaborate litanies celebrating the virtues of "she crabs," various vegetables, fruit, and delicacies. Most of the vendors used to come from James Island. Their equipment ranged from baskets carried on the head up through wheelbarrows, and pushcarts, to wagons with a huge vari-colored umbrella, decorated with advertising, over the driver's seat. Some of their cries were incomprehensible; one old woman used to call out something that sounded like "Annie buyee." When imitated by the unfeeling young, she proved a dead shot with an Irish potato.

Long ago there used to be a "honey man"—not in the sense of the words as now applied to privy cleaners—and there was a knotted and gnarled mauma named Chloe who exercised the profession of midwife and peddled "groundnut cakes" with a hoarse croak. These chewy disks of molasses and peanuts were once a cent apiece, germs and all.

Labor Day was the occasion on which these vendors had their festival. They paraded down King Street. Of late years the custom has become tourist-infected, with prizes given for the most original entries. In my childhood it was simple and almost primitive. The vendors then were picturesque, some ragged, and plentiful, and they were around from early morning to the middle of the day.

Supper, oddly enough, for a city that eats so fully, was often a slim meal in my childhood. There were a lot of superstitions among the old people concerning what it was proper to eat at night and what would invariably be fatal. Among the reputedly lethal articles of nocturnal diet were such harmless things as cheese and bananas; there was probably just as little reason for the others being included, whatever they were.

And of course there were the fruit cakes and puddings and

other desserts, each one a prized recipe or "receipt" and loyally supported against all others. One particularly horrible dessert was made of ginger and sweet potatoes, cooked to a sticky, semi-transparent jelly that looked like solidified sea water. But there were many good sweet things to eat. For instance, the incomparable sugar figs, the red variety that are eaten skin and all, grew virtually wild in Charleston. There were lemon figs, which had to be skinned, and pound figs, great black ones; and there were persimmons, which some people consider insipid. Children used to like Chinese jujubes, which grew here and there. These were tiny russet fruits, the size of a small olive with a similar pit; the pith was crisp and not unlike apple flesh. They were the color of fine polished calfskin. If you really were hard up, there were sugarberries, or hackberries (I am speaking of juvenile appetites now) lying around. Each one was the size of a small currant, and beneath the skin there was a sweet layer about one-thousandth of an inch thick. The rest was a large seed.

A traditional Charleston sweetmeat is peach leather. This is made of strained peach pulp rolled into thin sheets and left to dry in the sun. When it is of the toughness suggested by its name it is rolled in sugar. Also traditional, and now no more, was the stick candy made by a Frenchman in his store on King Street. And there was another little candy store, of which only a remnant is left now, where wonderful benné seed candy and fruit drops were sold.

The experimenter may be able to obtain a few cook books. The best known is *200 Years of Charleston Cooking* by Lettie Gay and Blanche S. Rhett. *The Carolina Housewife,* a much older compilation, and *The Southern Cook Book,* also old, are both out of print.

The great cooking of Charleston has always been private, although there are tales of the old Planters Hotel and of the Mansion House, kept before the Civil War by a colored

AN OLD WORLD STREET IN CHARLESTON—ST. MICHAEL'S
PLACE

ALL THAT REMAINS OF MIDDLETON PLACE. THE SOUTH
FLANKER, OCCUPIED BY THE OWNERS OF MIDDLETON PLACE
GARDENS

OLDEST EXTANT BUILDING, THE LITTLE POWDER MAGAZINE
ON CUMBERLAND STREET

LONGITUDE LANE

woman named Eliza Lee. Nowadays Charleston is not so well
prepared for restaurant diners. I did not sample the cooking
at the Fort Sumter Hotel, which is said to be good, because
the hotel had just reopened when I was about to leave, returning to public use after its war experiences. The cooking
in the other big hotel, the Francis Marion, was good but not
outstanding in the spring of 1946, when food was after all
hard to obtain. There are two good sea-food restaurants,
the one called Henri's, alongside the Market Hall, and the
Oyster Bay, on King Street just about Calhoun. The Villa
Margherita, once famous for its cookery and the steepness
of its prices, is now in the care of the United Seaman's Service,
and the luncheon I had there was not notable. There is an inn
on Church Street, which takes its name from being lodged in
the Brewton carriage house, where good lunches and dinners
are served. But, though more natives than formerly now go
out occasionally to dinner, the citizens don't yet make a practice of dining out. (Neither do most New Yorkers, according
to Simeon Strunsky.) And, in Charleston, who with a capable
cook and houseman would want to go out to a public place?
Usually you are not so far away from home that you can't
get back there for a meal. And if you want your rice and
gravy and the accompanying non-essentials to be just right,
have them in your own home or at somebody else's. Charleston, to sum it up, is no New York or Paris when it is a matter
of paying a check for your dinner. Furthermore, you may not
be able to have anything stronger than beer or wine with
your food. You can buy all the liquor you need in the numerous liquor stores, but the law does not permit the serving of
strong drink in public places.

It is true that this chapter is headed food and drink, but
although there are a number of recipes for punches and such
concoctions, most people in Charleston appear to drink the

usual cocktails and highballs. The only characteristic drink I know of at present is the artesian water, and not everyone will care for that. It has an odd metallic flavor not without a suggestion of the pluff mud which distinguishes Charleston's waterside, and the trusting reader may try it if he likes.

CHAPTER TWENTY-ONE

Catastrophes

When the Reverend Mr. Vedder, in pronouncing his disapproval of the acquittal of Dr. McDow, spoke of Charleston as a city of disasters, he was not indulging in rhetorical exaggeration. Really, the city ought to have a phoenix on its official seal. There are not, as there were at Troy, seven cities one above the other, but Charleston has had to rebuild itself several times since the settlement was removed from the east bank of the Ashley to the west. In the words of the artist Charles Fraser, "It would be scarcely too figurative to say that there are few buildings in Charleston that do not rest upon the ashes of former ones."

It would not have been difficult for the citizens, on many occasions, to have indulged in civic self-pity and point themselves out as ill-fated and marked out for disaster; but they did this only at the end of their first two decades. After other acts of God, and after that perilous time too, they simply cleaned up the mess and returned to what was left of their business.

Charleston's catastrophes come under the headings of fire and flood, war, tempest, disease, and earthquake, and they constitute almost a history in themselves.

The fires have been numerous and spectacular. The first

outbreaks came in the last years of the seventeenth century, but the blaze of 1740 is the first of the major conflagrations. It began at two o'clock on the afternoon of Tuesday, November 18, and raged for six hours. The militia and the crews of ships in the harbor aided in the work of demolition and in patrolling. The fire came close to razing completely the areas south of Broad Street and east of Church; one of the residents, named William Wright, reported that he had lost "a long piece of gold, near a foot in length and the breadth of a gold button." Like the Irishman who measured the back yard, he was not very exact about his dimensions.

Four years prior to this disaster, a group of Charlestonians had gathered together to found a "society" for protection against losses resulting from fires. It is believed to be the first of its kind established in the United States. In Revolutionary times and shortly afterward there were more fire insurance companies and branches, and their quaint plates may still be seen attached to a few houses, the "Pirate" house on Church Street for one. And the museum has a number of these old plates.

In 1778, when the British were preparing to besiege the city, a bad fire broke out. It is often suggested that this was of deliberate origin. According to Crouch's *Country Journal,* one of the phases of the *Gazette,* the trouble started in a kitchen at four o'clock on the morning of January 15. The fire, encouraged by a fresh northeast wind, destroyed "all Union (*i.e.,* State) Street, the south side of Queen Street from Mrs. Bayley's house to the Bay, most of Chalmers Alley, all the Bay except fifteen houses from Queen Street to the Granville Bastion. Much of the North side of Broad Street, and also the south; all Gadsden's Alley, Elliott Street, excepting three houses; Bedon's Alley, the east side of Church Street from Broad Street to Stoll's Alley, excepting five tenements, all Tradd Street east of Church." The *Journal* also

notes "the crackling of flames, the dreadful columns of smoke
... the roar of explosions; the crash of falling houses, the
shrieks of the unhappy sufferers." And there was looting to
make matters worse. The Charleston Library Society's collection of books and instruments was lost, and over two hundred and fifty dwellings were destroyed, some of them
irreplaceable. The loss may have reached one million pounds
sterling.

In 1796 another fire came to plague the citizens of the
Republican city, with losses not quite as widespread as those
described above, but bad enough in all conscience. The old
Beef Market, located where the City Hall is today at the
corner of Broad and Meeting streets, was destroyed, and we
learn that "B. F. Pritchard, an apprentice to W. P. Young,
printer and bookbinder, was blown up during the prevalence
of this fire." Other notable fires occurred in 1800, when one
Martin Miller "attempting to stop a leak in a cask of brandy,
in closing which a candle was held too near the liquor, which
immediately caught and in a few minutes communicated to
some gunpowder." The depressing chronology goes on: 1810,
a bad fire; 1835, another which destroyed St. Philip's Church
and many other buildings. That, by the way, was the year of
the "Great Frost," when temperatures as low as two above
zero were recorded. The suffering must have been dreadful
in a city built for ventilation and unaccustomed to more than
a few freezing days per year.

Then came the Great Fire. That was in 1838. This time
the flames literally swept the city. The assistant engineer,
Frederick Schierle, was killed while blowing up buildings to
arrest the progress of the flames, and Colonel Steedman, naval
officer of the port, also met his death in the performance of
his duty. The light of the flames was reported to be visible
eighty miles away. The fire did major damage to one thousand buildings with a total property loss of three million

dollars. We can sum it up with the banner headlines in the *Courier:*

GREAT FIRE! ONE THIRD OF CHARLESTON IN RUINS!

It was after this visitation the comments of travelers became less and less flattering when they remarked on Charleston's appearance. Shabbiness after a fire of that extent is hardly to be wondered at; and there was a bad outbreak in 1842 to add to the destruction.

But Charleston was not through with fires. In 1861, with Union forces not very far away and General Pemberton bumbling around in an effort to prepare its defense, another fire broke out, this time at the foot of Hasell Street, and before it was finally extinguished had traveled to the foot of Tradd Street. It swept one hundred and forty-five acres of the city, and destroyed, among others, such buildings as the great Cathedral of St. John and St. Finbar, which remained in ruins until the late nineties; Institute Hall, where the Ordinance of Secession was ratified; St. Andrew's Hall, the Circular Congregational Church, and the Charleston Theatre. Add to this that unending bombardment by the Federal forces and it is not difficult to believe those descriptions of the pitiable appearance of the town after the Civil War. Worse damage might have been done, at that, for Pemberton's idea was to build bombproof shelters in the devastated area and abandon the city to bombardment. Richmond did not take kindly to the plan, and Pemberton was removed from Charleston.

The explosion of the gunpowder at the North Eastern Railway Depot, and a 100-building fire in 1876, happily close the list of the disasters of this kind. A more modern fire department was instituted in the early years of Mayor Courtenay's tenure of office, and the city has since been able to cope with any blaze that has come along.

Less spectacular to relate, but of course much more injurious to the city, were many epidemics, which ravaged it for over a hundred years after its founding. What eighteenth century city was ever free of these visitations? Yellow fever was raging in Charleston in 1699 and 1706, both of them years in which the French and Spanish were on the point of attacking the city. It came in with the ships from the West Indies. It has been suggested that it was sometimes mistaken for malaria, the curse of the Low Country, which made the region uninhabitable by whites for half the year. It was the cause of the planters' building their great town houses in Charleston, which shows how a germ can influence a civilization. Malaria also decimated the troops of the American General Howe, during the Revolution, and greatly aided the British General Prévost. And yellow fever, remember, was the immediate cause of the establishment of the Orphan House in the early years of the Republic.

The town did not escape smallpox, either. In 1738, for instance, a vessel brought the disease into port, whence it was promptly communicated to the luckless Indians. It is estimated that the epidemic at that time killed off one third of the Cherokees. If it arrived on a slave ship, as is possible, it is just one more count against the brutal slavers. It is believed that the same source was responsible for an outbreak in 1763.

These epidemics did not come unattended, either. One of the bugbears of Charleston weather is tempest and flood; those houses half a story above ground level are an indication. The first bad blow we know of came in 1699—following, in the years 1696 and 1698, the combined effects of smallpox, earthquake, and fire, and right upon the heels of a virulent outbreak of yellow fever. As if waiting for the best opportunity, the hurricane struck. Ships were flung ashore, wharves were swept away, and water rose to the second stories of the houses. Is it to be wondered at that the settlers talked of removing to Philadelphia?

We are indebted to the *Gazette* for a description of the hurricane of 1752, which was even worse than the preceding one. It came in September, after a summer of unbearable heat:

The most violent and terrible hurricane that was ever felt in this province happened on Friday the 15th inst. in the morning, and it has reduced this town to a very melancholy situation. . . . On the 14th in the evening it began to blow very hard, the wind being at N.E. and the sky looking wild and threatening. It continued blowing from the same point with little variation till about four o'clock in the morning of the 15th . . . at which time it became more violent and rained, increasing very fast until about nine, when the flood came in like a bore, filling the harbor in a few minutes. Before eleven o'clock all the vessels in the harbor were on shore, excepting the *Hornet* man-of-war, which rode it out by cutting away her mainmast. All the wharves and bridges were ruined, and every house and store, etc. on them beaten down and carried away (with all the goods etc. on them) as were also many houses in the town, and abundance of roofs, chimneys, etc. Almost all the tiled or slated houses were uncovered and great quantities of merchandise etc. in the stores on Bay Street damaged by their doors being burst open. The town was likewise overflowed, the tide at sea having raised upwards of ten feet above the high water mark at the spring tides, and nothing was now to be seen but the ruins of houses, canoes, wrecks of periaugers and boats, masts and yards, and incredible quantities of all sorts of timber, barrels, staves, shingles, household and other goods, floating and drifting with great violence through the streets and around the town.

Many people, adds the *Gazette,* "were up to their necks in the water in their houses."

However, at about eleven o'clock the wind veered and the waters fell about five feet in ten minutes, "without which unexpected and sudden fall every house and inhabitant of this town must, in all probability, have perished."

Houses were actually bowled over, and the new fortifications which Governor Glen had undertaken were destroyed.

Many of the townsfolk were actually drowned. Ships were actually in the streets, and the pest house on Sullivan's Island was floated up the Cooper River.

Charleston climbed out and dried off and got to work; and the flood marks the time when the present East Battery was begun. It took another hurricane, in 1804, to persuade the city to build the sea walls of stone.

There was no other major tempest until eighty-one years later. In 1885, on August 25, the hopeful city, having just two years earlier celebrated its centenary, was slumbering. At one-thirty that morning a twenty-five-mile wind arose, and there was a heavy downpour out of a thick sky. After four o'clock the wind blew harder, and the streets began to be littered. By seven o'clock in the morning the wind velocity had reached fifty miles per hour, according to a newspaper account reprinted in the all-inclusive *Yearbook,* and "the air was soon filled with flying missiles." Tiles and slates were hurled over the city. Bricks and mortar flew. Tin was stripped from roofs and left to bang and pound the timbers. If you know the sound effect of crumpling sheets of tin, imagine it in such quantities. We shall never know how hard the wind blew in that storm, for the anemometer cups in the observatory blew away at fifty-six miles per hour, but the speed of the wind has been estimated at eighty miles, which is no zephyr. The wind was so noisy, in fact, that according to the newspaper account even thunder "scarcely deepened its volume."

At eight o'clock the gale was apparently doubled in force. Trees snapped off or were uprooted. The waterfront was destroyed. An iron ship crashed through the pilings of the new Ashley River bridge. Water burst over the Battery wall like a waterspout, and White Point Gardens and all streets near the waterfront were submerged. The spire of the Citadel Square Baptist Church crashed to the ground.

Within an hour the wind died down, and there was a calm.

But after forty minutes it rose again, this time from another direction, and raged destructively, though in somewhat less force than before. When it was all over the town was a trash heap. In the process of clearing away the debris, over ten thousand cartloads of "vegetable trash" alone were taken away. Charleston went to work to make the necessary repairs, and within a few weeks was offering its aid to Washington, Ohio, which had just suffered a similar disaster.

The townsfolk may very well have asked themselves, "What next?" They did not have to wait long to find out.

On September 1, 1886, a casual and hurried reader of the *News and Courier* (and as the sequel will show, a highly suppositious kind of deaf hermit of a reader) might have noticed nothing strange about the paper's first page. He would have glanced carelessly over the optimistic trade reports, and skeptically at the promise of renewed electric lighting. Such matter occupied the first three pages. Except for a gloomy account of the ravages to Sullivan's Island resulting from the storm of a year earlier and a report on the bad effects of the blizzard of January on truck farming, the tone of the news was bullish. The leading editorial commented on oddities and contradictions in the news.

Near the head of the second column of the editorial page was a brief piece headed "The Earthquake Last Night," just nine lines of conventional editorializing. Only on page eight was there a detailed report of one of the great disasters of history.

There had been an earthquake late in the seventeenth century, but Dr. George Milligen had said of the city in 1763: "Earthquakes are unknown or so trifling as to have passed unnoticed." The sardonic chuckle of posterity must have roared in his eighteenth-century ears when he wrote that down. There were earthquakes in 1811 and in 1812 which set St. Philip's chimes ringing; another in 1843, and a shock in 1857 which was sufficiently severe to frighten some of the inhabitants into holding prayer meetings. But there had been nothing like this.

Warnings had come earlier from Summerville, about twenty-two miles away, and a perceptible tremor had occurred in the city on August 28th. Nevertheless, Charleston was serene on the night of August 31st. In the office of the *News and Courier* members of the staff were busy putting the paper to bed. This is how the news editor told the story:

At ten minutes past ten o'clock the men who were at work in the office of the *News and Courier* were startled at hearing a rumbling sound.

At first it was thought to be a very rapid street car coming down Broad Street. The sound grew in intensity, and was accompanied by a rumbling, crashing and shaking of the building. The men jumped from their seats and rushed to the doors, looking for some way to escape from the building. The building was swaying to such an extent that the men could with the greatest difficulty hold their footing. As they rushed down the back stairs they were enveloped in clouds of dust, and the whizzing of flying bricks was in their ears. The air was filled with cries and shrieks and the rumbling, crashing sounds of falling buildings.

Broad Street was instantly filled with men, women, and children, in all conditions of dress. Men in their shirt sleeves, women and children in their night clothing, just as they rushed from their beds to escape impending destruction. There was a scene of the wildest confusion for a few minutes, but the exertions of a few cool-headed men soon brought affairs to a state of order.

Shortly afterward came another severe shock. "This again," say the faithful news editor, "threw the people into great fright and their screams and shrieks were again heard on all sides. Many fell upon their knees and prayed aloud for mercy. ... The colored people were frantic in their behavior."

But the first shock had done the damage. In thirty seconds it had laid the city in ruins. Over six thousand buildings had been wrecked. The pillars of the Hibernian Hall had been thrown down and broken into bits. The interior of St. Philip's was mangled, and the spire was "a total wreck almost." The quake split St. Michael's in four places and the entire structure sank eight inches into the ground. Buildings wrecked and damaged included the Court House and the Guard House at Meeting and Broad, afterwards replaced by the Post Office. Contemporary drawings and photographs reveal a scene of horror, as if a giant demolition squad had been at work tearing down walls and ripping roofs off wholesale.

There were four more shocks that night after the first terrible upheaval of the earth, but they contributed chiefly fright. Thousands had been made homeless; ninety-two had been killed, generally those who had rushed outdoors. Hordes of the homeless camped out on the Citadel Green and in City Hall Park. The Negroes, who were probably not more frightened than anyone else but were doubtless less afraid to show it, held prolonged prayer-meetings; and the sulphurous fumes that filled the air suggested the end of the world to the superstitious.

The newly reorganized fire department was superior to the occasion, and for all the devastation and destruction, fire was confined to about twenty buildings, chiefly on King Street between Broad and Queen.

Along with the tragedy there were freaks and absurdities. In one badly shaken house an oil lamp continued to burn steadily in its place, untouched in the general overturning. A Negro family, whose frame house was uninjured, slept peacefully through that terrible night and awoke in astonishment at what they saw. And on one of the nights of vigil an alarm clock, innocently going off in a house near the Citadel Green, gave everyone a great fright. And the intrepid news editor of the *News and Courier,* forced to spend the night in the park, was taken for a corpse. A "quick turnover" proved that he was not.

Next morning Charleston was up and around, surveying

the damage. It was obvious that the city was hard hit; 90 per cent of the buildings in the entire town had been damaged. The *News and Courier* was, as noted, published as ûsual, and since all communication was cut off, had a scoop on the disaster which must have created a lot of envy among the journalists of the time. In one of its lists, published that day, appeared the name of "Mrs. E. Galliott, colored"—certainly a result of the confusion. The paper continued to print news of the disaster for several months, with side stories of all sorts, descriptions of the behavior of the homeless people, and lists of casualties and damages.

Charleston immediately got busy on the work of restoration. Many shops were opened on the second of September. Six hundred and forty thousand dollars was contributed to the relief of the stricken city. One of the contributors was Edwin Booth, who sent one thousand dollars in the care of a friend. The South Carolina Railroad provided a hundred freight cars to make temporary quarters for the homeless. The United States Government furnished tents.

Curiosity seekers came to view the devastated town, and some of the strange sights, like the great craters opened in the ground above the city. From these, sand of all colors was spouted out. It was later collected and sold to souvenir hunters at one dollar per phial. A pamphlet, describing the quake in detail and showing engravings of many buildings as they looked afterward, announces that this sand is for sale by the publisher.

This enterprising businessman obtained a considerable volume of advertising for his pamphlet; one caption, under the picture of the block of burned buildings on King Street, obligingly refers the reader to "the Morris card below," thus keying in the advertisement of a tinsmith and roofer of the vicinity. Other trades took advantage of the space offered; one advertisement announced "C.G.G. The Young Man's

Friend. Price fifty cents per bottle." This would appear to show that the supposed arrival of the millennium had not deterred some of the population from the ordinary worries of life.

There were two miracles connected with the event. One was that the three-million-gallon reservoir of the water works was unharmed. The other is related in the newspaper:

> On the top of the ruins of the porch of the Main (police) Station was seen a Cross, the emblem of Christianity, which shone with resplendent brightness. There was never a cross on the building as far as was known [mind you, the police station!] and the appearance of this one soon attracted attention as it stood out of the ruins.

The city as a whole reacted to the disaster with firmness and even with humor. One manufacturer of large machinery, when interviewed concerning his opinion of the city's prospects for resuming business, pointed to the open space where the wall of his establishment had been and remarked that it would be all the easier now to deliver his products. Some of the temporary camps were named "Camp Duffy," "The Queen's Camp," and "Artesian Park."

By October 31st the quake had lost out as news. On that date there was a brief recapitulation of the damage to public buildings and the story about the Negro preacher who invoked help of the Lord and asked that He come Himself and not send His Son "because this ain' no time for children." There was a letter, too, about the probable cause of the disaster, which modern science ascribes to a geological fault, a result of Charleston's "geologically young" setting. Charleston was in the very center of the disturbance, which had reached as far as the Middle West.

But this little freak of nature, which had cost Charleston five million dollars and untold hardship and grief, was not weighing the citizenry down. "Yesterday afternoon," said the

News and Courier of October 31st, "King Street presented its usual ante-earthquake appearance. Mingling with the crowds from the matinee were the blue uniforms of the Porter Academy and the familiar gray of the Citadel cadets." The matinee, by the way, was the operetta by Audran, *Le Serment d'Amour.* The paper further reports that the day before 13,000 bales of cotton and 3,000 tons of phosphate rock were among the exports "in spite of the earthquake."

Sixty years later there is virtually no trace of the calamity. The city's chief memento is in the form of plates and bars on the outsides of many of the houses. Almost a distinctive feature of Charleston architecture, these hold the steel rods which were inserted through the houses to steady the upper floors if the thing ever happened again. Some of the bolts on the outside have even been used decoratively.

Another memento is the letter of sympathy from Queen Victoria, kept in the City Hall.

This, one would say, is enough for any city. But there was more. On August 27 and 28, 1893, almost seven years to a day after the earthquake, another fearful cyclone lashed Charleston. It was worse than the one of 1885; the wind was actually recorded at 120 miles per hour. The Battery was undermined, piers were stripped bare, and the damage was frightful. One full-rigged ship, the *Astoria,* was found afterwards on the Stono River, completely deserted. She contained among other things a piano and female wearing apparel. All birds were blown right out of the city and none were seen until four days after the storm.

All the trees re-budded and remained green at the end of the year, which seems almost symbolic of Charleston's long defiance of catastrophe.

Except for a storm and flood in 1911, there was no further damage of the sort until 1938, when a one-minute tornado struck with terrific force. Roofs were torn off houses, chimneys toppled wholesale, and one whole section of Negro shacks in the path of the tornado was flattened with much loss of life. The effects of the tornado might have been even greater had it not providentially occurred at breakfast time, when most of the people were still in their houses.

As soon as the danger was past, everyone was out on the streets to survey the damage. Among those who were out were two clergymen, each anxious about the prominent church of which he was rector. A notably fine window had been blown out of one church, and in the same way the other had lost an eyesore. "Condolences," said the rector of the latter church. "Congratulations," replied his brother of the cloth.

Which is one more proof that Charleston can take it.

There is, by the way, a magnificent description of one of these tropical storms in *Porgy,* which gives a brilliant picture of the force and fury of such blows. No matter-of-fact accounts, like the preceding, can match its word-painting. And anyone who reads it will most likely read the entire novel, which is all to the good.

ROOFS, CHIMNEY POTS, AND REAR PIAZZAS

GABLES, SHUTTERS, AND CHIMNEYS

CHAPTER TWENTY-TWO

Roundabout

It is a pleasant diversion to think, now and then, of the various ways in which history can be told. In any city which qualifies by age for the term historic, the possibilities are many. There are streets and their names; houses—you couldn't go very far back in Charleston by that method, however, on account of those fires—and there is the biographical method, the study of the development of intellectual culture. There are the lesser biographies, too, of people who were odd or did odd things, and there is the story of commerce, that of topographical development, and that of the little things of government, its petty men and its pilferers, and the history of crime.

Those Charleston streets, for instance. Ashley Avenue commemorates the leading spirit among the Lords Proprietors. Tradd Street was named after the first white child born in the colony; his name is otherwise extinct in Charleston. King, Queen, George, Hanover; Church; Atlantic, Water, East Bay, Broad, Line—some of these tell their own story. There are Bull, and Pitt, Laurens, Gadsden, Pinckney, Rutledge Avenue, to commemorate great men; Anson, a reminder of that great seafarer; Coming, after the landholder who ceded the land at Oyster Point for the new settlement, and who gave

273

the glebe lands of St. Philip's, from which comes the name of Glebe Street.

Meeting Street is so called for the White Meeting House that stood there in the early days. Wentworth Street is called after the family name of Lord Rockingham, who was friendly to the interest of the colonies. The two builders of the old Exchange are remembered by Horlbeck Alley (not very gloriously); Bee and Cannon Streets recall Confederate generals; Murray Boulevard, the philanthropist who made it possible.

Sometimes the old names of streets have to be referred to to bring out their story. There is, for instance, the street known officially as Charles. It was originally Archdale, after that Lord Proprietor who came over in the early eighteenth century to pour oil on the troubled waters of faction. Not so long ago, because the pretty old street, which has some fine tumble-down houses and two handsome churches, had achieved a bad reputation for itself, the name was changed. Of course no one pays any attention to the change. Officially it may be Charles Street but architecturally, historically, and sentimentally it is Archdale.

Boundary Street, when it ceased anyway to be the boundary, was renamed Calhoun in honor of that statesman; Mazyck, bearing the name of one of the merchant princes, became Logan after one of those Confederate heroes; Friend Street was renamed to honor the Legaré who was a great scholar and statesman; Union's alteration to State shows the change of feeling in the city. There is a Sixth Avenue, but no one has yet suggested calling it Avenue of the Americas.

Stoll's Alley, in the district where the great wholesale stores once stood, is named after a hardware merchant; Vanderhorst after one of the great landholders. There are a number of streets which one of the landholders, a certain Wragg, named after his daughters—Ann, Charlotte, Judith, and the like. And there are oddities—Do As You Choose Alley, Longitude Lane,

and Zig-Zag Alley, which deserves to be called that. Its queer
bend was the result of that arrangement of creeks that honey-
combed the original land, and it remained when reclamation
came too late.

As for that long process of reclamation, an interesting
thing to see would be an animated drawing of Charleston's
topographical development, its gradual growth and filling in.
One would like to know just how the city looked when a
swimmer could go right to where the City Hall stands now,
and Mr. Hollybush's farm was at King and Broad streets,
and Henry Laurens, on his lands away uptown, had all those
fruits and exotic plants set out. Such a device might also
show Vauxhall, at the corner of Broad and Legaré streets,
where Alexander Placide, the pantomimist, amused the citizenry with plays and music.

Charleston has, by the way, a long musical history. There
were concerts as early as 1732, and the first known announcement of a musical event was printed in 1734. Joseph Lafar
opened a music store there in 1786, and the Siegling Music
Store, on King and Beaufain streets, is an establishment that
has been in the hands of the same family since 1800.

As early as 1762 the St. Cecilia Society was founded—in a
year when Haydn was a man of thirty, when Mozart, a child
of six, was beginning to astound all Europe with his precocity,
and Beethoven was not yet born. The original purpose of the
society was the giving of concerts, and it continued to fulfill
its purpose until finally it became difficult to obtain sufficient
musicians; the orchestra was gradually reduced to a quintet,
and in the end Terpsichore took over and the Society became
frankly an institution for the giving of balls and the establishment in Charleston society of a dividing line over which
all the wealth of the Indies could not push a family if those
on the other side of the line were not desirous of having
them. It is not impossible to get into the St. Cecilia, however;

DuBose Heyward, in *Mamba's Daughters,* devotes an interesting episode to the election of a Northern businessman. He also makes the famous ball seem rather like a drunken shindig, an impression which was confirmed by a daring newspaperwoman who crashed the gate. There are, however, certain handicaps which no one can overcome. No actor and no divorced person may belong.

The love of music, which brought the St. Cecilia Society into being, has persisted in Charleston. A house without a piano of some kind is relatively rare; there is an active choral society, and a symphony orchestra which practises in a kitchen building on Rutledge Avenue. To my knowledge, however, the city has produced only one nationally known musician, William Lawrence, who toured with the tenor Roland Hayes. A girl descended from one of the Santo Domingo families became a well-known singer in France. Recent hearings brought to light a talented Negro girl who is being encouraged. But, after all, professionalism is no sign of a community's musical health. A musical tradition that goes back as far as the year of Haydn's birth is a fairly long one in America.

Here are some items of the city's commercial history. Announcing the offer for freight or charter of the ship *Pochohontas* (sic), an advertisement in the *Courier* offers the following:

> For sale, very low, received from
> Rotterdam by said vessel:
> 100 pieces Platillas
> 12 pieces Rouans
> 13 pieces Oznaburghs, Linens
> 9 pieces Boozles

One might make a guess at some of the items, but what on earth are "boozles"? Could they be bustles?

Another advertisement lists in part such goods as "Chellars, Blue Romalls, Cushlettes, Alligars, and 30 Elephant's Teeth, of large sizes," and adds, "all entitled to drawback." We have certainly lost touch with our ancestors. For every gadget or plastic we could puzzle them with, they could probably spell us down with some article we had never heard of.

Another story, of a quasi-commercial type, is to be found in one of the early issues of the *Courier*. It tells how a certain Withers remained in a drain for three months while tunneling to within a short distance of the vaults of the South Carolina Bank, then at the corner of Broad and Church where the Chamber of Commerce now stands. We wonder if he ever came to the notice of Sir A. Conan Doyle, whose *Red-Headed League* one immediately recalls.

And then for those ghost stories and oddities: there is one ghost associated with a house on Tradd Street, who should be mentioned if only because of his very unwraithlike surrender to progress. This specter used to arrive quite regularly in an equipage, but nowadays the sound of his coming is that of an automobile. No doubt, being so committed to up-to-date means of locomotion, he will come in a helicopter one of these days.

A recent prowler was not a ghost at all. In the spring of 1946 that part of Charleston south of Broad Street was visited by a nocturnal wanderer who became in a few weeks a figure of legendary proportions. His chief stunt was to insinuate himself into bed with ladies, even if a husband were present. He prevented all identification by the neat trick of unscrewing all the electric light bulbs before he set to work. There were various descriptions of him, one of which attributed his noiseless progress to the fact that he wore heavy woolen socks without shoes. There were reputedly authenticated cases of attack, carefully concealed from newspaper readers and probably much multiplied by gossip. Humorists spoke of the prowler as Goldilocks. The well known psychosis of Southern women (and men) was somewhat prone to ascribe all these mysterious doings to a Negro, but it was also said that the stockinged prowler went around in blackface and also that he was the relative of a well-known citizen. There was such a nailing down of windows as Charleston had not seen for many a year and much replacing of bolts and locks and oiling of firearms. The police were unsatisfactory to those hoping for a revelation; it was finally reported that the stranger had gone off to Charleston's maritime rival Savannah, which did not appear to arouse any sympathy. Bit by bit lights ceased to turn on all night in the houses, amateur sleuths discontinued their vigilante activities, and that was that. We wonder what sort of shrift that prowler would have got from Mrs. Rebecca Motte, who had stood off the British officers from her attractive daughters.

Eccentrics have been fairly plentiful. One distinguished old gentleman of long ago used to take his tea out on the sidewalk undisturbed. An elderly lady, too feeble for the stairs of one of the huge old houses, was known to haul up her supplies in a basket, which she let down with a rope. A businessman not so very long ago was notable among the unsympathetic young for the odd habit of twirling a collar button as he walked through the street and counting his steps. There was an eccentric mulatto who led every funeral to the cemetery. One religious lady founded a society of Catholic boys and girls which she called "The Angel Adorers" and who assisted at Benediction clad in white flannel robes. Some of them were far from angels or anything like it. And who can forget the gentleman whose hobby was crocheting and who brought his handiwork around to show it to the ladies?

A colored man known as Crook-neck Dick was pointed out as one who had so stubbornly resisted hanging that he had been freed and was the worse only by a wry neck for his experience in nearly reaching the great beyond. Another, with a peculiarly peaked cranium and known by the unflattering nickname of Egg-head Eddie, was whispered to have mortgaged his peculiar brain case to the "students"; in other words for dissection *post mortem*.

A certain Stonewall Jackson, a perfectly harmless tramp, was noted for living on bananas and sweet condensed milk and for wearing only new unlaundered shirts, although he wore them a long time. Once he was arrested for vagrancy and lodged in the jail, whereupon the sympathetic ladies of the city fairly overwhelmed him with dainties. According to the story, Stonewall stubbornly refused to eat any of it except the fruit and purely vegetarian foods, and the credulous mur-mured that these feeding prejudices arose from the fact that he had been a castaway and had survived all the other members of the crew. I have no hopes of authenticating this story, but you can't always tell by what seems incredible. I have told else-where of the old lady who insisted on taking her own coffee pot with her when she went visiting. One indignant reader expressed herself about this in a bookstore; she declared that it was preposterous.

Charleston has its historical eccentrics too, beginning in the early eighteenth century with the mystic, Hugh Bryan, who bedeviled Dr. Garden (the clergyman) by such pranks as proclaiming that he would divide the waters like Moses and who was ducked to restore him to reason. Alexander Cumings, who had some success in pacifying the Indians, must have been a rather queer fish from all accounts. The British officer who was called "Mad Archy" Campbell, and who captured Isaac Hayne, met a pretty young lady in Tory Row, wagered his Arab steed that he would marry her with her consent in three days and did so by kidnapping her and forcing the parson at Goose Creek to marry them at pistol point.

And here is a theatrical note of 1870, which shows the od-dities of local outlook:

The greatest sensation that we ever saw in the theater was occasioned by Mrs. Julia Dean Hayne, not on account of her acting, though that was generally acknowledged to be good, but rather on account of her having married Dr. Hayne, a member of one of the best families of Charleston.

Charleston has usually been fairly tolerant in racial affairs. It has heard Blind Tom and the Black Patti; and Dorothy Maynor's recital at the Morris Street Baptist Church was duly announced by the Carolina Art Association. Residential segregation was never compulsory. And the tale is told of a Negro physician, apparently a skilled practitioner, who was called in to attend the mistress of a prominent white family after other physicians had failed. His treatment successful, the grateful family made him a present of a fine pair of gray horses and a carriage, in which he proudly went for rides with his wife and daughter.

This tolerance was not in evidence in the famous case of the Grimké sisters, Sarah and Angelina. They were aristocratic Charlestonians, daughters of a judge and descendants on their mother's side of Governor James Moore and Landgrave Smith. Sarah began her career of eccentricity as a religious mystic and later, with Angelina, became one of the last three Quakers in Charleston.

Angelina, in defiance of the law which her father upheld, taught the Negro servants of the family to read and write. Later rebelling against the institution of slavery, she joined the New York Anti-Slavery Society and wrote "An Appeal to The Christian Women of the South." Copies of the pamphlet sent to Charleston were seized by a mob and burned. The mayor of the city informed Mrs. Grimké that Angelina could not return to Charleston, even for a visit, and both sisters became exiles. They enjoyed the friendship of various Northern men of letters and became chronic enthusiasts—or, more plainly, cranks.

Their final affront to Southern sensibilities was delivered after the war. In the year 1868, they noted the name Grimké on the commencement program of a Negro school in the North. They made inquiries and found that both boys of that name were natives of Charleston. A visit to the school convinced the sisters that these boys were their own nephews. Of course, at that time, mentioning the paternity of partly white Americans was a social indecency, but the Grimké sisters did not hesitate to do what they thought proper. They accepted the relationship, treated the youths as social equals and aided in their education.

The Grimké sisters were considered "eccentric," and that is the only excuse for their inclusion at this point.

CHAPTER TWENTY-THREE

Plus ça change . . .

They say Charleston doesn't change, but you, a long-exiled native, have heard of many things that seem like changes.

You have heard about the tourist boom, the war boom that has driven the population of the city up to unprecedented figures, and there's that Santee-Cooper project that furnishes 600,000,000 kilowatts a year, doing away with the necessity for the old coal ranges that you remember; your family sneered at gas. You have read that the city had in 1944 a payroll of $100,000,000, and that everybody is busy, and that Negro servants enjoy a rate of pay that was unheard of in your time, and that Northern millionaires have been taking the city away piece by piece, gateways, balconies, even entire houses, the way August Belmont took away the old race track pillars to Belmont Park before you were born.

It may be true. You know, for a certainty, that Charleston has changed over the centuries; that people long ago gave up the custom of having an Indian supply them with game, and that ladies finally dared to go out unescorted, and that the Negro maumas stopped wearing those colored turbans. And all those rumors of changes and changes! You are prepared to believe, in spite of what people say about its never changing, that the old city is unrecognizable.

Then you meet a Charlestonian up North, and you know that they talk just the way they did, and it sounds pretty good to you. You tell him that you haven't been back for many years, and he smiles widely and tells you, as if in confidence, that the old place is just the same. "It hasn't changed a bit" is the motto of those who have come away to be dazzled in vain by splendor. But when you pin them down to particulars, that's another story. Old Mr. So-and-so? He's dead. And such and such a place? Oh, you wouldn't know that now; it's all built up. Is the So-and-so Store still on Such-and-such Street? Oh, no, man. The —— chain has a store there now.

You finally go down there to see for yourself, and coming down from the North Charleston station, for the fast trains all put you off miles away from downtown, you see all those housing developments, and you turn off and see the great new Citadel, and you begin to wonder if that business about the city's unchanging qualities is not some illusion of the inhabitants, caused by the fact that they see these things happen gradually and that the old types keep reappearing one generation after another.

You find that straw matting has lost its vogue as a floor covering, and you wonder what the world is coming to. And then you meet someone who asks you about your mother, calling her "Miss" and her first name, and you are reassured. You look, however, in vain for a joggling board, that curious piece of piazza and garden furniture made of a long flexible plank supported between two uprights, and you know that even a place as accustomed to resist change as old Charleston does become altered in this restless country.

You see a lot of superficial alterations, and when you run across a spot that seems unchanged since your childhood, the relief is simply overwhelming.

You begin with the house where you were born. There it is. It looks a good deal smaller than you expected, and somehow this seems like a rebuff. Smaller? No, it's really larger. There's a whole new wing added at the rear.

And the house you lived in after that, which you remember a good deal better because you stayed there until you were four years old? Well, that has shrunk too; and they've masked the piazzas except for a bit at the back, and the house has been made over into apartments. You wonder about the front bedroom in which you first saw your small brother, and the great center room upstairs that was a kind of dormitory; you remember a Christmas morning, away back in the dim past now, on which you had a row of paper soldiers mounted on wooden blocks, and a sheet or two of paper caps for a little cast-iron pistol, and a coffee-cup and saucer with the alphabet running around the rim; and somebody in the family had a little magic lantern with an oil lamp in it that showed glass slides.

You look at the garden. They *must* have widened the street; it's a very narrow space from that fence to the side of the house. And the fig trees are gone. So is the little stable where the cow was kept and the horse. Somebody has been awfully ruthless here and that front room where you sat in the sunshine and petted a large plaster dog that came from the store where they sold pianos and victrolas . . . well, something's been done to all of it.

You haven't given up yet. You go to look at the house in which you spent the greater part of your childhood, seven or eights years of it. It's an apartment house now, you've been warned. But there is the familiar coping, and the pillars with knobs on top that seemed perilously high when you perched up on them, and the driveway; but a great tree you never saw before has grown up on the little front lawn. You go into the back yard, and the peach tree you planted yourself, and that you heard years before was a great one full of fruit, is no

more. There's not even a stump of it left. The chicken houses
are gone, and the fig trees that hung over the fence at the back,
and they've done something to that downstairs floor where you
look in after ascertaining that there's no one at home. After
that you're unwilling to see any more. Right next door there
used to be a great old house built of brown bricks. It was a
boarding house, the property of maiden sisters and their
bachelor brother, and when you first read *Père Goriot* that was
the Maison Vauquer.

Many times you had played in the yard with the children
who were staying there, and looked at the big garden that occupied most of the plot. You knew about it, but the new apartment house there is a blow all the same.

You walk along "the Pond," and all the poisonberry trees
are gone. There are oleanders everywhere, which is a great
improvement, as you grudgingly admit; there in the northwest
corner is a man fishing for mullet with dough for bait, which
seems right and fitting. But where is the lumber mill that you
used to watch, to see the logs piled up? There's a playground
there now, looking just as if it had a right to be, too.

Broad Street; now, that's a little better. You recognize those
houses and they don't seem greatly altered. There's a familiar
face. It has a mustache on it now but the eyes and head are
unmistakable. It belonged to a little boy as you remember it;
now it belongs to a man grown. You hadn't realized that you
were that old. Why, you and that boy used to steal his
mother's blackberry wine, the last you recall of him. Now he's
a solid citizen. You talk briefly about old times, which are
a good deal more interesting to you than to him. Three of
the old group you knew are dead; three more are established
professional men.

You part from him and potter onward, determined to see
this thing through to the bitter end. There's the house where
you attended private school. The big hackberry trees that

grew outside the abandoned churchyard next door, where the Hessian soldiers may have drilled, have disappeared, and so has the huge tree that grew right through the wooden fence, The high fence itself has been taken down, and you look into the little yard where, somehow or other, you managed to cram enough boys to play baseball, three or four on a side. Only too certain that the bench with the bowl of water and the always gritty soap are no more, you pass on. There are ghosts in that old house, and what is worse, they are ghosts of children.

Now for the Boulevard. You can clearly remember when they began to fill in the river and marsh. Before that there was a wharf at the foot of the old street; you used to go with your nurse to the colored boatman's house, and once, when a ring had become too small for your finger, he filed it off to the accompaniment of loud screams from you. They piled up sand and silt there, and all over that white expanse, that was almost like a beach, you picked up shark's teeth of all sizes. You played baseball on the empty lots, until the salty sand made the ball too heavy and soggy to handle; you flew kites there. The father of some boys you played with built box kites; he had one of the first houses built on the new land. Well, it's all built over now, and a broad asphalt driveway has replaced the old oyster-shell road that hummed when your bicycle tires rolled over it. The old wharf at the foot of Tradd Street, too, where the fishermen came in, is lined with submarine chasers and other gray navy craft; the old mill has been put to new uses, and the house set slightly askew to the street, where your grandparents once lived, is an official dwelling of some sort. A drowned man was washed ashore there once, and the gentleman who flew the box kites wouldn't let his sons or you go down to see the fascinating spectacle, for which you silently cursed him. Somebody, in those days, was always shutting the door in the face of opportunity.

You take a hopeful look at King Street, and of all things, the old monument-works and the sail- and awning-maker have departed. Ladeveze's candy store, where the finest peppermint and fruit sticks in the world were made, has disappeared. The old cycle shop is still there; that's a comfort, at any rate. The Chinese laundry is gone, though, backscratchers, punk sticks, and all. There's a new theatre where the old Academy of Music stood. You saw "The Birth of a Nation" there, and shuddered and wept by turns at that brazen and indecent piece of propaganda. ... And now for the "art" store, where they sold passe partout and cameras and film and such things, and which was so dark you wouldn't have been surprised if they did their developing right there in the front. Yes, it's there, but how changed. And Louis Cohen's old dry goods store, where you had your first thrilling ride in an elevator—well, they've replaced that, too.

There is still a hardware and house furnishings store where you used to buy buckshot for your slingshot and cartridges for your rifle, but the wax man, eternally on the point of chopping wood, is gone from the window. Legerton's Book Store still stands, and the familiar druggist's store, too, but the clothing store, where the wax dummies with iron feet melted down in the hot weather, has passed on and is a chain establishment. Where is Onslow's candy store? Oh, that's gone, too.

And then, little by little, you think over all the things that you remember and wanted to see again and never will. You go back to the West End, and you look in vain for the lot where you used to play ball, and the piers under which at low tide the fiddler crabs went scurrying aimlessly about, and the little shack where a gentleman of color sold cheap root beer and told the young bloods unprintable stories. There's the old Bennett Rice Mill, put to official uses. No use to search for the oyster-shell road with the tiny footbridge over the marsh where you rode a bicycle and felt like a daredevil.

Jenkins' Band is still around; they were in that Boy Scout parade the other day. That makes you think of the band that played on the streetcar when the races were on. There aren't even streetcars now. The "blue car" that was really blue you can't remember; but you remember when the cars were yellow, and then green, and some of the older people still called it the "blue car," to the dismay of strangers who might easily have waited until doomsday for it.

That's right, the band was called "Metz's." Come to think of it, it played for dancing, too, in the days when a band or an orchestra of the conventional type could still play for dancing. And what was by courtesy called "Metz's Orchestra" helped to kill silence in the vaudeville theatre. Four pieces. Piano, clarinet, cornet (or was it a violin), and the drums played by that extraordinary trap-drummer, who was said to have refused a flattering offer from Sousa. Many a comedian has landed on his seat to the crash of Freddy Seel's bass drum and cymbals; many an acrobat has completed a dizzy turn to the crescendo of Freddy's drumsticks.

Nostalgia. . . . You remember the days when Wigg's little ice-cream wagon, painted that pale golden yellow that used to distinguish wagons and streetcars—almost the color of vanilla ice cream—went slowly up and down past the children playing on the Pond, and rang its bell. You ran home and got a tumbler, and for ten cents it was filled right up to the brim. You recall the old "groundnut cake" woman, a decrepit mauma, with that wonderful chewy black molasses candy full of peanuts spread out on a flat basket tray. Her feet hurt. The feet of all old colored people hurt, from rheumatism and from wearing cast-off shoes, and their eyes were very sad and very wise. They don't wear turbans any longer, and they don't balance impossible burdens of laundry and vegetables on a little pad that fits their heads, and they're not called "Dah" by their white charges. They meet you at the corner, occasionally, with a basket of flowers; you're old enough now to appreciate the beauty of old faces that were young when you were a child.

Customs change. They still have dinner in the early afternoon, but the young swains don't yodel on the pond at night, or sing and play the tinkly, melancholy tunes of Hawaii as they did in the days when to the sentimental and romantic young "Aloha Oe" seemed the most sublime song in the world.

And that matter of the bridges. You remember the bridge across the Ashley as a rattle-trap affair of wood, that gave out a noise like musket fire when wagons and automobiles crossed it. On the James Island side, there was a farm to which you used to go for picnics, and where you were thrown by the blind pony that belonged to the boys on that farm. Right there, where the old house stood, you picked up, not far from the porch, a moldy pocketbook containing the unheard-of sum of three dollars and twenty-five cents, mostly in silver, but there was a single dollar bill so decayed that it had to be exchanged at the bank for a new one. It was a long time before anybody could convince you that there was no opportunity in Charleston. And since you have the memory of the club bore, you can recall the exact items of baseball equipment you bought with that fortune, particularly the bat with gaudy red stripes that was entirely too big for you to swing. It cost twenty-five cents, as much as the favorite baseball of small boys, a slightly undersized sphere with the fascinating trade name of "Lively Bounder," which it certainly was—the original rabbit ball, and invariably the cause of a ground rule that over the fence was out.

Well...there is a suburban development right where that farm used to be; and there is a new and rather imposing steel and concrete bridge in place of the old one. As for the poor colored soul who no doubt had grieved bitterly over the loss of that three dollars and twenty-five cents and of which you didn't think at the time, it's probably not grieving about any-thing now.

As for that other bridge that vaults up almost into the sky across the Cooper River, you don't remember it at all. When you were a child, a trip to Sullivan's Island or the Isle of Palms was more of an event than it is now. There was no long bridge to deliver you there almost at once. You had to take the ferry to Mount Pleasant. The ferry boat was an ancient affair, probably acquired from some operator who had found it no longer fit for use on the Great Lakes, and it rejoiced in the singularly inappropriate name of *Sappho*. It creaked mis-erably and its smell was a composite of all the smells that afflict ferry boats—salt water, tar, rotting wood. Later it was supplemented or replaced by a somewhat newer vessel, the *Lawrence,* which seemed a great improvement.

Once safely in the ferry slip at Mount Pleasant, which, as has been often pointed out, is no mount at all, but as flat as the back of a Dutchman's head, you were done with the first leg of the trip. There remained a journey in the streetcar, which finally would reach the Isle of Palms after stopping at what seemed to you innumerable "stations" along the way; once, when you were going to visit relatives who lived near Fort Moultrie, the motorman went past the station, and your little grandmother, a relic of spacious days, made the motorman back the car for her.

Sullivan's Island is considerably more built up by now, but the jungle is just as thick as ever where it hasn't been cleared. The Isle of Palms beach, which you remember as virtually empty except for the pavilion and an abandoned ferris wheel, is a marvelous stretch of sea and sand some twelve miles long, with wide beaches of clean, fine sand, packed down so hard that it feels almost like cement, and kind to your feet—unlike a good many bathing beaches in the North where you will cut your feet to ribbons if you don't wear bathing shoes.

You miss the little boys who used to clean chimneys—or did you really remember them, or merely miss hearing about them? You do remember the little lamplighter, who went patiently around every evening at dusk, when cocoa was simmering in the grate and toast was browning in the rack, and with his taper put a little star at the top of every lamppost. You understood very well about *Leery* in Stevenson's poem; you had seen him. And you remember the carbon arc lamps at the street corners that crackled and hissed in the still of the evening; and the old carbons that were thrown down by the repairmen and used by small boys for crayons as long as the charred part lasted.

They told you, too, that a good deal of the zip had gone out of the Christmas celebrations. During the war, of course, no one had fireworks, for the fireworks companies were all busy making instruments of death. You remember the years when, about the first of December, the seed stores and greengrocers and fruiterers, having piddled around most of the year with such uninteresting items as garden seeds and vegetables, really got down to brass tacks and justified their existence with the sale of fireworks. For at least a month—from December first to New Year's Day—the lesson of thrift was wasted on the young. What boy could have been a miser when those sawdust boxes were bursting with "spitfires" and cannon crackers, and small and large Roman candles and skyrockets and, best of all, the little red-wrapped packages of Chinese crackers? Christmas was really Christmas then. The booming commenced about five o'clock in the morning and for the rest of the day, or even the week, noise reigned. Your eyebrows were singed, your fingers were rubbed sore from the triggers of cap pistols, and your ears throbbed with warnings of lockjaw from the old folks.

There are, apparently, no more goat carts, the delight of white and colored small boys alike. Goats with gilded horns and bells, and brilliant red carts; shabby stinking buckgoats with soapbox wagons hitched by bits of string—no more of either. There are no cows in the back yards, either, as there were when you were a small boy, and there are apparently few chickens, although you did see some. There are still a good many bicycles, ridden by children and grownups.

In fact, everything hasn't changed. An annex does cover the little park behind the Post Office, where they used to keep deer and which in earlier days was frequently the scene of duels. Negro women stand on the Post Office steps and sell flowers, a recent custom, dating only from the nineteen-twenties, and the old Schuetzenplatz, where the German rifle clubs held their outings, has vanished. But you go around, here and there, and you see the house where you played with So-and-so, and it looks pretty much the same; and you find that people still have stoves unashamedly in their living rooms, even if they are oil heaters of a new type and not the old Franklin stoves you knew; and although you can't buy "gun-gers," those indigestible pieces of gingerbread, yet the ground-nut cakes for which you paid a penny are sold at an exorbitant price in a tourist shop. And there is the old Exchange at the foot of Broad Street, and the City Hall, and St. Michael's, and the South Carolina Society Hall, and the Pitt Statue, and there are the little pink primroses, the same as ever; and you see the old artesian pump near the museum, and you get the old familiar and indescribable smell from the river, and there in the harbor is Fort Sumter, just as it was; and in the morning you hear a fish vendor come down the street with a long-drawn and incomprehensible cry, and you have hominy for breakfast, and St. Michael's clangs the quarter hour, and you read the *News and Courier,* and it's all suddenly just like yesterday. You can take up where you left off, for there is a continuity about Charleston, and the city endures in more senses than one.

Bibliography

American Journal of Philology. Vol. 9, 1888.

Antiques Magazine. March, 1942.

BARING-GOULD, SABINE.—*Lives of the Saints* (Grant, Edinburgh, 1914).

BARRY, RICHARD H.—*Mr. Rutledge of South Carolina* (Duell, Sloan and Pearce, 1942).

BENNETT, JOHN.—*Apothecaries' Hall* (The Charleston Museum, 1923).

—— *The Doctor to the Dead* (Rinehart, 1946).

BOLTON, HERBERT E.—*Adventurers of New Spain: Part Two, The Spanish Borderlands* (Chronicles of America Series, Yale University Press, 1919).

BOWES, FREDERICK P.—*The Culture of Early Charleston* (University of North Carolina Press, 1942).

BRAGG, LAURA M., ed.—*The Charleston Museum Quarterly.* First Quarter, 1923 (The Charleston Museum, 1923).

BURTON, E. MILBY.—*South Carolina Silversmiths* (The Charleston Museum, 1942).

CARSON, JAMES PETIGRU.—*Life, Letters and Speeches of James Louis Petigru* (W. H. Lowdermilk, 1920).

CASH, W. J.—*The Mind of the South* (Knopf, 1941).

Charleston and Vicinity Illustrated (Walker, Evans and Cogswell, 1901).

The Charleston Yearbooks. Charleston, 1881—.

CHILDS, FRANCIS SERGEANT.—*French Refugee Life in the United States, 1790-1800* (Johns Hopkins University Press, 1940).

CRUM, MASON D.—*Gullah* (Duke University Press, 1940).

DEAS, ALSTON.—*The Early Ironwork of Charleston* (Bostick & Thornley, 1941).

The Dictionary of American Biography.

DOAR, DAVID.—*Rice and Rice Planting in the South Carolina Low Country* (The Charleston Museum, 1936).

DUMOND, DWIGHT LOWELL.—*A History of the United States* (Henry Holt, 1942).

———— *The Secession Movement, 1860-61* (Macmillan, 1931).

EASTERBY, J. H.—*A History of the College of Charleston* (Charleston, 1935).

ENGLAND, RT. REV. JOHN E.—*Works*. Vol. 3 (John Murphy & Co., Baltimore, 1849).

The Exposition. December, 1900-November, 1901.

The Forum. January, 1940.

FRASER, CHARLES.—*Reminiscences of Charleston* (Charleston, 1854).

FROST, MARY PRINGLE.—*The Miles Brewton House: Chronicles and Reminiscences* (Privately Printed, Charleston).

FROST, SUSAN PRINGLE.—*Highlights of the Miles Brewton House* (Privately Printed, Charleston, 1944).

GARDEN, ALEXANDER.—*Anecdotes of the Revolution* (A. E. Miller, Charleston, 1828).

Gateways and Doorways of Charleston (Legerton & Co., Charleston).

GONGAWARE, GEORGE J.—*History of the German Friendly Society* (Garrett & Massie, 1935).

GONZALES, AMBROSE.—*The Black Border* (State Publishing Co., Columbia, 1922).

Harper's Magazine. June, 1857; October, 1915.

HENDRICK, BURTON J.—*Statesmen of the Lost Cause* (Little, Brown, 1939).

HENNIG, HELEN KOHN.—*Great South Carolinians* (University of North Carolina Press, 1940).

HENRY, ROBERT SELPH.—*The Story of the Confederacy:* (Bobbs-Merrill, 1936).

HEYWARD, DUBOSE.—*Porgy* (George H. Doran, 1925).

———— *Mamba's Daughters* (Doubleday, Doran, 1929).

———— *Peter Ashley* (Farrar & Rinehart, 1932).

———— And Herbert Ravenel Sass, *Fort Sumter* (Farrar & Rinehart, 1938).

HUGER, ELIZABETH PINCKNEY.—*Statement of the Attempted Rescue of Gen. Lafayette from "Olmutz"* (Walker, Evans & Cogswell Co., 1881).

JEFFERSON, JOSEPH.—*The Autobiography of Joseph Jefferson* (Century, 1890).

JERVEY, CLARE.—*Inscriptions on the Tablets and Gravestones in St. Michael's Church and Churchyard* (The State Co., Columbia, 1906).

Journal of the American Association of Architectural Historians. October, 1942.

KING, W. L.—*The Newspaper Press of Charleston.* Charleston, 1882.

LEIDING, HARRIET KERSHAW.—*Charleston, Historic and Romantic* (Lippincott, 1931).

——— *Historic Houses of South Carolina* (Lippincott, 1921).

LESESNE, THOMAS PETIGRU.—*Landmarks of Charleston* (Garrett & Massie, 1939).

LEWISOHN, LUDWIG.—*Upstream* (Boni and Liveright, 1922).

LOSSING, BENSON J.—*Pictorial History of the Civil War in the United States of America* (G. W. Childs, 1866).

LOWERY, WOODBURY.—*The Spanish Settlements Within the Present Limits of the United States.* Vol. 2 (Putnam, 1905).

McCRADY, EDWARD.—*History of South Carolina Under the Proprietary Government* (Macmillan, 1897).

——— *History of South Carolina Under the Royal Government.* The same. 1899.

——— *History of South Carolina in the Revolution.* The same. 1901.

MEADE, ROBERT DOUTHAT.—*Judah P. Benjamin* (Oxford University Press, 1943).

MILLER, FRANCIS TREVELYAN, ed.—*The Photographic History of the Civil War* (The Review of Reviews Co., 1912).

MORSE, S. F. B.—*Letters and Journals* (Houghton Mifflin, 1914).

The Nation. November 22, 1933; January 24, 1942; November 20, 1943.

NEVINS, ALLAN.—*Frémont, Pathmarker of the West* (Appleton-Century, 1939).

The New York Tribune. 1889, *passim.*

The News and Courier. Sept., Oct., Nov., 1886; Sept., Oct., 1878.

OLIPHANT, MARY C. SIMMS.—*The New Simms History of South Carolina* (State Publishing Co., Columbia, 1940).

Picturesque Charleston.—(Walker, Evans & Cogswell, 1935).

POYAS, ELIZABETH ANNE.—*Days of Yore* (W. G. Mazyck, 1870).

———— *Our Forefathers* (Walker, Evans & Cogswell, 1860).

———— *A Peep into the Past* (Privately Printed, Charleston, 1853).

RAVENEL, BEATRICE ST. JULIEN.—*Architects of Charleston* (Carolina Art Association, 1946).

RAVENEL, MRS. ST. JULIEN.—*Charleston, the Place and People* (Macmillan, 1906).

———— *Eliza Pinckney* (Scribner's, 1896).

RHETT, BLANCHE S.; GAY, LETTIE, and WOODWARD, HELEN.—*200 Years of Charleston Cooking* (Cape & Smith, 1930).

RHETT, R. GOODWYN.—*Charleston: An Epic of Carolina* (Garrett & Massie, 1940).

RICHARDSON, EMMA B.—*Charleston Garden Plats* (The Charleston Museum, 1943).

———— *The Heyward-Washington House Garden*. The same, 1941.

RUTLEDGE, ANNA WELLS.—*Catalogue of Paintings and Sculpture in the Council Chamber, City Hall, Charleston, South Carolina* (City Council of Charleston, 1943).

RUTLEDGE, ARCHIBALD.—*Home by the River* (Bobbs-Merrill, 1941).

SALLEY, ALEXANDER S., ed.—*Narratives of Early Carolina* (Scribner's, 1911).

SIMONS, ALBERT, and LAPHAM, SAMUEL, JR.—*Charleston, S.C.* The Octagon Library of American Architecture (Press of the American Institute of Architects, 1927).

SIMONS, KATHLEEN DRAYTON MAYRANT.—*Stories of Charleston Harbor* (The State Co., Columbia, 1930).

SMITH, ALICE R. HUGER, and SMITH, D. E. HUGER.—*The Dwelling Houses of Charleston* (Lippincott, 1907).

SONNECK, OSCAR G.—*Early Concert Life in America* (Breitkopf & Haertel, Leipzig, 1907).

———— *Early Opera in America* (G. Schirmer, 1915).

The South Carolina Historical and Genealogical Magazine. 1900-1946.

STEVENS, WILLIAM OLIVER.—*Charleston: Historic City of Gardens* (Dodd Mead, 1939).

STONEY, SAMUEL GAILLARD, and WOOTTEN, BAYARD.—*Charleston: Azaleas and Old Bricks* (Houghton Mifflin, 1939).

STONEY, SAMUEL GAILLARD, and others.—*Plantations of the Carolina Low Country* (The Carolina Art Association, 1938).

———— *This is Charleston* (The Carolina Art Association, 1944).

TOWER, RODERICK.—*The Defense of Fort Sumter* (Publication sponsored by Fort Sumter Hotel, Charleston, 1938).

VERNER, ELIZABETH O'NEILL.—*Mellowed by Time* (Bostick and Thornley, 1941).

VON KOLNITZ, ALFRED H.—*A Panorama of Three Centuries Viewed from Charleston's Famous Battery* (Historical Commission of the City of Charleston).

WALLACE, DAVID DUNCAN.—*The Life of Henry Laurens* (Putnam, 1915).

WERTENBAKER, THOMAS JEFFERSON.—*The Old South* (Scribner's, 1942).

WHITE, LAURA A.—*Robert Barnwell Rhett, Father of Secession* (Century, 1931).

WINTER, WILLIAM.—*The Life and Art of Joseph Jefferson* (Macmillan, 1894).

INDEX

299